THE POLITICS OF FEDERALISM IN NIGERIA

Published by
Adonis & Abbey Publishers Ltd
P.O. Box 43418
London
SE11 4XZ
http://www.adonis-abbey.com

First Edition, February 2007

Copyright © J. Isawa Elaigwu 2007

British Library Cataloguing-in-Publication Data
A catalogue record for this book is available from the British Library

ISBN: 9781905068432

The moral right of the author has been asserted

Cover Design   Ifeanyi Adibe

Printed and bound in Great Britain

THE POLITICS OF FEDERALISM IN NIGERIA

Adonis & Abbey
Publishers Ltd

Table of Contents

1

INTRODUCTION:
THE POLITICS OF FEDERALISM IN NIGERIA

The Federal Principle

Federalism is essentially a compromise solution in a multinational state between two types of self-determination—the determination provided by a national government which guarantees security for all in the nation-state on one hand, and the self-determination of component groups to retain their individual identities on the other. Federalism emanates from the desire of people to form a federal union without necessarily losing their identity.[1] Thus, federalism is an attempt to reflect the diverse political, social, cultural and economic interests within the broader framework of unity. It therefore attempts to satisfy "the need for cooperation in some things coupled with right to separate action in others. Only federalism fulfills the desire for unity where it coexists with a determination not to smother local identity and local power".[2]

Federalism emphasizes non-centralization of powers. Each component unit of a federal system has its powers and functions delineated and guaranteed in a constitutional document. As the doyen of federalism, K.C. Wheare wrote, federalism is "the method of dividing powers so that the general and regional governments are each, within a sphere, coordinate and independent".[3]

There is greater inter-dependence among component federal units and less autonomy for subnational units than Wheare had anticipated; but he was correct to emphasize that the division of powers should be such that "whoever has the residue, neither general nor regional government is subordinate to the other".[4]

In essence, this is what distinguishes a federal system from a unitary system of government. In the latter, "the state governments are legally subordinate to the central government". It also differs from confederacy in which the "Central government is legally subordinate to the state government".[5] Thus, in a federal system of government, the very structures and their concomitant functions and authority should reflect dual legal *sovereignty* in areas of jurisdiction of the federal and subnational political units.

In practice, no country has been able to embody all these federal principles in its traditional definition. In fact, it is generally agreed that federal systems vary in content from one country to another. The particular political colouring that a country's federal government takes, is often reflective of its historical experience, its political, cultural, social, and economic environment and the disposition of its people at a particular point in time. There is no ideal model of federalism. Federalism responds to local problems. The old Whearist model of federal association in terms of relations among component units does not exist anywhere in the world now. As Justice Ranjit Sarkaria of India correctly observed:

> The classical concept of federation which envisaged two parallel governments of coordinate jurisdiction, operating in isolation from each other in watertight compartments, is no where a functional reality now with the emergence of the Social Welfare State, the traditional theory of federalism completely lost its ground. After the First World War, it became very much a myth even in the old federations... By the middle of the Twentieth Century, federalism had come to be understood as a dynamic process of cooperation and shared action between two or more levels of government, with increasing interdependence and centrist trends.[6]

The complexity of modern governance, the need for homogeneity within the state, as well as the nature of foreign trade (among other reasons) have contributed to the increase in the power of central government in most federal states, except perhaps in countries such as Belgium.

The United States of America is regarded as one of the best examples of federal government in practice. The United States (U.S.) example, which is buttressed by various discourses documented by its founding fathers,[7] has experienced adjustments over time in response

7

to new problems and political emergencies. Thus, U.S. Federalism in the 1890s or even in the 1930s is different from federalism in the U.S. of 1990 or 2000. This process of adjustment is normal. As integrative processes in a nation-state positively advance, adjustments will also become necessary in intergovernmental relations. In addition, the complexity of modern government (thanks to technological revolution) makes the traditional concept of federalism inappropriate, especially after the Second World War. Thus, as mentioned earlier, a greater degree of interdependence of component governments in a federal state has become inevitable. In the same vein, the traditional concept of 'independence' or 'autonomy' of component units has also changed. The very process of interdependence implies some erosion of that traditional concept of independence of component units.

Given the U.S. experience, which in itself is very interesting and complex, many Western writers give the impression that unless the practice of federal government of other countries approximate the U.S. experience, they are not yet operating 'federal government'. This has led to the use of the term *quasi-federalism*. While the U.S. experience has reflected the cardinal principles of federalism, the fact that the adoption of the federal compromise is a response to the peculiar problems of a particular nation-state operating within a particular environment, makes differences in federal experiences inevitable. The important point is that the cardinal principles of federalism are constitutionally guaranteed and/or practised. Perhaps Ivor Duchacek hit the nail on the head when he observed that:

> Using the American measuring rods, we are, however, far from suggesting that the United States federalism should be considered the only 'true' or 'pure' one. Neither do we suggest that its birth and evolution are relevant to other countries that in the twentieth century may contemplate the adoption of a federal system. Some of the characteristics and aspects of the United States federalism are so anchored in the American soil that its experiences and lessons can hardly be transplanted elsewhere. Furthermore, its record of preserving unity with diversity is much less impressive than some textbooks on American Government would have one believe.[8]

8

The experiences which led to the adoption of federalism in the U.S. differ from those of Western Germany (after 1945), Australia, Nigeria, Switzerland and Canada. The practice of federalism in each of these countries would reflect the local settings and the peculiar nature of these countries. We shall return to this issue later.

The Military

The military, in liberal literature, is expected to be apolitical and professional, submitting itself to the supremacy of civilian rule.[9] At independence, Western liberal social scientists expected the Third World to emerge as examples of democratic polities, beyond the Western Hemisphere. Their hopes soon turned into frustrations with the spate of military interventions in politics. Again, theorists of law and order lionized the role of the military both as modernizers and as institutions of national integration and state-building.[10]

This view arose from the belief that military institutions in developing countries were the most unified or cohesive institutions. The military was also described as the most modernized state institution, and was ascribed positive qualities such as being *austere, prudent, disciplined, self-abnegating, incorruptible, puritanic and nationalistic.*[11] With the benefit of hindsight, we now know that these views emanated from myths which buttressed the Western military. We know that the military in most developing countries are not as unified or as cohesive as described, even though their internal structures may give semblances of coherence. The military in countries such as Nigeria, Burundi, and Uganda have demonstrated how clearly social cleavages, such as ethnicity, can implode into the barracks and become articulated by the military. As a result, one military regime gets over-thrown by another set of military officers.

Studies in Latin America, Africa, and Asia have demonstrated clearly that military regimes may not be the best economic managers in the state; nor are they austere.[12] Similarly, in many countries where the military intervened in order to 'eliminate corruption' and 'clean up the mess' created by politicians, its messianic political physician role has often been aborted. Often they became patients of the same vices they came to cure. Their self-abnegating and patriotic credentials have also been seriously tarnished or questioned by their performance. This is not to say that some military administrations in the Third World did not perform efficiently. In Nigeria, for instance, the military has contributed substantially to the processes of state and nation building. However, set side by side with their declared intentions, their performance in office has often fallen below expectations. Again, this varies from country to country. In Singapore, authoritarian regimes had launched that country on the path of economic development.

Given our argument that the military is not necessarily a cohesive organization in the Third World, the question arises as to how we can make general statements about the military as an institution. It is true that since January 1966 *coup d'etat* in Nigeria, the events, which followed, did not show the Nigerian military as a cohesive institution. Apart from geo-ethnic dimensions to the coups of January and July 1966, the fratricidal civil war that followed, statements and actions of some serving and retired military officers, at one time or the other, questioned the military's claim of institutional cohesiveness and patriotism. Yet, in Nigeria's forty - five years of survival as a state, the military ruled or administered the country for about thirty years. While the political pendulum may swing between the *ballot box* and the *bullet box* or *the barracks*, there has been a demonstration of some kind of institutional cohesiveness, for the military to have ruled Nigeria for so long, albeit, occasionally overthrowing fellow military rulers.

As we shall show later, in its administration of the country, the military has been fairly sensitive to Nigeria's social, political, economic and cultural environment. It has also sensitized itself to the often aggressive egalitarian and democratic values of the average Nigerian. A look at Nigeria's over thirty newspapers and myriads of magazines (even under military rule) will shock any visitor; for occasionally it is liberty turned into licentiousness. As Ali Mazrui observed of the Nigerian press, "freedom sometimes has even gone mad..."[13] Generally, Nigerian military rulers have been more sensitive to these irrepressible libertarian Nigerian traits than the civilian rulers of some democratic countries in Africa such as Kenya under Moi, not to mention countries under military rule.[14] There were many cases of intolerance of the members of the media by military rulers, but the media remained undaunted under all military regimes in the country.

The Military and Federalism

With this background, let us now discuss the relationship between military rule and federalism. In much of Western Political Science literature, federalism is regarded as incompatible with military rule. Reasons adduced for this includes the fact that military rule does not provide avenues for popular participation in plebiscitarean forms.[15] Military rulers are not elected and therefore are not accountable to the electorate.

These arguments are very valid. From the experiences of the various military administrations in Nigeria between 1966 and 1999, none of the leaders was elected. The military came to power by virtue of their monopoly over the instruments of violence. This does not belie the fact that very often many Nigerians such as students, politicians, bureaucrats and businessmen often encouraged the military to take over the reins of government and salvage the nation from the recklessness of politicians. In 1982, this writer witnessed nation-wide demonstrations by Nigerian students in which they called on the military to come back into the political arena. The utterances and actions of university lecturers, as well as those of opposition politicians at state and federal levels, were open invitations to the military to intervene in politics.

However, according to the 1960, 1963, 1979, 1989 and 1999 Constitutions of the country, the procedures for attaining political power were clearly spelt out. Thus, when the military takes over political power through a coup, it has engaged in an illegal act, no matter how messianic the motive may be. The essence of a democratic polity is that the rulers should be elected and thus made accountable. The military does not and cannot claim to be democratic.

Since military rulers are not elected, that power of accountability, which rests with the people, has been taken away from them. This becomes clearer when you get to the appointment of lieutenants of the military Head of State. Given the complexity of the Nigerian situation, all military Heads of States have had to appoint military governors for subnational states. In line with the hierarchical chain of military command, these governors are directly responsible to the Head of State and Commander-in-Chief. This also runs counter to the grain of federal principles. Finally, all military administrations in Nigeria had suspended the legislature and any other institutions for popular participation. Given this setting, a principal question arises—that of the autonomy of component units as embedded in the principle of federalism. Some of the issues, which bug the minds of analysts, include:

♦ how can the military's *hierarchical* structure be compatible with the virtually *pyramidal* structure of the federal system?

♦ how can the *autonomy* of the component units be guaranteed when they have no control over their leader? and

♦ without avenues for popular participation, how can the *people* who desire the 'union but not (necessarily) unity', have inputs into decisions which affect their lives?

We shall use the Nigerian case to respond to these basic questions and more.

Two points need to be stressed at this point. The first deals with length of military rule. Retired Major-General Joseph Garba, Nigeria's one-time Minister of External Affairs, observed that "military rule is an aberration". In Nigeria, after about thirty years of military rule, is military rule still "an aberration"? Or are Nigerians so used to the Western model of civilian supremacy that they have not bothered to ponder over the possibilities of political adaptation of the concept of 'civilian supremacy' to their own setting?

The second salient point is that while there have been arguments about the incompatibility of military rule with federal government, almost all governments in Nigeria have adopted one form or the other of 'federalism'. Even under the military, an attempt by General Ironsi to experiment with a unitary system generated violent protests in the form of communal instability, which Nigeria had never witnessed before 1966. In addition, except for the Decree No. 34 of May 24, 1966, which renamed the military regime 'National Military Government' – all leaders or heads of the central military government had insisted on being known and called as the 'Head of the Federal Military Government' (HFMG). Only General Ibrahim Babangida opted for the label, President of the Federal Republic of Nigeria.

Our argument, therefore, is that even military regimes with *mobilizational* styles and hierarchical structures of command have not been able to ignore the centrifugal forces in Nigeria's socio-political setting and the necessity of effecting a compromise between the demands of centrifugal and centripetal forces in the multinational state. The reasons for this sensitivity of the military to the ticklish and potent issues of sub-national identity and autonomy are to be found in the nature of the Nigerian society – its complexity.

We contend that participation through plebiscitarean form is not the only form of participation. As Henry Bienen[16] showed clearly in the Kenyan case study, the *Kenya African National Union* (KANU) did not offer as much avenue for participation as the regional administrative structures. The political party was moribund between elections. Thus, the mere existence of political parties does not necessarily guarantee popular participation.

There are many dimensions of participation. It may be suggested that political participation takes at least two forms. It could be *political access*, an *input* into the political system from below. People come to participate in decisions, which affect their lives—through representations, expression of opinions, and involvement in community programmes. It is essentially access to decision-making units from below. Participation may also involve anomic activities such as riots and rebellions.

Yet participation also has an output form. This is the *mobilization* of the people by government for specific activity. Thus, when the military government mobilized people for activities such as *Operation Feed the Nation* in 1976, voter registration and census exercises, it was mobilizing people for participation. The point of initiation was at the top.

Our argument is that military rule is not necessarily totally incompatible with federalism. The nature of military regimes may be hierarchical and the constitution may be so amended that you may not have a strictly federal constitution; but that does not mean you cannot have a 'federal' government. As K.C. Wheare wrote:

13

If we are looking for examples of federal government, it is not
sufficient to look at constitutions only. What matters just as much is
the practice of government.[17]

The crucial issue is the "working of the system". In Africa, after
independence, most inheritance elites were faced with the problems of
consolidation of political power at the centre. For those who wanted to
centralize political power, federalism, which also exhorted sub-national
self-determination, was an inappropriate political grid within which to
operate. Moreover, the expenses of a federal system certainly out-
weighed the administrative expenses of the unitary system of
government.

From the literature on state building, the impression is often
created that the centre can penetrate the periphery with little regard for
heterogeneity at subnational level. According to Apter,[18] a
'mobilizational system' is typified by hierarchical authority structure
and its emphasis on organization, with 'minimum accountability'. On
the other hand, a 'reconciliation system' emphasizes pluralism and the
desire to reconcile diverse interests – it 'mediates, integrates, and above
all, coordinates rather than organizes and mobilizes'.

In Nigeria, the military leaders found that a model of government
that provided for mobilization or 'politically induced change from the
centre' without regard to the interests of subnational units was
unsatisfactory in its operation, and the reaction to Decree No. 34, 1966
illustrated this.

General Yakubu Gowon, Nigeria's father of *military federalism*,
captured the reasons for the sensitivity of military rulers to the problem
of subnational identity and form of government when he told the *Ad
hoc Constitutional Conference* in Lagos on September 12, 1966:

Discounting the experience of pre-independence days, the incidents of
May last in Northern Nigeria following the tendencies to extreme
unification during the period after January 17, points to one and only
one thing, that a country as big as Nigeria and comprising such
diversity of tribes and cultures cannot be administered successfully
under unitarian form of government unless such a government is to
be enforced and maintained by some kind of dictatorship.[19]

14

Thus, in reaction to the Unitary Government Decree of General Ironsi, Gowon issued another Decree reverting Nigeria to the amended federalism under the military as existed on January 17, 1966.[20] The military's sensitivity to Nigeria's complexity and commitment to federalism can be further illustrated. Gowon believed that a unitary form of government was not suitable to Nigeria, and not only consistently declared his bias but also acted out his bias in his relations with his governors. [21] As the General once remarked:

> I was...bearing in mind the set-up of the country – the old regional set-up, the various ethnic groups in the country. Our variety was such that you could not get the best out of people under unitary system of government. You probably could, but at the expense of one group or the other or being dictatorial and by forcing certain issues. I did appreciate that you could not do that in Nigeria and get away with it.[22]

After the creation of twelve states, General Gowon again emphasized this belief in the federal compromise. "I believe in a federation with a strong centre, but with states having enough powers to manage their own affairs".[23]

Similarly, General Murtala Mohammed who succeeded Gowon was sensitive to this issue. In addressing the Constitution Drafting Committee on December 18, 1975, he declared:

> We [the Supreme Military Council Members] are committed to a Federal System of Government...[24]

His successor, General Olusegun Obasanjo, described Nigeria as a:

> ...cast iron, which had to be gently anvilled and slowly bent to prevent the breaking or doing damage to the bodywork, not to talk of the ever-present fatal damage to the ornamentor.[25]

Given this perception, Obasanjo was also committed to the Federal solution and handed over government to civilians in 1979.

General Buhari never announced a political transition programme, but ruled in the context of a *military federalism* along the line pursued

15

by his military predecessors, even if his style was markedly different. He was the Head of the Federal Military Government, with military governors posted to the states, with relative autonomy to perform their duties, even if under close supervision.

Apparently, this was one of the reasons for Buhari's ouster. On his own part, General Babangida believed that on the basis of events in Nigeria's history, Nigerians had arrived at a consensus that a *Federal solution* was a political imperative. Thus, in his address to Constitutional Assembly on May 11, 1988, he advised the Assembly not to:

> ...indulge itself in fruitless exercise of trying to alter the agreed ingredients of Nigeria's political order, such as federalism, presidentialism, the non-adoption of State religion, and the respect and observance of fundamental human rights.[26]

And in his Address to the Constitution Review Committee which had provided a draft constitution for the Constituent Assembly, President Babangida said;

> ...I wish to emphasize our firm commitment to the Presidential system of Government and Federalism.[27]

Having realized the complexity of the heterogeneous Nigerian society, the military leaders adopted a compromise solution between Apter's 'mobilization' and 'reconciliation' models. The disadvantage of the mobilization system with its emphasis on coercion and non-accountability is compensated for by the 'reconciliation' elements of the reconciliation system. Under military rule, therefore, except for the brief periods mentioned before, Nigeria has always practised one form or the other of 'federal' government, no matter how warped or adulterated.

Our argument is clearly one, which recognizes the value of the U.S. Federal experience. However, we argue that federations are formed in different ways and for varying reasons. This is where perhaps Wheare probably erred in assuming the federations would emerge from an association of states, which are in search of security. As mentioned above, (and as shown in this volume), Nigeria's experience was

16

different. Another author, Nicolas Gillet, shows that the "factors in the Swiss environment which have militated towards federation include the history of country... and geographical factors... and the obstacles set by the differences of religion and language".[28]

Similarly we argue that the federal compromise in each country would reflect its local environment and its peculiar circumstances or problems. Thus in Western Germany, the *Bundesrat* or the equivalent of the U.S. Senate is not directly elected. In fact, Laendar premiers or prime ministers and ministers represent their states in the *Bundesrat*, which is usually chaired by Laendar prime ministers in rotation. In essence this may violate the principle of autonomy or independence of component units. However, the peculiar German circumstances necessitated that adjustment. Western Germany operates a federal government and not a quasi-federal government.

It may be pertinent to recapture Wheare's words here again that if we are looking for examples of Federal Government, "it is not sufficient to look at constitutions only." What matters also is the "practice of government." In this context therefore, we suggest in this book that:

1. federalism and militarism are not necessarily incompatible bedfellows; the major differences in the operations of federalism under civilian and military regimes in Nigeria are to be found in the style and structures of administration;
2. the reasons for Nigeria's adoption of the federal compromise are historical and multidimensional;
3. if federalism is a mechanism for effecting political compromise in a multinational state, it is embedded with its own seeds of discord;
4. in Nigeria's federal structure, there is a delicate relationship between the centre's demand for control and the demand by the subnational units or states, for autonomy;
5. on the horizontal plane, echoes of the past are very much around even if heard from within different structures, and these seem to detract from the goals of national unity or integration; and
6. the future threat to the survival of Nigeria, if any, may not come from the vertical relations between the federal centre and subnational states, but from the horizontal relations among Nigerians as the centre becomes increasingly a big political prize to win, especially as the

17

crises of allocation of scarce but allocatable resources increase in tempo and in the aggressiveness of such demands.

Notes and references

1. See some other literature on federalism Carl Freiderich, *Trends of Federalism in Theory and Practice* (London: Pall Mall, 1968); Daniel J. Elazar, *The Politics of American Federalism* (Lexington Mass, -D.C. Heath, 1969); Richard Leach, *American Federalism* (1970); A.B. Akinyemi, P.D. Cole, and W. Ofonagoro (eds) *Readings on Federalism* (Lagos: Nigerian Institute of International Affairs, 1979); Ronald Watts, *Administration in Federal Systems* (London: Hutchinson Educational, 1970); James Sundquist, *Making Federalism Work* (Washington, D.C.: The Brooking Institution, 1969) and *Publius: the Journal of Federalism* (Centre for the study of Federalism, Temple University, U.S.A.); Eme Awa, *Issues of Federalism* (Benin: Ethiope Publishers, 1977); Kenneth W. Thompson (ed.) *The U.S. Constitution and Constitutionalism in Africa* (New York: University Press of America, Inc., 1989); Dan J. Elazar, *Exploring Federalism* (Tuscaloosa: The University of Alabama Press, 1987); Vincent Ostrom, *The Political Theory of a Compound Republic* (Lincoln: University of Nebraska Press, 1987); and D. Elazar, *Governing Peoples and Territories* (Philadelphia: Institute for the Study of Human Issues, 1982). J. Isawa Elaigwu and E.O. Erim, (eds.) *Foundations of Nigerian Federalism: Pre-Colonial Antecedents. Second Edition* (Jos: IGSR, 2001); J. Isawa Elaigwu and G.N. Uzoigwe (eds) *Foundations of Nigerian Federalism: 1900-1960* (Jos: IGSR, 2001). J. Isawa Elaigwu and R. Akindele (eds) *Foundations of Nigerian Federalism: 1900-1995* (Jos: IGSR, 2001).

2. Shridath Ramphal, The Commonwealth Secretary-General, "Keynote Address to the International Conference on Federalism," at the Nigerian Institute of International Affairs, Lagos. Published in A. B. Akinyemi, P. Cole, and W. Ofonagoro (eds.) *Readings on Federalism* (Lagos: N.I.I.A., 1979) pp. xiii-xv.

3. K.C. Wheare, *Federal Government* (London: Oxford University Press, 1964), p. 10.

4. *ibid.,*

5. Roland Watts, *op.cit.* p. 5.

6. Ranjit Sarkaria, *"Foreword"* in S.C. Arora (ed.) *Current Issues and Trends in Centre-State Relations: A Global View* (New Delhi: Mittal Publications, 1991), p.3.

7. See, *The Federalist Government Papers* for interesting discussions on the experience.

8. Ivor Duchacek, *Comparative Federalism: The Territorial Dimensions of Politics* (New York: Holt, Rinehart and Winston, 1970), p. 202.

9. I have argued, in J. Isawa Elaigwu, "Military Intervention in Politics: An African Perspective." *Geneve-Afrique: Journal of the Swiss Society of African Studies,* Vol. xix, No. 1 (1981), pp. 19-38, that the concept of civilian supremacy is alien to Africa.

10. See Samuel Huntington, *The Soldier and the State: The Theory of Politics of Civil-Military Relations* (New York: Vintage Books, 1957); Morris Janowitz, *The Military in the Political Development of New Nations: An Essay in Comparative Analysis* (Chicago: University Chicago Press, 1964); W.F. Gutteridge, *Military Regimes in Africa* (London: Methuen and Co. Ltd., 1975); Alfred Stepan, *The Military in Politics: Changing Patterns in Brazil* (New Jersey: Princeton University Press, 1971); Jose Nun, "A Latin American Phenomenon: The Middle-Class Coup" in *Trends in Social Science Research in Latin American Studies* (Berkeley: Institute of International Studies, University of California, 1965), pp. 55-59; Harold Z. Schiffrin (ed.) *The Military and State in Modern Asia* (Jerusalem: Jerusalem Academic Press, 1976), p. 2.

11. See. S.E. Finer, *Man on Horseback: The Role of the Military in Politics* (New York: Praegar, 1962).

12. Ali Mazrui, *Soldiers and Kinsmen: The Making of a Military Ethnocracy in Uganda* (Berkeley Hills: Sage, 1975); Samuel Decalo, *Coups and Army Rule in Africa: Studies in Military Style* (New Haven: Yale University Press, 1976). The case of competition and imprudent financial management among military rulers is often as bad as those of politicians whom they overthrew. Also see P. Huntington, "Political Change in the Third World" in Myron Weiner and Samuel P. Huntington (eds.) Understanding Political Development (Boston: Little, Brown, 1987); M. Weiner, "Political Change: Asia, African and Middle East" in Weiner and Huntington, *op.cit.* pp. 33-64; and Jorge I.

Dorminguez, "Political Change: Central America, South America, and the Carribean" in Weiner and Huntington, *op.cit.* pp. 65-102.

13. Ali A. Mazrui, "The American Constitution and the Liberal Option in Africa: Myth and Reality" in Kenneth Thompson (ed.) *The U.S. Constitution and Constitutionalism in Africa* (New York: University Press of America, 1990), p. 14. Professor Mazrui observed:

...I heard things said by people in power in Nigeria under Shagari that you wouldn't normally hear elsewhere. Freedom sometimes has even gone mad, not just calling the President a pirate, a thief and a robber, which he was called, but sometimes talking in terms of outright revolution.

14. See O. Obasanjo, *Not My Will* (Ibadan: Ibadan University Press, 1990) pp.44- 45 - for an interesting insight, "On another occasion, when President Mobutu sent a ministerial delegation to me to complain on vicious attacks on him by the Nigerian press and requested me to control the Nigerian press. The Nigerian Tribune gave me a perfect answer. That day the Nigerian Tribune came up with a very rude and vicious criticism of my administration on its front page with a caricature of and an unpleasant comment on myself ...I gave a copy to him to give to his President in reply to his complaint. I could not have provided a better reply to President Mobutu who is very sensitive about press." (p. 44-45).

15. See the typical definition: "A federal state is one in which sovereignty, supreme political power, is split between a central federal government and local or provincial governments which thus maintain some degree of independence. In practice the term is not usually applied to a federal state, which may have these characteristics, but to states in which democratic elections are held at both levels."Nicholas Gillet, *The Swiss Constitution: Can it be Exported?* (Proistol: Yes Publications, 1989), p. 15.

16. Henry Bienen, *Kenya: The Politics of Participation and Control* (Princeton, N.J: Princeton University Press, 1974). Bienen demonstrated clearly that while Kenya had a political party, it was the bureaucracy and the regional administration, which offered channels and opportunity of participation for Kenyans.

17. K. C. Wheare, *op.cit.* p. 20.

18. David Apter, *The Politics of Modernization* (Chicago: University of Chicago Press, 1965), pp. 359-421.

19. Federal Republic of Nigeria, 'Ad Hoc Constitutional Proposals: Verbatim Report' (National Hall, Lagos, September 1, 1966), p. 2 (Unpublished Mimeograph). The 'May last' incident refers to the May riots of 1966 in the Northern Region, essentially (and ostensibly)

against the Unification Decree No. 34, 1966 introduced by General Ironsi.

20. This was contained in Decree No. 52, 1966.

21. See an account of this in J. Isawa Elaigwu, *Gowon: The Biography of a Soldier-Statesman* (Ibadan: West Books, 1986).

22. My interview with General Gowon, July 1978.

23. General Gowon's interview with *Drum* (Lagos) March 1968.

24. Address by General Murtala Mohammed, Head of the Federal Military Government and Commander-in-Chief of the Armed Forces, to the Constitution Drafting Committee, December 18, 1975.

25. O.Obasanjo, *Not My Will* (Ibadan: Ibadan University Press, 1990), pp. 130-131.

26.*Inaugural Address by General Ibrahim Badamasi Babangida to the Members of the Constitution Assembly at Abuja on Wednesday, May 11, 1988.* p.4.

27.Federal Government of Nigeria, *Portrait of A New Nigeria: Selected Speeches of IBB* (Precision Press) p.36.

28.Nicholas Gillet, *op.cit,* p.18.

2

NIGERIA UNDER COLONIAL RULE

In September 1957, the Prime Minister of Nigeria, Alhaji Sir Abubakar Tafawa Balewa, told the House of Representatives:

> I am pleased to see that we have all agreed that the Federal system is, under the present conditions, the only basis on which Nigeria can remain united. We must recognize our diversity and the peculiar conditions under which the different tribal communities live in this country. To us in Nigeria therefore unity in diversity is a source of great strength, and we must do all in our power to see that this Federal system of Government is strengthened and maintained.[1]

How and why did Nigerian leaders come to accept federalism as the "only sure basis on which Nigeria can remain united"? Were they striving to attain a model of government propounded by some political theorists, such as Wheare?[2] Or was federalism chosen because of the empirical situation in Nigeria?

In this chapter we show how the colonial history of the area, which later came to be known as Nigeria, affected that country's political history; and how federalism as a form of government in Nigeria was the result of social forces at work within that country. It was not an attempt to realize the ideals of a model of government; it was a compromise solution to some of the political problems, which emerged in the terminal period of colonial rule.

Similarly, the creation of additional subnational units in Nigeria was the result of centrifugal and centripetal forces in the country. It may be argued that the creation of additional subnational states and the adoption of federalism in Nigeria are interrelated and spring from the same source: Nigeria's ethnic pluralism and the mutual fears and suspicions of domination of one group by another in a competitive setting. It was this fear of domination and lack of mutual trust which led to the adoption of a federal system of government, and the issue may be better understood if one looks at Nigeria's political

22

history. How did the pattern of colonial administration in Nigeria affect her political development?

Amalgamation and Ambivalent Integration, 1914 – 1946

The "present unity of Nigeria, as well as its disunity, is in part a reflection of the form and character of the common government—the British superstructure – and the changes it has undergone since 1900".[3] By 1900, what later came to be known as Nigeria comprised three colonial territories under the umbrella of British colonial administration, but administered separately, receiving orders direct from the metropolis: London. These were the Colony of Lagos and what came to be known as the Protectorates of Southern Nigeria and Northern Nigeria.

In 1906, the Colony of Lagos and the Protectorate of Southern Nigeria were unified under a single administrator. In 1914, the Colony of Lagos and the Protectorate of Northern and Southern Nigeria were amalgamated as the Colony and Protectorate of Nigeria.[4] In 1939, Nigeria was divided into the Colony of Lagos, and the Northern, Eastern and Western Groups of Provinces, with each group of provinces having a Chief Commissioner who was responsible to the Governor in Lagos.

If the amalgamation of 1914 was aimed at creating a political fusion of the North and the South, it did not have the objective of building a unified State for the purposes of establishing an indigenous government. In this, British colonialism was not unique; many colonial regimes did not often give thought to the granting of independence to their subjects and as such, gave little thought to the form of government and administration which would best suit the people in a particular territory. Thus, between 1914 and 1946, very little effort was made to integrate Northern and Southern Provinces. They were administered separately, and the colonial officials in these administrations zealously fought to keep each group of provinces separate. This led to the quip that "if all Africans were to leave Nigeria, the Northern and Southern administrators would go to war".[5] Except for the amalgamation of some essential departments, such as customs, education, railways, police, and the prisons, little effort was made at integration.

Moreover, until the introduction of the Richards Constitution of 1946, which provided for a central Legislative Council, there was no central legislature in which the people of this territory could meet and deliberate on issues affecting the country as a whole. The Northern Provinces had no representation in the central legislature until 1947. Thus, the amalgamation of Nigeria in 1914 did not really lead to an effective integration of the colonial territory called Nigeria. The colonial administrators were ambivalent about such integration.[6] This separate political development of the North and the South must have been suitable for colonial administration but was not useful in the development of a State and a Nation, especially given the context of Nigeria's multi-ethnicity.

The Emergence of Federalism in Nigeria, 1946-1960

From Unitarism to Quasi-Federalism in Nigeria, 1947-1954

The Richards Constitution legally established three regions: North, East, and West. The constitution provided for a central legislature and regional legislatures (unicameral for Western and Eastern Regions, and bicameral for the North).[7] While the constitution for three regions took into account the diversity of Nigerian people, it was basically unitary in nature. Political power was concentrated in the hands of the Governor in Lagos, though the size of Nigeria and the local political differences from one region to the other, made it necessary for power to be devolved to the Lt. Governors in the regions and their subordinate officials.

The Richards Constitution drew considerable opposition from many Nigerian nationalists, particularly the National Council for Nigeria and Cameroon (NCNC) under the leadership of Herbert Macaulay and Nnamdi Azikiwe. . This party organized protests and toured parts of the country to educate the public about some of the flaws in the constitution, and to express objections to it. . Basically, there were three main objections to the Richards Constitution by Nigerian nationalists:

24

1) the imposition of the constitution from above without due consultation with the Nigerian people; 2) the ambiguous role of chiefs in politics (nationalists were suspicious of chiefs whom they regarded as colonial government officials and anti-nationalists groups); and 3) the number of political units created in Nigeria.[8] Among criticisms from individuals, Awolowo's was more systematic and vigorous. He called for a federal system of government to allow various groups to develop at their own pace, and opposed the unitary elements in the constitution which, according to him, did not reflect Nigeria's ethnic pluralism.[9]

The opposition to the Richards Constitution necessitated a review. In this regard, Sir John MacPherson, the new Governor of Nigeria, undertook elaborate consultations at different levels of government in a way that had never been done in Nigeria prior to that period.

The result of this was the MacPherson Constitution of 1951. This constitution gave more autonomy to the regions. Bicameral legislatures were provided for in the Western and Northern Regions, while the Eastern Region was to have a unicameral legislature. Regional legislatures were empowered to send delegates to the central legislature, and they could have their bills vetoed by the central legislature. At the centre, twelve Nigerians became members of the Council of Ministers, with six members of the council being officials of the colonial government. The House of Representatives of 142 members was to have 136 Nigerians.

It may be argued that up to this point, Nigeria was operating a unitary form of government. From 1951–1954, a quasi-federal form of government was established within the colonial framework. But once the regions had been created with powers gradually devolved to them and the prospects for self-government became only a matter of time, emergent nationalist identities crystallized around the regions.[10]

The very prospect of decolonization in Nigeria led to tensions among groups who competed for power in order to i) protect their group interests against possible invasion by other groups in the competitive process; and ii) take over the reins of power from the colonial government and control the dispensation of allocatable resources and patronage. This leads us to a brief discussion of emergent political parties and the growth of parochial ethnic or ethnoregional nationalism.

Political Parties and Ethnoregional Politics[11]

The first political organization resembling a political party in Nigeria was the Nigerian National Democratic Party (NNDP), founded in Lagos by Herbert Macaulay in 1923. It was basically a Lagos-centreed party with no claims for immediate independence or self-government. In 1934, however, a group of "educated young radicals" formed the Lagos Youth Movement (LYM), and in 1936, this became the Nigerian Youth Movement (NYM). At this point, Nnamdi Azikiwe, (an Ibo) trained in the United States had returned to Nigeria after some years in Ghana (then the Gold Coast) as an editor of a newspaper. Azikiwe joined the NYM.[12]

In a very short time, the NYM became drowned in ethnic and personality clashes. In 1941, Azikiwe broke with the NYM over an intra-NYM election tussle between Mr. E. Ikoli and Mr. Akinsanya, which he claimed, was influenced by ethnic rivalries. Together with Mr. Herbert Macaulay, Azikiwe (popularly known as Zik) formed the National Council for Nigeria and Cameroons (NCNC) in 1944. At this point in time, the support of NCNC came mainly from Yoruba Nationalists in Lagos and from non-Yoruba youths. It was not an ethnic party.

Meanwhile, Obafemi Awolowo had formed the *Egbe Omo Oduduwa,* a Yoruba cultural group in London in 1945. This cultural group formed the basis of the Action Group (AG) party in 1951. While members of the *Egbe Omo Oduduwa* were also members of the party, the cultural group was not. The AG was not exclusively Yoruba in composition; it drew upon the support of some Ibo-speaking members of Western Region. As members of the NYM, Azikiwe and Awolowo had been opposed to each other, up to the point where Azikiwe resigned from the movement. In a matter of time, the AG became the spokesman for pan-Yoruba nationalism, while looking for support among minority groups in other regions.[13]

Nnamdi Azikiwe became the President of the NCNC after the death of Herbert Macaulay. His membership of the *Ibo State Union* (led by Z.C. Obi, a wealthy Nnewi merchant in Port-Harcourt) gave the impression that he was fanning Ibo interests, though his party remained basically multi-ethnic in composition. In Northern Nigeria, a late-starter in political organization, the formation of the *Jam'iyyar Mutanen Arewa* (the Northern Peoples' Congress or NPC) as cultural group in 1949, was a reaction to nationalist awakening in the Southern part of Nigeria. Its reluctance to transform into a political party had resulted in a splinter group, which in 1949 became a political party known as the Northern Elements Progressive Union (NEPU), under the leadership of Aminu Kano. It was basically anti-traditionalist and was a party of commoners in the predominantly Hausa-Fulani area under aristocratic Native Authorities. It wanted to get the North to participate in Nigerian politics and to protect its interests against invasion by Southern groups.[14] It was therefore ironic that finding itself in opposition in the Northern Region and short of funds, NEPU allied itself with NCNC, a basically Southern-based party.

An interesting trend at this time was the appeal to ethnic loyalty and the crystallization of ethnic identity around the regions. After the 1951 elections, the AG became the dominant party in the West (with a strong NCNC opposition) in the predominantly Yoruba Western Region, while the NCNC controlled the government of the predominantly Ibo Eastern Region. The NPC soon became the party of the dominant Hausa-Fulani Northern Region. Thus, gradually, Nigerian political parties became identified with particular regions and often appealed to the ethnic groups in those regions for support in their competition with parties from other regions. In part, Azikiwe's lack of a regional base in Nigeria's ethnoregional politics had led to his exclusion from the Western legislature. That he returned to his home region in the East later was a realization of the ethnoregional basis of Nigerian Nationalism.

Furthermore, the Yoruba-Ibo rivalry that ensued in the South only accentuated the pace of aggressive ethnic nationalism. Statements reflecting inter-ethnic animosity were often made with reckless abandon. One of such statements was made by a member of the *Egbe Omo Oduduwa*, who said:

> We were bunched together by the British who named us Nigeria. We never knew the Ibos, but since we knew them we have been friendly

27

and neighbourly...we have tolerated enough from a class of Ibos and addle-brained Yorubas who have mortgaged their thinking caps to Azikiwe and hirelings.[15]

This statement was a reflection of Yoruba feeling: an appeal to members of that group to organize so that "Yorubas will not be relegated to the background in the future".[16]

The election of Azikiwe as the President of the Ibo Union and his speech at the 1949 Ibo State Union Conference may be regarded as an appeal to his ethnic bedfellows for support in the emerging Yoruba-Ibo competition for jobs in the modernizing sector. In his speech, Azikiwe had told the conference that:

it would appear that the God of Africa had specifically created the Ibo nation to lead the children of Africa from the bondage of the age... The martial prowess of the Ibo nation at all stages of human history has enabled them not only to conquer others but also to adapt themselves to the rule of the preserver... The Ibo nation cannot shirk its responsibility. [17]

No matter the intention of Azikiwe, the speech could not have been more ill-timed. It came at the height of Yoruba-Ibo competition and was quickly used to dismiss Azikiwe's pan-Nigerian claims.

Once nationalists turned to their ethnic bedfellows to canvass for support in competing with members of other ethnic groups, Nigerian Nationalism became interpreted as ethnic nationalism. This trend continued because of the fragile sense of identity of Nigerians with the concept of the Nigerian Nation. Thus, Awolowo described Nigeria as a mere geographic expression. "There are no 'Nigerians' in the same sense as there are 'English', 'Welsh', or 'French',"[19] A similar statement was made by Alhaji Abubakar Tafawa Balewa, the deputy leader of the NPC, when he told the Legislative Council in 1948:

"Since 1914 the British Government has been trying to make Nigeria into one country, but the Nigerian people themselves are historically different in their backgrounds, in their religious beliefs and customs and do not show themselves any signs of willingness to unite... Nigerian unity is only a British intention for this country".[19]

In the absence of any strong sense of unity, the process of decolonization created a feeling of suspicion and fear as ethnic groups interacted with one another in a competitive process. Emergent identities crystallized around the regions as effective units for competition. Intra-regional ethnic differences were often "driven under the carpet" to present a homogeneous front for competition with other regional groups, and political parties assumed regional labels (consciously or unconsciously). As Aminu Kano (one of the participants in the constitutional conferences) told the writer:

> I think regional grouping was a result of sudden awakening. I think there was a period of sudden awakening in Nigeria, but the awakening was misdirected. That is to say, it was a crude form of interpretation of awakening... The sudden realization of 'we can take power' resulted in ethnic grouping and therefore regionalism.[20]

If the very process of decolonization spurred regionalism, regionalism also determined the form of government Nigeria was to have: a federal system grafted on mutual fear and suspicion among Nigerian groups.

Federalism and the Politics of Compromise

The sense of distrust of Nigerian leaders for one another and the existence of centrifugal forces in the country were amply demonstrated in the constitutional conferences of the 1950s. A few issues will serve to elaborate this point.

In 1950, the Northern members of the conference threatened to secede unless the North was granted an equal number of representatives in the House of Representatives as the Southern Regions in accordance with "democratic principles"[21] of government. After much deliberation, the North was given 68 seats, the West 34, and the East 34 — a compromise solution in order to maintain a single country. There was no doubt that the Northern delegation wanted to maintain numerical superiority over the South to counterbalance their fear of domination of skills by the more educated Southern peoples.

The 1953 constitutional conference demonstrated the persistence of centrifugal forces in Nigeria's process of decolonization. The Western delegation threatened to opt out of Nigeria if Lagos and the Colony

29

were not merged with the Western Region[22]. Given the trend towards greater autonomy of the regions, the two other regions did not look favorably at the prospect of a region controlling the port of Lagos. Only a compromise solution which allowed for the merger of the colony with the Western Region and the maintenance of Lagos as federal territory saved a serious confrontation between the colonial administration and the Western Region delegates (particularly after Awolowo's telegram to the Colonial Secretary).[23]

The mutual fear of one another diluted the demands of some nationalists for a more unitary form of government or a federal system with a very strong centre. The regions opted for greater autonomy with the promise of self-government and the subsequent removal of colonial umpireship. This was demonstrated by the Northern delegation's refusal of Chief Anthony Enahoro's proposal for independence in 1956. The North was afraid of independence in 1956 against the background of the wide educational gap between the North and the Southern Regions, which it feared would only give the South the opportunity to dominate the North. As Ahmadu Bello put it while explaining his opposition to self-government in 1956:

> We in the North are working very hard towards self-government although we were late in assimilating Western education... With things in their present state in Nigeria, the Northern Region does not intend to accept the invitation to commit suicide.[24]

The North opted for self-government "as soon as practicable". This decision by the Northern delegation alienated many Southerners who derided the delegation outside the Hall, after the conference, and on their way home. The Kano riots of 1953 were directly related to this deteriorating relationship between the North and the South.

A federal system of government "is the result of a compromise between centrifugal and centripetal forces. It rests on a peculiar attitude on the part of the people of the federating units who desire union but not unity".[25] Nigerian leaders demonstrated their desire for "union but not unity" by opting for a federal system of government. The 1954 Constitution only legalized this feeling.

30

Under the 1954 Constitution, a federal system within the colonial framework came into existence. The regions were given more autonomy in decision-making. Not only had regional assemblies sprung up, regional bureaucracies had also become established. Even the Marketing Board became regionalized. The regions maximized their autonomy at the expense of the centre, which was still under colonial control, though Nigerian ministers had become members of the Council of Ministers with the introduction of a *diarchy* in 1952.

By 1956, the three major leaders had become grafted in their respective regions, which had increasingly become centres of power. Nnamdi Azikiwe had returned to the Eastern Region as Premier; Awolowo was Premier of the Western Region; while Ahmadu Bello took on the title of the Chief Minister of Northern Nigeria. Secure in the regions, the leaders jealously guarded any erosion of regional powers; even Nnamdi Azikiwe, who had supported a strong centre, equivocated.

However, in 1957, the role of colonial administrators became increasingly supervisory as Nigeria passed through the terminal colonial period. The central legislature became a parliament, while the Prime Minister (who came from the majority party, the NPC) formed his cabinet. Regional representatives to the central legislature were no longer elected indirectly but directly.[26] In this same year, Western and Eastern regions attained self-government while self-government in the North was delayed until 1959—a reflection of the differential pattern of social mobilization among groups in Nigeria.

Thus far, we have seen the centrifugal forces at work in Nigeria and the adoption of the federal system as a compromise solution in Nigeria's political evolution. However, the aggressive ethnoregionalism between 1951 and 1959 gave a false impression of homogeneous regions. The regions were by no means homogeneous units, as each had a number of vocal and politically active minority groups. The North's largest groups were the Hausa, Kanuri, and Fulani. But there were over 100 other ethnic groups in the region, most notably the non-Muslim groups in the Middle Belt, including the Tiv, Idoma, Berom, Northern Yoruba in Ilorin and Kabba divisions, the Igala, Igbira, and others.

In the East, the Ibo formed the major ethnic group. But there were other vocal minorities such as the Ogoja, Efik, Ibibio and Ijaw. Similarly, the West was dominated by the Yoruba in population, but there were minority groups such as the Edo, Itsekiri, Urhobo, Ika-Ibos, Ijaw and many other smaller groups.

Thus, if the major ethnic groups used the regions to protect their interests, the various minority groups opted to stay out of those regions in order to protect their interests against domination by the major regional ethnic groups. Clearly Nigeria's multi-ethnicity not only raised the issue of the form of government (federal or unitary) suitable for the country, but also the appropriate number of sub-national units required in order to cope with aggressive ethnic competition. The fears of minority groups of domination by major ethnic groups led to increasing demands for separate political units within Nigeria as independence drew near. This is our next focus, and it underlies the demands for the creation of additional subnational units in later years.

The Politics of Minority Participation

The fears of domination by minority ethnic groups emanated from 1) the multi-ethnicity of Nigeria, 2) the size and nature of composition of subnational political units, and 3) the desire by each group to protect its interests as political power passed from the British to Nigerians. The demand for changes in the size and number of political units in Nigeria may be traced back to the 1940s. It is probably fair to say that behind these demands lies:

> the desire of the generality of Nigerians to crystallize a political union which would have a central authority to govern and to protect the whole country while recognizing the dissimilarities in language and culture among its diverse elements. This desire aims at a balanced federation, which is cooperative but ensures that no linguistic group would be able to dominate any other groups.[27]

In 1943, Nnamdi Azikiwe proposed the division of Nigeria into eight units within a federal framework of government.[28] But the Richards Constitution of 1946 established three regions and drew opposition from various nationalists. Among its bitter critics was

Awolowo, who in 1947 suggested the division of Nigeria into ten units,[29] along ethnic and linguistic lines. The NCNC had in 1948, (in its *Freedom Charter*) argued for ethnic groups as the basis for the federation. In response to this, the Ibo Union changed its name to *Ibo State Union* "to organize Ibo linguistic groups in a political unit".[30] Other ethnic groups responded by forming their own union, such as *Edo National Union* and the *Warri National Union*. Of all ethnic associations in Nigeria, the *Ibibio State Union* was the oldest.

However, it was the implementation of the 1951 Constitution and the prospects of regional and national self-government which:

> ...accelerated the drift towards subgroup nationalism and tribalism. Educated Nigerians who aspired to fill the new positions of power and status opened up to Nigerians by that constitution realized that their most secure base of support would be the people of their own group. The indirect electoral system strengthened this realization... In the struggle that ensued, tribalism was the dominant note; but when appealing to the people for support, the competing parties strove to out do each other in the use of nationalist slogans.[31]

Thus, in 1951, a movement for the creation of the Midwest State (comprising Benin and Delta Provinces) in the Western Region began, under Chief Anthony Enahoro. The demand continued through 1953; and in 1955, a resolution was passed through the Western House of Assembly supporting the creation of the "Midwest State".[32]

Similar demands were being made for the creation of the "Middle-Belt Region" in Northern Nigeria. In 1950, David Lot founded the Middle Zone League (MZL) to unite the people (Berom, Tiv, Idoma, Igala, Northern Yoruba, Nupe, Jukun and others) in the Middle Belt area. In 1953, under the pressure of the NCNC, the Middle Belt People's Party (MBPP) was formed to demand a separate Middle Belt State from Northern Nigeria. In 1955, the MZL and MBPP formed the United Middle Belt Congress (UMBC).

Meanwhile, in the Eastern Region, the Calabar, Ogoja, and Rivers Provinces had started demanding a separate Calabar-Ogoja-Rivers (COR) State.[33] They protested against domination by the Ibo and neglect by Eastern Region Government in the distribution of amenities.

An interesting aspect of minority politics of participation was the role played by the three major political parties and their leaders: the NCNC, AG, and NPC. The NPC had a clean-cut policy of a "one North, one people, irrespective of religion, rank, or tribe". It opposed the splitting up of any part of the North and embarked on a policy of *provincialization*, that is, devolving more regional decision-making authority to the provinces. In response to Southern fears about Northern domination, it suggested the fusion of the two Southern Regions as a solution to this fear of domination.[34]

The Action Group had supported the creation of a "Midwestern State" in 1955, but only on condition that the Yoruba elements in Benin and Delta Provinces agreed to it. This was a virtual veto, because the exclusion of these Yoruba people from a new "Midwest State" clearly undercut the argument for the viability of the remaining section as a state.[35] On the other hand, in 1953-54, the AG encouraged the separation of Southern Cameroons from the Eastern Region and cooperated with the Cameroon National Congress to realize it.[36] In 1953, Awolowo proposed the division of Nigeria into nine states: four in the Northern Region; two in the Western and three in the Eastern.[37]

In 1955, the AG called for the merger of the Yoruba in Ilorin and Kabba Provinces in Northern Nigeria with their linguistic kins in the West. Hence, after the Constitutional Conference in London in 1957, the UMBC and the AG "came to an understanding". The Action Group promised support to UMBC, which agreed to exclude Ilorin and Kabba divisions from their proposed State.[38] In the East, the party urged the creation of Calabar-Ogoja-Rivers State.

In the same vein, the NCNC played politics with minority participation. In the North, it urged the MBPP to demand an autonomous Middle Belt Region in 1953. Azikiwe and the NCNC supported the creation of "Midwest State" from the Western Region. In his electioneering campaign in 1957, Azikiwe, as the Premier of the Eastern Region, declared his belief in the right of minorities (including Calabar-Ogoja-Rivers Provinces) to self-determination.[39] Election fever hardly evaporated before Azikiwe changed his mind, in the light of the AG support for the creation of a COR-State from Eastern Nigeria. In October of 1957, Azikiwe declared that the situation in the Eastern Region was exceptional and that the East "can no longer stand

34

dismemberment as a sacrifice either for administrative convenience or for national unity".[40] Thus, by the 1957 Constitutional Conference in London, it was clear that the new leaders in the regions were opposed to the creation of states. It would seem that arguments with regard to the viability of new states were just rationalizations for positions already taken by a majority of Nigerian leaders.[41] They had come to see the regions as the most effective platforms for ethnoregional competition.

The Willink Commission, 1957-1958

In the light of increasing demands by minority groups for the settlement of the issues of the creation of additional states before independence, the focus of the 1957 Constitutional Conference in London changed. Whereas Nigerian leaders had gone to London with the hope of settling finally the issue of independence, the British Colonial Office succeeded in deflecting the focus to the issues of minority participation. This was ironic because the British government did not want to get itself saddled with the problem of creating additional states in Nigeria before independence. But the issue provided an excuse to delay the granting of independence in 1958.

In fact, the British government's opposition to the creation of states came out in its declaration that even if additional states were to be created, not more than one state would be created in each region.[42] A commission was therefore appointed to look into the fears of minority groups. Again, the terms of reference of this commission, chaired by Sir Henry Willink, illustrated British opposition to creation of additional states. The commission was appointed with the following terms of reference:

> 1. to ascertain the facts about the fears of minorities in any part of Nigeria and to propose means of allaying those fears whether well or ill-founded;
> 2. to advise what safeguards should be included for this purpose in the Constitution of Nigeria;
> 3. if, but only if, no other solution seems to the Commission to meet the case, then as a last resort, to make detailed

recommendations for the creation of one or more new States, and in that case:

a) to specify the precise area to be included in such State or States;

b) to recommend the Governmental and Administrative structure most appropriate for it;

c) to assess whether any State recommended would be viable from an economic and administrative point of view and what the effect of its creation would be on the Region or Regions from which it would be created and on the Federation.[43]

On November 23, 1957, the commission arrived in Nigeria to begin its public sittings in each region. These ended on April 12, 1958.[44] Thereafter it compiled a report, which was handed over to the Colonial Secretary.

a) Minority Fears and Grievances

The Willink Commission visited all the existing three regions and submitted its report on some of the basic fears and grievances of minority groups. As the commission noted, it was

> ...generally the object of the party giving evidence to persuade us of the necessity of a new state rather than to press for any form of constitutional safe-guard; this led to the presentation of a complex case in which not only fears for the future but existing grievances were indicated, usually with the implication that what was uncomfortable today was likely to become intolerable tomorrow.[45]

Each regional minority expressed the fear that independence would make it difficult for *autocratic regional governments* to be changed because of their dependence on the votes of majority ethnic groups. In the West, minorities feared AG dependence on a Yoruba majority; in the North, minorities expressed anxiety about Hausa-Fulani domination through the NPC; while minority groups in the East feared Ibo domination through the NCNC.

There were also *social fears and grievances*. Fears were expressed in the West about a "deliberate intention of obliterating the separate language, culture, and institutions of the Midwest..."[46] Similarly, complaints were made in the Northern Region by minority groups about Hausa language and its teaching in schools. The use of contemptuous phrases to describe minority groups was also mentioned.

Minority groups also expressed anxiety about discrimination in the economic field. Minority groups in the West complained about the regional government's concentration of public investment or finance on cocoa (the main cash crop of Yoruba areas) to the detriment of rubber and timber – the main cash crop of the Midwest. In the East, there were minority areas – particularly Efik and Ibibio. The Ibo were also accused of non-observance of local customs in market-places.

Another source of suspicion and fear among minorities was *discrimination in public posts and provision of public services.* The "Midwest" minorities complained about negligence by the government of the Western Region in the provision of roads, schools, hospitals, and water supplies. The same complaints were made in the East by minorities from Rivers, Calabar and Ogoja Provinces, and by the Middle Belt peoples in the Northern Region. However, while minority groups in the East and West expressed fears about discrimination in the recruitment into public offices, that was not the case in the Northern Region. Actually, the Middle Belt peoples supplied most of the skilled manpower for the Northern Civil Service because of their headstart in Western education through Christian missionary schools. In fact, this was one of the reasons for the "dilution" of the strength of support for the creation of states in the North. Many educated people from the minorities (unlike in the Eastern and Western Regions) did not experience discrimination in recruitment into the Civil Service of the Northern Region, which was the main employment agency. Thus, their sense of alienation from the Northern Regional Government was less than their fellow minorities in the two Southern Regions. The desire for new states in the North was often diluted by the fact that the minorities dominated the Civil Service in the region, and therefore some of the educated elements who could have led the crusade for the creation of additional states became lukewarm. They had vested interests in the Northern establishment as compared to the civil services of a new state about which they were unsure. Moreover, there were efforts by the ruling dominant groups in the Northern Region to co-opt people from the minority rather than to alienate them.

The fifth set of grievances of minority groups dealt with *changes in the legal system* in the regions. In the Eastern Region, the minority groups opposed the law (Sections 3 and 4 of the Customary Courts of Law, 1956), which gave the Minister the power to "appoint, dismiss, or suspend" County or District Courts. Such control of courts created apprehension among minorities. In the Northern Region, the vague distinction between the executive and the judiciary in the Native Authority set-up made the minorities uneasy about the future. Moreover, there were complaints about the propriety of trying non-Muslims in Muslim courts and according to Muslim law.

The *maintenance of public order and individual rights* in the regions accounts for the sixth grievance of minorities. In the Northern Region, minority groups questioned the impartiality of Native Authority Police and Alkali Courts on the political scene. Emirs' bodyguards were mentioned as one of the instruments of intimidation to compel respect for the Emir's person and office, and to prevent political criticism. Prisons were also used, it was claimed, to harass and intimidate people. Prisoners were ill-treated in Native Authority Prisons, particularly if the prisoners were from the opposition party and were in jail for the criticism of the established Native Authority.

Similar complaints of intimidation and victimization through the use of "strong-arm groups" in the name of public order were reported about Eastern and Western Regional governments. Local Government police and local courts, according to the commission's report, "as instruments of policy are an important factor in the fear, which were found to be widespread, that a government of the future might have no intention of permitting criticism or giving place to a rival party unless expelled from office by force."[47] In the Eastern Region, the activities of the *Zikist National Vanguard* amounted as it was claimed, to an intimidation of opposition political parties. In response, the COR-State Movement formed its own militant branch.

A seventh minority complaint in the regions related to the role of *traditional rulers* and the relationship between *Native Authorities* (local governments) and the regional government. There were accusations in the West that in places where the local government was in sympathy with the opposition in the Regional House, the government took actions to win over such councils, or where this was impossible, obstructed the wishes of local councils entirely. In the East, minority groups complained about the regional government's insufficient attention to local chiefs (the Ibo had no history of great chiefs, except in Onitsha and a few areas). They feared a "tendency of the present government, which would no doubt be accentuated later, to centralize powers of local government."[48] It was a fear of regional government's erosion of local autonomy in self-government system reforms.

In the North, there were complaints in non-Muslim areas which formed part of Muslim Emirates about the Emir's appointment of Chiefs for them contrary to their traditions (as in Ilorin and Southern Kaduna). There were also complaints that chiefs and emirs who acted as judges in some courts were too closely identified with the government to be impartial in the dispensation of justice.

Finally, there were expressions of fears by *religious minorities*. In the Northern Region, fears were expressed regarding the future by Christian bodies, which "stated clearly that they did not wish for political separation: they did express the hope that the new constitution would embody a statement on human rights which would give minorities the freedom to practise their religion and which would specifically lay down that there should be no obstacle to a person changing his religion."[49] The government of the North did bring pressure on chiefs to change their religion from Christianity to Islam. To a lesser degree, there were complaints about religious intolerance in the Western Region, as well.

Thus, in general, fears by minorities were in anticipation of what would happen after independence if they remained in the existing political framework of three regions. Needless to say, all the regional governments denied many of the above allegations as sources of fears. For our purposes, the above expression of fears by minority groups is important because they explain the demands for the creation of additional subnational units in order to protect their interest. It is important to note that political, economic, social and cultural forces were at play in the demands for the creation of additional states in Nigeria. It was not an attempt to meet an ideal structure of government, on the theoretical level of analysis. We shall take a brief look at proposals of states to be created, and then at the recommendations of the committee.

b) *The Proposals for New States*

In each region, the commission "found either a minority or a group of minorities who described fears and grievances which they felt would be more intense when the present restraints were removed and who suggested as a remedy, a separate state or states."[50] The committee received suggestions for the creation of about fifteen states, but below we shall discuss only the major ones: in the Western, Eastern and Northern Regions.

i) The Western Region and Creation of New States

There were suggestions for the creation of mainly four new states in the Western Region. In the Yoruba-speaking area, there were agitations for the creation of Central Yoruba State (Oyo and Ibadan Provinces), and an Ondo Central State (Ondo Province only). The commission rejected these suggestions because there were no "minorities of permanent nature" here and because most of the agitations were based on AG-NCNC conflicts and not minority ethnic group fears. The suggestion for a Lagos and Colony State was also rejected because it represented "no discernible minority interest."

The fourth and most controversial case was that for the creation of the new Midwestern State. While there were minorities of a "permanent nature" here, controversies arose over what areas should constitute the state. The *Midwest State Movement* suggested that the "Midwest State" include Benin and Delta Provinces, with boundary adjustments to include Ijagba and Sobe in the use of two criteria for the creation of states:

1) language and ethnic homogeneity, and 2) popular support or opposition by the mass of the population.

On the basis of the first criterion of ethnic homogeneity, the AG suggested that Ibo-speaking peoples of Asaba and Agbor should be added to the Eastern Region: the Ijaws west of the Niger should join their kinsmen in the East and the two minorities with Yoruba dialect (Akoko-Edo of Afemmai and the Itsekiri of Warri) should remain in the Western Region. This also implies that the Ilorin and Kabba Yoruba of

40

the North should be merged with Yoruba West. On the basis of the second criterion, the Action Group suggested the exclusion of Ishan and Afemmai divisions from the proposed Midwestern State because of their opposition to the Midwestern State idea. If accepted, what remained of the Midwest could hardly form a State.

Hence the commission concluded that "even if public opinion were taken as the sole criterion, it would not be justifiable to set up a Midwest State in the form demanded by the Midwest minorities and others whose enthusiasm was extremely moderate."[51] A Midwest State of Edo-speaking people would not be viable and could hardly compete with other regions, and a "separate state would accentuate and underline tribal division," reported the commission.

ii) *The Eastern Region and Creation of New States*

Four new states were proposed in the Eastern Region: the Ogoja State, Cross-River State, Calabar-Ogoja-Rivers State (COR-State), and the Rivers State. The NCNC government expressed no opposition to the creation of additional states as long as these were done in other regions and were based on four principles. These principles for the creation of new states were:

a) the principle of self-determination (majority support for separate state);
b) the principle of relative ethnic homogeneity;
c) the principle of geographical contiguity of such new state; and
d) the principle of viability – that each state, as nearly as possible, should be a self-contained economic and administrative unit.

There was a proposal for an Ogoja State to coincide with Ogoja Province. The commission rejected this idea because of the presence of Ibo minorities in such a state, which would create similar problems to those under discussion. The suggestion for a Cross-River State was rejected because of little evidence in the support of such a state. The commission agreed that the Rivers Province was neglected by a government "which did not understand their needs". It objected, however, to the creation of a Rivers State because (1) of the separation of Ogoni from Brass and Degema by water; (2) Port Harcourt was (regarded by the commission as) an Ibo town;[52] and (3) Ahoada and

41

Port Harcourt would, the commission believed, "create a problem as acute as that with which we are asked to deal at present and would be sharply resented by Ibos of the Central Plateau".[53] Instead of a state, the commission suggested ways to "help the Ijaws and others of the coastal strip to receive sympathetic consideration in their peculiar problems". We shall deal with the recommendations later. Suffice it to say at this point that the commission rejected the idea of a Rivers State.

With regard to a Calabar-Ogoja-Rivers (COR) State (Calabar-Ogoja-Rivers Province, excluding Abakaliki and Afikpo), the commission noticed that: 1) Ibos would constitute a minority in such a state; 2) "many of the other tribes expressed at least as much fear of Efiks and Ibibios as of Ibos",[54] and 3) since Ibos were an expanding people, such a state surrounding them would likely "exclude them from the public service and from other outlets for their energies and ambition", and therefore lead to greater tension rather than a relief. It was therefore "unable to recommend any new state in this region."

iii) *The Northern Region and New States*

In the Northern Region, there was the suggestion for a Middle Belt State, and the revision of boundaries to permit the Yorubas in Ilorin and Kabba divisions to merge with the West. The main controversy was over the component units of the proposed state. The UMBC (with AG prodding) had changed from its stand of a Middle Belt State including Ilorin, Kabba, Benue and Plateau Provinces, Southern Bauchi, Southern Zaria, Niger Provinces as far as Kontagora town, and Numan Division and the districts of Muri and Wurkum.[55] The UMBC wanted to exclude Ilorin and Kabba divisions from the Middle Belt state and then include the whole of Niger and Adamawa Provinces in it.

As expected, the NPC regional government, with a policy of "one North, one people, one destiny", opposed the creation of any state in the North. In fact, it co-opted some Middle-Belt leaders into its leadership; thus, the UMBC wing under David Lot (founder of the Middle-Belt Zone League – MZL) allied itself with the NPC.[56] In the same way, the Idoma State Union (comprising mainly Native Authority Officials) supported the NPC position.[57] The Northern government pointed out that the region's concept of diversity in unity was working: the Muslims, Christians, and adherents of traditional

42

religions were living together happily. It pointed out that there was a growing sense of loyalty to Northern Region and that Middle-Belt people were receiving more than a fair share of the capital services such as schools, roads, railways, and hospitals. To the NPC, a separate state would not only be impossible to administer, it would create manpower problems for the rest of the region if the skilled men in the Middle-Belt were withdrawn into new state services.

The commission found strong support for additional states in "limited areas" such as among the Tiv in Benue Province, Yagba in Kabba Province, the Berom of Plateau, and a few other groups. It therefore recommend that no state be created in Northern Region because a state which "consisted only of the areas where there is strong support would be extremely difficult to administer" and that it did not consider that such constituted a "practical proposal."[58] It suggested that as the importance of the federal government grew, the NPC would be forced to appeal to Northern minorities in order to control the centre. "This we believe will constitute a better safeguard for the position of minorities than the creation of separate state".[59]

We shall now turn to the main recommendations of the commission.

c) *Recommendations to Allay Fears of Minorities*

The committee agreed that in all the regions "minorities or groups of minorities" expressed their fears and grievances and felt these "would become more intense when the present restraints were removed, and suggested a separate state or states". It came to conclusion that in each region "separate state would not provide a remedy for the fears expressed", even though some of the fears expressed were genuine.[60]

It rejected the creation of additional states, particularly because; 1) of the difficulty in drawing a clean boundary which "does not create fresh minority"; 2) the proposed states would become so small and unviable by the time they had been pared down to an area in which it was possible to "assert with confidence that it was desired". However it would seem that the commission's greatest objection had to do with item 3 (c) of its terms of reference: the effect of new states on existing regions and the federation. The report stated:

The powers left to their Regions by the decision of 1953 are considerable and, as we have said elsewhere, we do not regard it as realistic to suppose that any of the Regions will forego the powers they now have. Some years ago, before the relations between the Federation and the Regions crystallized, it was possible to conceive a large number of states with smaller powers, but a new state created today would have to compete with the existing Regions and the cost in overheads, not only financial but in resources — particularly trained minds would be high.[61]

From the above quotation, it would seem that once federalism had become accepted to Nigerian politicians and regionalism had become a good base for inter-regional competition, each region guarded its powers jealously— both in its relations with the federal government and other regions. The criterion of "viability" as a basis for new states, as suggested by the regions, may be regarded as a rationalization of the existing regions did not undercut the new region; it only created temporary difficulties.

However, the commission decided to make recommendations in order to allay fears among minority groups.

i. *The Police Forces and Magistrate Courts* were regarded as the main protectors of individual's rights against repression by "strong arm groups". While it recognized that the maintenance of law and order should be in the concurrent legislative list, the federal government should take over the control of the local police. If the police "became a solely regional force" the protection of individual rights would disappear. The ultimate responsibility for law and order was that of the federal government though regions were to maintain law and order in their areas. "There should be no regional police force,[62] and local police forces should be absorbed gradually into Nigeria Police Force."

ii. *Social Areas* were created to allay the fears of minorities because of their "special position." This was to be on the concurrent list. In the Niger–Delta (with its problems of poor communication) this special area covered the Rivers Province, except Ahoada and Port Harcourt, including Western Ijaw Division in Western Region. The Development Board, to be chaired by a federal official, was to have officials of Western and Eastern Regions. The federal government was to

44

contribute one-third of the capital cost, and one-third recurrent cost, up to ten years. Eastern and Western Regions were to contribute to this fund. This board was to undertake the development of the area, and its existence was to be reviewed over time, depending on desirability of its continuation.

iii. *Minority Areas* were created to allay fears of the people. These were: 1) Benin Province (with Urhobo Division, but excluding Akoko-Edo and Asaba) – to be called "Edo Area", and 2) Calabar Province – to be know as "Calabar Area." Each minority area was to have a council, with a chairman from the area, nominated by the Regional Government. A substantial number of members of the council were to be elected or nominated by local bodies. These councils had the functions of fostering the "well-being, cultural advancement and economic and social development of minority area and bring to the notice of the Regional Government any discrimination against the area."[63]

Iv. *Fundamental Rights* were to be inserted into the constitution for the protection of individuals and minority groups.[64]

*v. Boundaries Adjustment: Ilorin and Kabba.*There were to be no boundary changes between Northern and Western Regions, "except as a result of a plebiscite," which could only be held with general approval by the Constitutional Conference, with full knowledge that such results would be binding. At least 60% of the votes was required to make it binding.

vi. .*Muslim Laws* should not be applied to non-Muslims in the Northern Region; a regional service of *Alkali* (under a Judicial Service Commission) was to be established; and improved arrangements were to be made to facilitate appeals and ensure copies of court records not delayed."

These were the main items of the Willink Commission recommendations. The British Government, aware of the problems of creating additional states in Nigeria before independence, was anxious to hand over the problem intact to Nigerian leaders. Thus, when at the 1958 Constitutional Conference in London agitations for the creation of additional subnational units continued, the British Government came out with what virtually amounted to a political *blackmail* or *whitemail*. If

Nigerians wanted additional states, independence would have to be delayed for a couple of years. Of course, given the unwillingness of some Nigerian politicians to resolve the issue of the federal structure, British opposition and the threat to delay the attainment of independence of Nigeria, were enough excuses for them to sweep the issue of the creation of states under the carpet.

Nigerian leaders opted for independence in 1960, but with a formula for the creation of additional states to be inserted in the constitution.[65] With the shelving of the issue of states creation before independence, Nigerian leaders stored a rich legacy of problems which cast thick shadows over the political system after independence. Two basic but inter-related issues remained unsolved and were "shelved" to the independence period:

> 1. *The fundamental imbalance in Nigeria's political structure* remained. The disproportionate size of the Northern Region in relation to the two Southern Regions was to heighten the embers of suspicion, fears and aggressive ethnoregionalism, after independence.
> 2. *Fears by minority groups of domination by majorities remained* unresolved in the context of Nigeria's three-regional structure.

Fears of minority groups in the regions, as reported by the commission, may be summarized under eight main headings:

1) domination of government by a regional ethnic majority;
2) social fears and grievances;
3) discrimination in economic spheres;
4) discrimination in recruitment into public posts and in public activities;
5) changes in legal system in the regions;
6) the maintenance of public order and individual freedom;
7) traditional rulers and local (Native Authority) governments; and
8) religious intolerance.

Notes and references

1. Tafawa Balewa, *Mr. Prime Minister* (Lagos: Government Printer, 1964), p. 2.

2.   K. C. Wheare, *Federal Government,* 4th Edition (New York: Oxford University Press, 1964).

3.   James S. Coleman, *Nigeria: Background to Nationalism* (Berkeley: University of California Press, 1959), pp. 45- 46.

4.   Ahmadu Bello, *My Life* (London: Cambridge University Press, 1962). Sir Ahmadu Bello observed that:

Lord Lugard and his Amalgamation were far from popular amongst us at that time. There were agitations in favour of secession; we should set up our own; we should cease to have anything to do with the Southern people; we should take our own way. (p. 135)

5.   J. S. Coleman, *op. cit.,* p. 47.

6.   Lord Hailey, *Report on Nigeria: 1940-41,* with a minute by H. E. the Governor, January 1942 (London, 1942), pp. 19-20, quoted in T. N. Tamuno, "Separatist Agitations in Niger," *Journal of Modern Africa Studies,* 8, 4 (1970), p. 566. Tamuno claims that while the Commissioner of the Northern Provinces and "his officials and Emirs encouraged separate development of the Northern Provinces vis-à-vis the Eastern and Western Provinces, officials in Lagos and the colonial office sought to discourage such tendencies" (p. 566). Eme Awa, *Federal Government in Nigeria* (Berkeley: University of California Press, 1964), claims that it seemed unlikely that existing Chief Commissioners would welcome a change that would strip them of substantial political and administrative power" (p.17).

7.   J. P. Mackintosh, *Nigerian Government and Politics* (London: Allen and Unwin, 1966). K. Ezera, *Constitutional Developments in Nigeria* 2nd Edition (Cambridge: C. U. P., 1964.)

8.   Coleman, *op. cit.,* pp. 271- 284.

9.   Obafemi Awolowo, *Path to Nigerian Freedom* (London: Faber and Faber, 1947), pp. 137-129.

10. Clifford Geertz (ed.), "The Integrative Revolution: Primordial Sentiments and Civil politics in New States," in *Old Societies and New States* (Glencoe: The Free Press, 1963) p. 150, was correct in observing that:

...whereas in most of the other new states final phases of the pursuit of independence saw a progressive unification of diverse elements into an intensely solidarity opposition to the colonial rule, open dissidence emerging only after the inevitable waning of revolutionary comradeship, in Nigeria tension between the various primordial groups increased in the last decade of dependency.

11. *Ethnoregionalism* is used to refer to the crystallization of the identity of the major ethnic groups with the regional administrative boundaries. In Nigeria, there were three major ethnoregional groups: the Hausa-Fulani in the Northern Region; the Ibo in the Eastern Region; and the Yoruba in the Western Region. In such situations the desire was to protect the interest of the major ethnic group in that region... an administrative unit becomes the base for competition with other ethnic groups. See R. L. Sklar, *Nigerian Political Parties* (Princeton; Princeton University Press, 1963).

12. James O 'Connell, "Political Integration: The Nigerian Case," in Arthur Hazelwood (ed.) *African Integration and Disintegration* (London: Oxford University Press, 1967), pp. 115-184.

13. *ibid.,*

14. Interview with Aminu Kano, former Federal Commissioner for Health, Ikoyi, Lagos, 2 February 1974.

15. Oluwole Alakija, in *Egbe Omo Oduduwa Monthly Bulletin,* 1 (4 December 1948), quoted in Coleman, *op. cit.,* p. 346.

16. Minutes of the First Inaugural Conference of the Egbe Omo Oduduwa, June, 1948 (typed copy), in Coleman, *op. cit.,* p. 346.

17. *West African Pilot* (Lagos), 6 July 1949, in Coleman, *op. cit.,* p. 320.

18. Obafemi Awolowo, *op. cit.,* pp. 47-48.

19. *Legislative Council Debates,* Nigeria, 4 March 1948, p. 227 quoted in Coleman, *op.cit,* p. 320.

20. Interview with Aminu Kano.

21. B. J. Dudley, *Instability and Political Order: Politics and Crisis in Nigeria* (Ibadan: Ibadan University Press, 1973), p. 63. Also, in Nigeria, *Proceedings of a General Conference on Review of Constitution* (Lagos, 1958), p. 218; also quoted in T. N. Tamuno, "Separatist Agitations in Nigeria", *Journal of Modern African Studies* 8, 4 (1970), p. 568, in which the Emir of Zaria was quoted as having said that:

...unless the Northern Region was allotted 50% of the seats in the central legislature, it would ask for separation from the rest of Nigeria on the arrangements existing before 1914.

48

22. T. N. Tamuno, "Separatist Agitations in Nigeria," *loc. cit.,* pp. 187 -188.

23. Kalu Ezera, *op. cit.,* pp. 187-188, quoted Awolowo as having sent the Governor a telegram reading as follows:

> ...I challenge you to deny that the people of the Western Region have the right of self-determination and are free to decide whether or not they will remain in the proposed Nigeria federation.
>
> If you are unable to accept these challenges, then you can be rest assured that you have totally destroyed, in a considerable and important section of the Nigerian community, what remains of confidence in the British sense of justice, equity and fair play, and have also dealt a fatal blow to the Nigerian unity.

Reply to Awolowo's telegram by Colonial Secretary, November 10, 1953:

> ...any attempt to secure alteration of that decision by force will be resisted, and in this context, I am to observe that any attempt to secure the secession of the Western Region from the federation would be regarded as the use of force...

24. Ahmadu Bello, *op. cit.,* pp. 119-135. After the hostility to the Northern delegation at Southern railway stations, Sir Ahmadu Bello said "The journey was about finished for us."

25. Adebayo Adedeji, "Federalism and Development Planning in Nigeria, "in A. and H. M. A. Onitiri (eds.) *Reconstruction and Development in Nigeria: Proceedings of a Conference* (Ibadan: Oxford University Press, 1971), p. 103.

26. Interview with Aminu Kano.

27. Nnamdi Azikiwe reported in *Daily Times* (Lagos), 19 May 1975, p. 5.

28. *ibid.,* p. 5. Zik explained the criteria he used for his 1943 demands for additional states:

> When I proposed that Nigeria should become a federation of eight regions in 1943, I was political, and not sociological in my approach. I did not necessarily overlook the tribal factor but, in my innocence, I minimized it.

- See Azikiwe, *Political Blueprint for Nigeria* (Lagos: 1945) for his political speeches within this period.

29. Awolowo, *op. cit.*, (1947), – Republic of Nigeria, *The Struggles for One Nigeria* (Lagos: Ministry of Information, 1967), p. 23, states that:

In 1947, Chief Obafemi Awolowo, a Yoruba, in his book, Path to Nigerian Freedom, suggested the division of Nigeria into forty states, with cultural and linguistic affinity as the basis of division.

30. Awa, *op. cit.*, pp. 61-62; also Coleman, *op. cit.*, (1958), pp. 347-48.

31. Coleman, *op. cit.*, (1958), pp. 347-348.

32. *ibid.*, p. 390.

33. A good discussion of the case presented by the Rivers State is in Rivers State Nigeria: *Our Case: Flashback on the Visit of the British Prime Minister, the Rt. Hon. Harold Wilson, to the Rivers State of Nigeria* (Lagos: Ribway Printers, 1969), pp. 5–12.

34. Coleman, *op. cit.*, p. 393.

35. Awa, *op. cit.*, p. 63.

36. *ibid.*,

37. Federal Republic of Nigeria, *The Struggle for One Nigeria. op. cit.*, p. 24.

38. Nigeria, *Report of the Commission Appointed to Enquire into the Fears of Minorities and the Means of Allaying them* (London, HMSO, Cmd 505, 1958), p. 57. (Hereafter called the Willink Commission Report).

39. *Daily Times*. 13 March 1957.

40. Coleman, *op. cit.*, p. 395; and *The Struggle for One Nigeria op. cit.*, p. 25.

41. Awa, *op. cit.*, p. 63, notes that:

The relish with which the debate on the viability of new states was carried on gave a clear impression that the leaders did not really want to create new states and were merely using the viability issue as a bogy to scare agitators in the minority groups.

42. *Willink Commission Report*, p. 12.

43. *Willink Commission Report*, p. A2

44. The members of the Commission were Sir Henry Willink (the Chairman), Gordon Hadow, Philip Mason, J. B. Shearer, and K. J. Hilton, as Secretary.

45. *Willink Commission Report* p. 12.

46. *ibid.,* p. 13.

47. *ibid.,* p. 17.

48. *ibid.,* p. 43.

49. *ibid.,* p. 64.

50. *ibid.,* p. 87.

51. *ibid.,* p. 33.

52. It is interesting that the commission accepted Port Harcourt as an Ibo town. The creation of states in 1967 legally confirmed Port Harcourt as a non-Ibo town. In his address to Dr. Nnamdi Azikiwe on his visit to the Rivers State, Alfred Diete Spiff, declared:

> On this occasion, it is pertinent to draw attention to an issue, which has been deliberately confused, to the detriment of all concerned. For political reason, it has been held in certain quarters both within and outside Nigeria that Port Harcourt belongs to the Ibos. Geographical situation historical association and available legal documents are clear on the issue. The national right of the Rivers People to Port Harcourt is inviolable and non-negotiable. There can be no compromise on this issue.

Rivers State Government, *Building from the Scratch,* (Apapa – Lagos, Information Service, 1969), p. 29, Refer also to Howard Wolpe *Urban Politics in Nigeria: A Study of Port Harcourt* (Berkeley; University of California Press, 1974).

53. *Willink Commission Report* p. 51.

54. *ibid.,* p. 49.

55. This view of a Middle Belt State was presented to the commission at Makurdi by the Benue Freedom Crusade, *Willink Commission Report,* p. 21.

56. Coleman, *op. cit.,* p. 367.

57. The aggressive State proponents were predominantly members of The *Idoma Hope Rising Union* (IHRU).

58. *Willink Commission Report,* p. 72.

59. *ibid.,* p. 73.

60. *ibid.,* p. 87.

61. *ibid.,*

62. *ibid.*, p. 93. Though the regions were to share in the upkeep of the Federal Police Force, it was not until 1966, under the military, that Local (Native Authority) Government Police Forces were absorbed by the Nigeria Police. The same happened to the Prisons Department in 1966.

63. *Willink Commission Report*, p. 104.

64. These were sixteen in number. *Willink Commission Report*, pp. 104 – 105.

i) The Right to life; ii) Protection against inhuman treatment; iii) Protection against slavery or forced labour; iv) The right to liberty; v) The right to respect for private and family life; vi) The right to public hearing and fair procedure in criminal charges; vii) Protection against retrospective legislation; viii) Freedom of expression; ix) Freedom of peaceful assembly; x) Freedom of movement; xi) The right to marry; xii) Freedom of religion; xiii) freedom of religious education; xiv) The enjoyment of fundamental rights without discrimination; xv) Protection against discrimination; and xvi) The enforcement of fundamental right (the individual's right to "appeal to the high courts for protection and enforcement of any provisions as to the fundamental rights contained in the constitution and the high courts shall have the power to make all such orders as may be necessary and appropriate to secure the applicant the enjoyment of any of these rights". p. 103.

We shall be dealing with this in the next chapter.

3

THE CIVILIAN REGIME AND DUAL
FEDERALISM 1960 – 1966

In the previous chapter, we discussed how federalism was adopted as a compromise solution amidst centrifugal and centripetal pulls in Nigeria. We also looked at the structure of Nigeria and the demands of minority groups for participation.

In this chapter, we shall look at the working of Nigeria's federalism in the first five years after independence. Why did this attempt at democracy and federalism fail? How did the demands for the creation of more subnational units affect the political scene? Why did the military intervene in politics?

The Structure of Nigeria's Federalism

On October 1, 1960, Nigeria became an independent state. At the federal centre was a bicameral legislature: the House of Representatives and the Senate (the upper house). The Prime Minister, Alhaji Tafawa Balewa, formed his independence cabinet after the 1959 elections[1] in an NPC-NCNC coalition government. His political executives, (i.e. the Ministers) headed the different ministries of the federal bureaucracy, which was expected (in the British tradition) to be basically non-political. Nigeria started off by adopting the Westminster model of parliamentary democracy.

In 1963, Nigeria became a Republic with a ceremonial President, Nnamdi Azikiwe, who had assumed the role of a ceremonial Governor-General after independence. He lacked any political authority but expressed the symbolic capability of the new Nigerian nation.[2] In the regions (which had become four, with the creation of the Midwestern Region in 1963) were the Regional Governors.

The division of powers between the federal government and the regions reflected the autonomy of the regions. The 1960 and 1963 Constitutions provided for three legislative lists: exclusive list (powers allocated to federal government), concurrent list (powers allocated to both federal and regional governments), and residual list (powers allocated to the regions).

The exclusive list included external affairs, defence, currency, customs and excise, control of exchange rate, major communications networks (railways, shipping, posts and telegraphs and aviation), deportation and extradition, immigration, and certain educational institutions (the universities of Ibadan and Lagos, and their teaching hospitals, the Nigerian Institute of Social and Economic Research, the Pharmacy School at Yaba, the Forestry School at Ibadan, and the Veterinary School at Vom).

On the concurrent list were higher education, industrial development, antiquities, census, labour, tourism, water, power, prisons and other institutions for the treatment of offenders, quarantine, scientific and industrial research, and any matter that was incidental or supplementary to any subject mentioned in the above list. In this area, the federal and regional governments had legislative powers, but legislation by the federal government on any of these matters took precedence over regional legislation on such matters.

The regions were allocated residual powers in the constitution, that is to say, items not mentioned in both exclusive and concurrent legislative lists. Among such items were primary and secondary education, health, public works, marketing boards and secondary roads.[3]

It was not the constitution as much as the interpretation and implementation of certain items in it (by the regions who guarded their autonomy jealously as they competed for the control of the central government), which confirmed the fragility of Nigeria's governmental structure. As the regions became more autonomous, the very increase in their autonomy subjected the federal government to the strains of centrifugal forces and vindicated that federalism was a "desire for union but not unity."

Essentially, federalism is a "process of bringing about a dynamic equilibrium between the centrifugal and centripetal forces in a society,"

54

and it entails continuous adjustments between the federal government and the governments of the component units. These adjustments may be either in the direction of further "differentiation and autonomy or of integration and unity."[4] In this period, adjustments in federal structure were in the direction "further differentiation and autonomy." It was a federation based on mutual psychological fears of political and economic domination among component groups. As a form of government, federalism has a tremendous appeal in Nigeria, "because the problem which it is capable of resolving is precisely that of guaranteeing a collective sense of security to the historic communities or at least some of them. Judged from Nigeria's political history, this preoccupation has served to heighten the identity crisis driving more and more Nigerians into seeking refuge in integration."[5]

A look at how the federal system in Nigeria worked between 1961 and 1965 may provide a better insight into the problems of Nigeria's first attempt at federalism after independence.

The Politics of Insecurity and Aggressive Ethnoregionalism, 1961-1965

In dealing with the politics of regional insecurity in Nigeria, two factors must be borne in mind. One of these is the uneven pattern of educational development between the southern parts of the country (the East, the West, and Lagos) and the Northern Region. The other point is the imbalance in the federal structure in which the Northern Region was not only three times the area of the southern regions, but also accounted for about 54% of Nigeria's total population (by 1963 census figures).

Once formal western education became the passport for entry into governmental, political, and economic roles in the modernizing sector, those who had a head start in education obtained inherent advantages over those who did not. Thus, the Northern Region's educational lag behind the southern regions was a source of fear – of domination by *southern skills*. The *Northernization* policy of recruitment into the northern bureaucracy was an attempt to keep the south from swamping the service. As the Northern Premier once observed:

> We were very conscious indeed that the Northern Region
> was far behind the others educationally. We knew that
> individually the educated Northerners could hold their own
> against educated Southerners, but we simply had not got the
> numbers they had, nor had we people with the university
> degrees necessary as a qualification... for some of the higher
> post.[6]

It may be argued that, disadvantaged in education, the Northern
Region wanted to retain its advantage of population over the south. To
the southerners, the very disproportionate population of the north was
a threat to their sense of security. It ensured the north's indefinite
control of the federal centre. Thus, while the north feared southern
domination through skill, the southern regions feared northern
domination through population.

As long as it was "one North, one people, one destiny," its
advantage of population would act as a counterbalance against the
south's advantage of a headstart in education. Of course, the
disproportionate size of the region only accentuated the situation, as
differential rates of educational development complicated the problem
of mutual trust among groups.

There were illustrations of these fears of domination and
discrimination against one group by the other during the civilian
regime: the 1962 and 1963 census exercises, and the federal election, the
1965 Western Regional elections, and the inter-regional squabbles over
the iron and steel mining complex. Let us look at these briefly.

1. *The Change of Guards and Crisis in the West*

After the 1959 elections, Dr. Azikiwe became the President of the
Senate, later on the Governor-General, then finally the first President of
the new republic. Obafemi Awolowo had also resigned his premiership
to contest elections to the federal parliament. He became the leader of
opposition in the House of Representatives. Thus, of the three main
political guards, in the regions, two had moved to the federal level, but
Ahmadu Bello, (the leader of the NPC) remained in the region, while
his deputy, Abubakar Tafawa Balewa remained as the Federal Prime
Minister.

Meanwhile, the southern regions had hoped that getting the support of the minority groups in the Middle Belt area would dilute the preponderant effect of the NPC. This hope turned into frustration after the 1961 northern regional elections in which the NPC won 94% of the seats.[7] The NEPU virtually lost its foothold in the House of Assembly, thus meaning the exclusion of its NCNC ally from the position of an opposition in the Northern House. The UMBC (mainly among the Tiv) retained a minor opposition in the House, giving its AG ally a little foothold in the north. This NPC victory in the 1961 northern elections convinced the south that "under the independence constitution, there was not little to prevent the North from winning a working majority at the next federal election."[8]

After the 1959 election, we had observed that there had been some changes in the political "guards" in the East and West. Michael Okpara (the new president of the NCNC) stepped into Azikiwe's shoes as the Premier of the East. In the Western Region, Samuel Akintola became the regional Premier after Awolowo had moved to the federal parliament as the leader of the opposition.

In a short while, a crisis developed within the AG. The regional administration under Samuel Akintola complained about Awolowo's intervention in routine decisions of the party's regional government. But essentially, the Akintola-Awolowo conflict may be traced to differences in their approaches to Nigeria's brand of politics. Within the context of the politics of patronage, Akintola favoured cooperation with NPC to secure for the Western Region a share of the federal "booty", believed to be going to members of the NPC/NCNC coalition. On the other hand, Awolowo saw this as a betrayal of the AG's ambition to control the federal government as a party.[9] The first rift between the two leaders led to a physical fight in the Western House of Assembly.

The NPC/NCNC coalition took this opportunity to get through the federal parliament a resolution declaring a state of emergency in the Western Region.[10] Akintola emerged a victor, forming the United People's Party (UPP) which, in coalition with the NCNC (under Fani-Kayode), formed a new Western Region government after the six-month emergency period. In an attempt at Pan-Yoruba nationalism, the

Akintola (UPP)-Fani-Kayode (NCNC) government formed a new party: the Nigerian National Democratic Party (NNDP).

This period of the Western Region crisis coincided with the treasonable felony charges against some members of the AG, notably Awolowo and Enahoro. Both men and some others were convicted and imprisoned in 1963. Thus, meanwhile, the NPC-NCNC *honeymoon* of the coalition went on peacefully, as both parties allied to deal heavy blows at the AG. As Kirk-Greene observed, one clear lesson, which emerged from the exercise of federal government's emergency power, was that it violated "regional security", whereby "each party was quietly left to control its own region without interference... The apparently impregnable walls of regional power bastions could after all be breached by the heavy artillery of the centre."[11]

If the federal government's constitutional powers of coercion became clear, it also made it more intolerable for a single regional party to control the federal government. A northern predominance in the federal government would thus be a potential threat to all other regions, particularly with the politics of excusivity[12], which ensued later. Regional security became linked to the regional party control of the federal government.

2. *The Census Exercise and the Politics of Numerical Superiority*

Meanwhile, the political honeymoon between the NPC and NCNC in the coalition government continued. [13] Both parties had not only cooperated to deal a fatal blow to the AG and the Western Region, they had also seized the opportunity of the relative power vacuum in the West to create the Midwestern State out of that region in 1962-1963. However, no sooner had the West become a testing ground for the power of the federal coalition political parties than the period of honeymoon expired. The census issues of the 1962 and 1963 marred the initial period of NPC-NCNC coalition.

Given the imbalance in Nigeria's federal structure, numerical superiority became an important factor in Nigerian politics. The NCNC, the Eastern government, and many southern peoples had hoped that the 1962 census figures would give the south numerical superiority over the north. In such a situation, a coalition of the southern parties with a few seats from the disaffected areas in the north

58

would give the south the majority with which to control the federal government.[14] On the other hand, the Northern Region continued to fear the concentration of numerical and technical superiority in the south. Such concentration of power, to them would be "utterly disastrous".[15]

In addition, census figures were tied to revenue sharing among the regions. The 1962 census exercise was therefore politicized. Discrepancies in the actual figures led to its cancellation and the initiation of another census exercise in 1963.

In the 1962 census, the population of the Eastern and Western Regions had shown an average increase of about 70%. In five Eastern divisions (Awka, Brass, Degema, Eket and Opobo), increases of about 120-200% were recorded. The total for the south was then about 23 million. The southerners had hoped that, for the first time, the North would be in a minority with its 22.5million (on the basis of 30% increase). Mr. Warren, the officer in charge of the census, felt the figures for the north were "reasonable."[16] He dismissed the southern figures as "false and inflated," particularly in the five divisions of the Eastern Region.[17]

However, in its revised 1962 figures, the north claimed to have "missed out all of 8.5 million people, presenting a total of 31 million,"[18] giving it an increase of about 80%. In the light of these discrepancies, Prime Minister Balewa decided to abandon it and conduct a new census exercise.

In 1963, another census exercise was undertaken. It was probably as unreliable as the previous one, but was even more controversial. The 1963 official census figures showed the north with a population of 29.8 million, the East with 12.4 million, and the West and the new Midwestern Region with a population of 12.8 million. The figures for the north and the east increased by 67% each, while the West and Midwest together recorded an increase of about 100%.[19]

Clearly, the NPC-NCNC's coalition, which had started "souring" or weakening from the Midwestern Regional elections, showed an open rift between the two parties over the census issue. While Ahmadu Bello, the Premier of the North, accepted the census as "fair and reasonably conducted," Michael Okpara of the Eastern Region rejected the census figures, which he regretted disclosed inflations "of such astronomical proportions that the figures... taken as a whole, are worse than useless."[20] Together, the Midwestern and Eastern Regions rejected the figures, while the Northern and Western Regions accepted them. Actually, the Midwestern Region was as much under NCNC leadership as was the East, while Akintola's Western Region had not gotten over her gratitude to the NPC for the latter's support during the political crisis in the Western Region.

To the NCNC leadership, the census controversy was indicative of the Northern Region's determination to use its size to maintain its hegemony at the centre. The Premier of the East, Dr. Okpara's suit in the Supreme Court alleging irregularities in the census exercise was dismissed. This court judgement was more painful for him because of the impending elections.

3. *The 1964 Federal Election*

By 1963, it had become evident (after the Midwest elections and then the 1964 controversies over the 1962/63 census figures) that the NPC-NCNC coalition was going to break up. Disappointed from the census issue and afraid of the weight of Northern population, the NCNC teamed up with the AG and their Northern allies – the NEPU and the UMBC respectively—to form the United Progressive Grand Alliance (UPGA). Okpara made it clear that the NNDP government in the West was a "baby of the NPC set-up in the West by the second Afonja of our time. It is a manoeuver of the NPC to stifle democracy in the West."[21]

On the other hand, by mid-1964, Sir Ahmadu Bello had declared that even if his party failed to "get the required majority in the next federal elections, it will definitely not enter into any agreements on coalition with NCNC." After all, he observed, "the Ibos have never been true friends of the North and will never be..."[22] The NPC, the NNDP, and the Midwest Democratic Front (MDF) formed an alliance resulting in a party: the Nigerian National Alliance (NNA).

The UPGA had started the 1964 electoral campaigns with every hope, through a consolidation of votes in the south and inroads into the discontented areas of the north (the Middle Belt and Kano areas), to be able to win the elections. However, this hope faded when 66 NPC members from the Northern constituencies were to be returned unopposed to the federal parliament. UPGA leaders were upset and complained about lack of freedom to campaign, and the prevention of its candidates from filing their nominations in the Northern Region. Allegations and counter-allegations from both the UPGA and NNA accentuated the tension of the campaign period.[23] Aggressive ethnicity escalated, and thuggery became an effective instrument of campaigning, especially by the *Sarduana* and *Okpara Youth Brigades*.

Dr. Okpara and the NCNC protested about the election machinery. The NNA and the Prime Minister, on the other hand, saw nothing wrong with the arrangements. UPGA therefore advised its members to boycott the elections. Only in the East was the boycott total, because the government refused to implement arrangements for the elections. Hence, NPC cleared the Northern seats, the NNDP won 36 out of 57 seats in the west and the NCNC won the belated elections in the Midwestern Region[24] in Lagos, only a few people went to the polls.

Dissatisfied with the conduct of the elections, Azikiwe refused to ask Tafawa Balewa to form the government. He was accused by the north of being in league with the East.[25] His attempt to get the military to take over power temporarily was declined by the heads of the Armed Forces, who had been advised that they owed their allegiance to the Prime Minister for operational orders and not to the President.[26]

However, with the advice of the Federal Chief Justice, the Attorney General, and the Chief Justice of the Eastern Region, an arrangement was worked out whereby Tafawa Balewa was to form a "broad-based" government comprising all major political parties, and elections were to be held in the Eastern Region. [27] Dissatisfied with the situation, the Eastern Regional leaders were said to have threatened to secede from the federation.[28] The UPGA boycott was a mistake it lived to regret. It could have done better than it eventually did in the Western Region, given the erosion of Akintola's legitimacy. One thing became clear, the fear of northern domination by population had become part of the southern political belief system, much as northern fears of southern domination by skills acquired through western education had encouraged its leaders to oppose any break-up of the north. The atmosphere of political corruption, violence and thuggery, and aggressive ethnoregionalism, which had raised the political temperature of the federation beyond "normal" levels, was further accentuated by the 1965 Western Regional elections.

4. *The 1965 Western Regional Elections*

Many people in Western Nigeria "never forgave Akintola for his treachery against his former leader,"[29] and his alliance with the NPC only confirmed earlier accusations of his betrayal of Yoruba interests to the Northern leaders. Awolowo, though in prison, still retained the allegiance of many Yoruba, who regarded him as almost a "martyr."[30]

The 1965 Western elections provided the southern parties (AG-NCNC) the "last desperate attempt to challenge the hegemony of the NPC," whose inroads into the south threatened the security of many southern politicians. They thought that by "winning control of the WestSSa real possibility in view of the evident unpopularity of the Akintola regime—they would have the control of all three Southern Regions as well as Lagos."[31] This would then give UPGA members of the senate a majority with which to frustrate legislators by the NPC majority in the House. The senate comprised eight members selected by each Regional House, four from Lagos and four by the President.

In the campaigns, which ensued, accusations about the conduct of the 1965 elections were rampant. The opposition parties complained about difficulties in filing their nominations, while NNDP members were given easy access to filing nominations. Among allegations against the Akintola government was the availability of ballot papers to NNDP members before polling and the violation of regulations in vote counting and announcement of results. The NNDP in the situation was declared victorious, to the chagrin of many people in the region. Violence, thuggery, arson, and looting punctuated normal patterns of life in the Western Region.

In the light of pressures from his party, the Prime Minister saw nothing wrong in the West and regarded the Akintola regime as legal. Killings and intimidations of public officials drew repression from the government, and more repression gave momentum to greater breakdown of law and order in the region. That the Prime Minister declared no State of Emergency in the West, as in 1962, was attributed by many observers to be the result of the pressures from his NPC leader in the North (Sir Ahmadu Bello) and NPC predominance in the federal parliament. The military coup of 1966 only saved observers the speculations about the trend of Nigeria's political development, given the situation in the Western Region and the magnitude of fear and distrust in the Nigerian society.

5. *Economic Planning and the Politics of Allocation*

Another illustration of the parochial ethnoregionalism in Nigeria is the nature of economic planning. Often, the regions jockeyed for the location and the allocation of particular resources and/or projects in their area. The 1962-1968 Development Plans included the establishment of a steel and iron ore smelting industry in Nigeria. In the National Economic Council in 1964, the North requested the siting of the industry at Idah in the Northern Region, the Eastern leaders wanted it at Onitsha in the Eastern Region, while the Western Region demanded that it be sited at Ikare in the West.

Ethnoregional politics therefore had an economic basis: the control of the powers to dispense patronage and allocate resources. In the ensuing squabble, the Western Region withdrew its request (a sign of its weakness at this point in time). It was then decided that the industry be split between the North and the East, with a plant at Idah and another in Onitsha – a wasteful economic process. Thus, the politics of regional insecurity also gave momentum to imprudence in economic decision-making. The iron and steel industry is only an example of reckless economic decision-making as a result of ethnoregional politics in Nigeria.[32]

From the above discussion, it is clear that mutual and suspicious fears of domination among groups not only necessitated the call for the creation of more subnational units in Nigeria, but also provided excuses for the maintenance of Nigeria's lopsided federal structure and resistance to the creation of additional states. The huge population and the large area of the North created fear among Southern people and gave rise to their demand for its break-up. The regional self-interest of Nigerian politicians and their insecurity in relations with one another were behind the inability of the politicians to solve the problem of the federation's structural imbalance.

Federalism and the Persistence of Minority Problems

Protest by minority groups of domination and discrimination by majority groups in the three regions continued after independence. If southern politicians feared the size of the Northern Region, minority groups were displeased with the three-regional structure and had called for the alteration of that structure. In the Northern Region, opposition from the Tiv ethnic groups turned into riots from 1960-1961 and in 1964.

1. *The Midwest Region 1962-1963*

Meanwhile, the crisis in the Western Region in 1962 provided an opportunity for reconsidering the negative recommendations of the Willink Commission concerning the creation of the Midwest State. Chief Obafemi Awolowo was in prison, and Akintola's party in the Western Region was weak, having a hard time recuperating from the 1962 crisis. Though there were demands for the creation of states in the North and in the East, both Northern leaders (in the NPC) and Eastern leaders (in the NCNC) seized the opportunity to weaken the Action Group in the West. For the NCNC, a Midwestern State was a prospective foothold for the party, outside of the Eastern region. Moreover, most of the proponents of the state were NCNC members.

Another reason for the success of the pressure for the creation of the Midwestern State was the influence of men from the Midwest who supported its creation. Among such men were Chief Festus Okotie-Eboh (the flamboyant millionaire, Federal Minister of Finance), Chief Dennis Osadebey (who, by 1962 had become the President of the Senate), the Oba of Benin, and Sir Jereton Mariere. These men, who were mostly NCNC members, put pressure both at the federal and regional levels for the creation of the Midwest State.

In addition to this, Benin and Delta provinces formed a more compact territory than the proposed Middle Belt or the Calabar-Ogoja-Rivers States.[33] However, the Willink Commission refused to recommend the creation of a Midwest Region as proposed by Midwest State movement because it would "include some actively protesting minorities and others whose enthusiasm was extremely moderate."[34] It agreed that the "estimate of the fiscal and economical position of such a

State" was "optimistic," though the cost of setting up administration and headquarters would be high. Actually, the Midwest not only had cocoa, rubber, and timber, but natural gas and oil had been discovered there by 1957.

However, once a combination of facts external and internal to the Midwest had favoured its creation, constitutional measures had to be taken. As mentioned earlier, the issue of creating additional states in Nigeria had been "shelved" until after independence by providing a formula in the constitution for the creation of states. Any creation of additional states had to go through certain procedures:

> a) a resolution approving the proposal for such a new state by two thirds majority of all members of the federal parliament;
> b) a proposal to be submitted to each House of the legislature of two regions, including the region or regions out of which a new state is to be created or by each House of a two-thirds majority of the regions. (This was altered to a simple majority of the regions after the creation of the Midwest Region);
> c) an act amending the federal constitution to give effect to the proposal, which must be submitted to all regions and approved by at least two of them; and
> d) a referendum in the area covered with at least 60% vote in favour of such a state is required for the amendment of the law, so approved, to come into effect.[35]

The Midwest Region came into being formally on August 9, 1963, after all the above procedures had been completed. Essentially, "the creation of the Midwest was as much a product of special political circumstances existing in Lagos and Ibadan as it was a popular sentiment in Benin and Delta Provinces (which approved the creation of the region by 90% vote in the referendum). In the broadest sense, the new state was the consequence of an alliance of the East and the North, operating under conditions of instability in the West".[36]

An interesting corollary of the Midwest Region was the inability of politicians to create any other region until the military's structural reorganization of Nigeria in 1967. By the simple majority of the regions clause in (b) above, if NCNC had succeeded in controlling the West, it would have meant its control of majority of the regions: the West,

Midwest, and East. The NCNC could then have pushed through the proposal for the creation of additional states in the Northern Region. But the NPC majority in the Federal house would have blocked the new effort in the federal parliament, if the former, as was more likely then, decided to vote against it.[37] But NCNC had no such control over the west. Similarly, any NPC attempt to break up the East might have passed through the Federal parliament, but the North was unlikely to get a simple majority after the creation of the Midwest, to do so. Furthermore, both the Northern and the Eastern leaders had vested interests, given Nigeria's ethnoregional politics, in maintaining the boundaries of their regions.

2. *Other Minority Groups*

Once the Midwest Region had been created, other minority groups accelerated their demands for the creation of additional units. The Midwest Region further fragmented the south, but the North still remained intact. The 1964 elections saw the alliance of minority groups in the East – as represented by the Niger-Delta Congress, which wanted the NPC to support the creation of states in the East – allied with that party. Similarly, northern minority groups – represented by the UMBC which had teamed up with the NEPU to form the Northern Progressive Front (NPF) – allied with AG and NCNC, supported minority demands in the East, it rejected similar demands for the Northern region. Similarly, UPGA frowned on minority demands in the East while courting agitations for the breakup of the North.

By 1965, the Tiv protest in the Northern House of Assembly for Middle Belt State turned to a threat of secession by the Tiv of Benue province. In response to a debate on the Tiv riots in February of that year in the Northern House of Assembly, Isaac Shaahu (a UMBC member from Tiv Division) declared that:

> Because the Northern Peoples Congress does not want peace in that Division (Tiv) the only course we can take now since we are not wanted in the North is to pull out of the North and the Federation as a whole. We shall be joining nobody. We are 1,200,000 in population, bigger than Gambia and Mauritania, and we have the manpower and every other thing.[38]

While this may sound unreasonable in view of the geographical position of the Tiv (even assuming they could exist as an independent state), it was reflective of the mood of opposition by a minority group that had felt neglected within a region [39] and wanted some form of autonomy outside that region.

Towards the end of 1965, there had emerged agitations in Kano State for a separate state, in "the heart of Hausa North". It may be pertinent to remember that Kano was the main foothold of Aminu Kano's party, the NEPU. Similar agitations for additional states continued in the Eastern Region, even after the military coup. In February of 1966, there was a secessionist movement in the Eastern Region under the leadership of Issac Boro, Sam Owonaro and Nottingham Dick. These men were among many others who had become frustrated in their demands for the creation of a Rivers State out of the former Eastern Region.

After the military coup and the ascendance to power by General Ironsi, they "feared that the Ironsi regime, strongly supported by Ibos, prejudiced their long-standing demand for the creation of the Rivers State."[40] They declared a "Delta Peoples Republic" and were ready to defend it militantly. It took the army after a futile police effort, to bring a halt to this "mini-secession" in the East.[41]

On the whole, while it may be argued that Nigeria's federalism was a result of social forces within the society, its structures negated certain principles of federalism. According to Wheare, it is "undesirable that one or two units should be so powerful that they can over-rule the others and bend the will of the federal government to themselves".[42] indirectly, a single region's domination of the federal government was also a domination of other regions. The imbalance in Nigeria's federal structure accentuated fears and suspicions, which emanated from Nigeria's multi-ethnicity.

As Nurul Islam observed, the "greater the diversity in culture, language, and traditions of the federating units, the greater also are the centripetal tendencies to which a federation is subjected".[43] Between 1961 and 1965, Nigeria was subjected to many strains arising from these factors. The fear of domination in the country was linked to the federal structure (of the subnational units, the regions). The politicians affected a series of fragile compromises, but shied away from the major issues: the nature and structure of the federal system, which would provide security for all groups. A publication by the Military Government in 1967 provides a good assessment, in hindsight, of the civilian regime and its politicians. It stated that:

> In their common desire to win independence, many vital problems were left unsolved. One of these outstanding problems was the creation of additional states that would have provided a more lasting foundation for stability of the Federation of Nigeria. The British Government pointed out at the time that if new states were to be created, the new states must be given at least two years to settle down before independence could be granted. On reflection, Nigerian leaders have admitted that the British were right and they were wrong on this vital issue in hurrying to independence without solving the problem of stability of the Federation.[44]

With the benefit of hindsight, the military could see how wrong the politicians were. It took politicians a long time to realize it, and even so, after they had left the political stage and Nigeria was moving fast towards self-destruction. By the end of 1965, the gross political instability, which followed the negation of the "rules of the game of politics", had doomed the politics of participation, compromise and tolerance. Of course, when the political environment became polluted and there were no acceptable forms of political ventilation, Nigeria's "game of politics" became very dangerous – both for the "players" and the "spectators" in a political stadium in which one's loyalty and support was demanded in one form or another.

Thus, when the military sent the politicians packing on January 15, 1966, very few if any tears were shed. Most people were surprised, but at least there was a temporary sigh of relief as the military took over political leadership.[45]

Notes

1. K. W. J. Post, *The Nigerian Federal Election of 1959* (London: Oxford University Press, 1963). R. Sklar, "Contradictions in the

Nigerian Political System," *Journal of Modern African Studies,* Vol. 3, No. 2 (1965), pp. 201- 213; Eme Awa; *op. cit.*

2.   It is pertinent to note at this point that Azikiwe was never clear about the limitations on his power until the 1964 election crisis. A good account of this is contained in J. P. Mackintosh (ed.), *Nigerian Government and Politics* (Evanston: Northwestern University, 1966), p. 603; also N. J. Miners, *The Nigerian Army, 1956 – 1966* (London: Metheun, 1971), pp. 139 – 146.

3.   Nigeria, *The Nigeria (Constitution) Order-in-Council, 1960,* Statutory Instruments, 1960, No. 1652; and the *Constitution of the Federal Republic of Nigeria, 1963* (Lagos: Government Printer, 1963).

4.   Adebayo Adedeji, "Federalism and Development Planning in Nigeria", in A. Ayida and H. M. A. Onitiri (eds.), *Reconstruction and Development in Nigeria: Proceedings of a Conference* (Ibadan: Oxford University Press, 1971), p. 103.

5.   E. E. Essien-Udom, "Nigeria-Colony To Nationhood", *Afriscope* 2, 1 (1970), p. 21.

6.   Ahmadu Bello, *My Life, op. cit.,* p. 110.

7.   J. O. Connell, "The Northern 1961 Elections", *Nigerian Journal of Economic and Social Studies* (July 1962), pp. 181 – 185.

8.   H. M. A. Kirk-Greene, *Crisis and Conflict in Nigeria* (Ibadan: Oxford University Press, 1971), Vol. 1, p. 17.

9.   R. L. Sklar, "Nigerian Politics in Perspective", in Robert Melson and Howard Wolpe (eds.), *Nigeria: Modernization and the Politics of Communalism* (East Lansing: Michigan State University Press, 1971), pp. 43-68.

10.   Under section 65 of the Independence Constitution and section 70 of the Republican Constitution of 1963, a period of emergency could only be declared when 1) the federation is at war; 2) a resolution is passed by each House of Parliament declaring that a state of public emergency exists; or 3) a resolution of each House of Parliament supported by the votes of not less than two-thirds of all members of the House declaring that institutions in Nigeria are threatened by subversion. The parliament under such situations could make "law for Nigeria or any part thereof with respect to any matters not included in the legislative lists as may appear to parliament to be necessary or expedient for the purpose of maintaining and securing peace, order

and good government..." With a period of honeymoon between the N.P.C and N.C.N.C., a two-thirds majority in the parliament was easily got.

11. H. M. A. Kirk-Greene, *op. cit.* (1971), Vol. 1, p. 18.

12. The politics in which each major party in the regions wanted to control the central government to the exclusion of others.

13. It may be important to remember that all the three parties, the NCNC, the NPC and the AG, had become identified with particular regions: the East, the North and the West, respectively. The NCNC, still had many non-Ibo group as members, but had become identified mainly as the party of the Eastern Region. When Azikiwe returned to the Eastern Region and displaced Prof. Eyo Ita as the Chief Minister, Eastern minorities were furious. The selection of Michael Okpara as the successor to Nnamdi Azikiwe as leader of the party had led to accusations of Ibo dominance of the party, and by 1965, Yoruba-Ibo conflict in the party became open.

14. Awolowo had observed in 1963:

I believe that the problem of Nigeria cannot be solved until that of Northern Nigeria has been solved... If the Action Group and the NCNC, both of which have a monopoly of political following in the South, and at least one-third of the political followership in the North, could come together, then they would serve as a catalyst to the political situation in the North, entrench liberal democracy in the country, and infinitely increase the tempo of progress in the federation as a whole. I hold it as a fact that such a combination is sure to win a landslide victory at a subsequent election." Quoted in Walter Schwarz, *Nigeria* (London: Praeger, 1968), p. 152.

15. Similarly, Ahmadu Bello had expressed the same fear of a Southern coalition in *My life,* when he contemplated that:

Eighty years have passed since the last crisis and we see clearly now that Nigeria must stand as one and that, as things are, the existing external boundaries cannot readily be changed--nor can those of the regions... As things are in the present situation, the North has half the seats in the House of Representatives. My party might manage to capture these, but it is not very likely for the present to get any others; on the other hand, a sudden grouping of the Eastern and Western parties (with a few members from the North opposed to our party) might take power and so endanger the North. This would of course be utterly disastrous. It might set back our programme of development ruinously; it would therefore force us to take measures to meet the need. What such measures would have to be is outside my reckoning at the moment, but God would provide a way. You can therefore see that the political future must rest on an agreeable give and take between the parties. So long as all respect the common purpose, all will be well. (pp. 228-229).

16. Mackintosh, *op. cit.*, (1966), pp. 547-549.

17. W. Schwarz, *op. cit.*, p. 159.

18. *ibid.*, p. 160.

19. Mackintosh, *op. cit*, p. 552.

20. Quoted in *ibid.*, p. 552.

Population Figures, 1952/3, 1962 and 1963, in Millions (Revised)

	1952-53		1962		Revised 1962		Revised 1963	
	A	B*	A	B*	A	B*	A	B*
North	16.8	55.3	22.5	49.3	31.0	57.4	29.8	53.5
East	7.2	23.7	12.4	27.0	12.3	22.8	12.4	22.3
West	4.6	15.1	7.4	17.1	7.8	14.4	10.3	18.5
Midwest	1.5	4.9	2.2	4.8	2.2	4.1	2.5	4.5
Lagos	0.3	1.0	0.7	1.5	0.7	1.2	0.7	1.3
Total	**30.4**	**100.4**	**45.6**	**99.7**	**54.0**	**99.9**	**55.7**	**100.1**

(Adapted from Schwarz, *Nigeria, op, cit.*, p. 163).
*Totals do not add up in some cases because of rounding.
A= Population figures; B= Percentage of the total population

21. *Daily Express*, (8 June 1964), quoted in Mackintosh, p. 564.

Afonja had called for Fulani to help in his revolt in Yoruba land. This revolt was the beginning of the disintegration of the Yoruba Empire. That was how Ilorin and Kabba Provinces (later) became part of Northern Nigeria.

22. *Daily Express*, (July 20, 1964), quoted in Mackintosh, *op. cit.*, p. 564.

23. A good discussion of the election tempo is in J. O'Connell, "Political Integration: The Nigerian Case", in Arthur Hazelwood (ed.),

African Integration and Disintegration (London: Oxford University press, 1967), pp. 129-184.

24. In the Midwestern Region, the NCNC government called off its election boycott.

25. Mackintosh, *op. cit.*, pp.603-146.

26. N. J. Miners, *op. cit.*, pp. 139-146. While Azikiwe, as President, was nominally the Supreme Commander of the Armed Forces, the actual power to commit the forces to action lay with the Prime Minister. It took the election crisis to unveil how little power Zik had in the constitution. He was reported to have threatened to resign rather than appointing Abubakar as the Prime Minister.

27. Schwarz, *op. cit.*, pp. 173-178, has a good discussion on the background discussion, which went on at this time.

28. Azikiwe's *State House Diary* had accused Okpara and his Eastern colleagues of threatening to secede on December 26, 1964 (see *Daily Times*, January 13 , 1965). However, Mackintosh (p. 604) reported UPGA leaders as accusing only the President (Azikiwe) of having "contemplated breaking up the federation because he had felt that attacks on him and on the Ibos were becoming intolerable." Yet, Okpara was quoted on the same day as having said that "if this is how the NPC wants to run the election, then this country is finished, and that disintegration was inevitable if the NPC continued to act in ways that would undermine unity of Nigeria". *Daily Express* (December 22, 1964). It was reported that Ahmadu Bello welcomed that idea of Eastern Region's secession, if given the time to "divide our assets" *(Daily Express*, December 30, 1964), all on p. 604; Mackintosh, *op. cit.*,

29. Miners, *op. cit.*, p. 137.

30. It is interesting that after his release from prison in 1966 by Lt. Col. Gowon, Awolowo was chosen as the "Leader of Yoruba", even though there were substantial numbers of Yorubas who never liked him and deprecated him for his "unforgiving" nature despite his public pronouncement about burying old animosities.

31. Schwarz, *op. cit.*, p. 178.

32. The squabble over revenue allocation is another case in point, particular after the Binn Commission recommendations in 1964.

33. David Abernethy, "Nigeria Creates a New Region", *Africa Report*, March 1964, p. 9.

34. *Willink Commission Report, op. cit.,* p. 32

35. *Report of the Resumed Constitutional Conference,* 1958, Nigeria, p. 21. The Nigeria (Constitutional) Order-in-Council, 1960, Second Schedule, chapter 1, section 4 (5).

36. Abernethy, *loc. cit.,* The Northern leaders were to use this as an example of their support for self-determination of minority groups. At the Ad Hoc Constitutional Conference in 1966, the Northern Delegation in its opening speech said:

This North has never objected to the genuine wishes of the various groups of the country. The North did not object for instance to the right of the people of the Southern Cameroons, the former Northern Cameroons and the Midwest to determine their destiny either within or outside the Nigerian association.

- Northern Nigeria delegation, "Opening Speech," *Ad Hoc Constitutional Conference,* Lagos, September 1966 (unpublished).

37. See B. J. Dudley, *Instability and Political Order: Politics and Crisis in Nigeria* (Ibadan: Ibadan University Press, 1973), pp. 74-75, for a discussion of this possibility.

38. Nigeria, Northern House of Assembly Debates (Kaduna), February 26, 1965, col. 65, quoted in Tamuno, *loc. cit.,* p. 576. The Tivs had a long history of opposition to British rule, such as riots in 1960. Thus, the 1964 and 1965 events were nothing new.

39. See J. M. Dent, "A Minority Party – The United Middle Belt Congress" in Mackintosh, *op. cit.,* pp. 461-507, for a fuller discussion of the Tiv people, and UMBC in its relations with the Northern regional government. Also Schwarz, *op. cit.,* pp. 234-244, for a brief discussion of the Tiv and its leader, Mr. J. S. Tarka, in the Nigerian Political scene.

40. T. N. Tamuno, "Separatist Agitations in Nigeria since 1914," *JMAS,* 8, 4 (1970), p. 577. There were rumours that the NPC had supported this group of agitators in the Eastern Region before the military coup to create some semblance of disorder or breakdown of law and order in that region. A State of Emergency as was declared in the West could then be applied in the East. The validity of these rumours could not be confirmed.

41. Boro, Owonaro and Dick were condemned to death for treason. Their sentences were commuted to life imprisonment, but they were later granted pardon after the creation of states (including a Rivers State) in 1967 by Lt. Col. Gowon. They volunteered for military

service to fight against *Biafra*. Boro and Dick lost their lives in active service, on the federal side.

42. Wheare, *op. cit.*, p. 50. The Northern delegation to the *Ad Hoc Conference, 1966,* argued that:

In a young country as large as Nigeria where the ethnic groups are not homogenous, where the cultures differ and where values are not necessarily the same from one part of the country to the other, the text-book rules for political association between the various groups will not necessarily be applicable. "Form of Association for Nigeria," by the Northern Nigeria Delegation, mimeograph (unpublished), Cabinet Office, Lagos, September 1968, p. 1.

43. Nurul Islam, "Comment on Adedeji's Paper," in A. Ayida and Onitiri, *op. cit.*, p. 3.

44. Federal Republic of Nigeria, *The Struggle for One Nigeria. op. cit.*, p. 3.

45. There was a sigh of relief all over the country even in the North. Many Northern politicians who returned after the coup were jeered at–some had to take refuge for a while to hide their faces.

4

THE QUEST FOR A MODEL OF GOVERNMENT

The issue of centrifugal pulls from the regions or the assertion of the regional autonomy did not end with the exit of civilian politicians. The military soon inherited the problems of a weak centre relating to strong regions. What was the reaction of the military?

Unitarism, Confederalism and Federalism

1. From Military- Federalism to Unitarism

On coming to power in January 1966, the military regime under General Ironsi suspended the legislative and executive institutions in the regions and at the centre. Thus, the federal parliament (House of Representatives and the Senate), the offices of the President, and Prime Minister, with his cabinet, were suspended. The Regional Houses of Assembly and of Chiefs, the offices of the Premier, and the Governors of all the four regions were also suspended by Decree No. 1, 1966.[1]

The above decree also gave the Federal Military Government "power to make laws for the peace, order, and good government of Nigeria or any part thereof, with respect to any matter whatsoever."[2] This decree defined the powers of both federal and regional governments. The Military Governor of a region was not to "make laws with respect to any federal matter included in the Exclusive Legislative List"; also he could not "make any law with respect to any matter included in the concurrent legislative list," except "with prior consent of the Federal Military Government." But the "Military Governor of a Region shall have the power to make laws for peace, order and good government of that Region."[3] So were powers distributed in the practice of *military federalism* under General Ironsi.

At the centre (the federal level) were two institutions: the Supreme Military Council (SMC) and the Federal Executive Council (FEC) under

75

the Chairmanship of the Head of the Federal Military Government.[4] These two bodies were basically military, except for the presence of the Inspector-General of Police, and later, the Federal Attorney-General in the Federal Executive Council. The Federal Executive Council was responsible for legislation with regard to federal matters. It was to "exercise general direction and control over every department of the government of the federation."[5] On the other hand, the Supreme Military Council (SMC) was to be the highest legislative and decision-making body for the whole country.

In the Regions, the Governor was responsible to the Supreme Commander, who appointed him (unlike the former Premiers). Each Regional Governor combined the functions of the former Regional Governor, the Premier, the Legislator and the Council of Ministers. He had near-absolute powers. Technically, the suspension of institutions of popular representation and the appointment of regional military governors by the Head of the Federal Military Government (HFMG), gave the impression of a unitary system of government. These were violations of the principles of federalism. In actual practice, however, the regions remained virtually as autonomous as they had been in the civilian regime – except that the military governors who now had both executive and legislative powers were directly responsible to the HFMG. This apparent "quasi-federalism" fits into our model of 'military federalism'. It is interesting to note that the central government retained the word 'federal' in its name – *The Federal Military Government*.

After the three months of vacillation, General Ironsi set up a *Constitutional Review Study Group*, which was to study the constitutional problems of Nigeria and submit a report to a Constituent Assembly to be established later. Under the Chairmanship of Chief Rotimi Williams, this committee was "to identify the constitutional problems in the context of one Nigeria."[6] The General promised the nation that the form of government to be set up would only be established after due consultation with the people, to be followed by a referendum. General Ironsi also set up another commission under Mr. F. Nwokedi (Sole Commissioner) to make proposals for the Unification of Civil Service.[7] An Economic Commission was also established under Chief S. O. Adebo.

76

Yet, on May 24, 1966, without waiting for the report of the Williams Commission, Ironsi opted for centralization under unitarism. This was given political expression by Decree No. 34, 1966, which made Nigeria a Unitary State.

> Nigeria shall on the 24th May 1966... cease to be a federation and shall accordingly as from that day be a republic by the name of the Republic of Nigeria consisting of the whole territory, which immediately before that day was comprised, in a federation.[8]

The former regions were abolished, and Nigeria was reorganized along territorial areas called group of provinces. Each former region was to be known as *group of provinces*. A *National Military Government* was established in place of the Federal Military Government. The Government was

> ...intended to remove the last vestige of intense regionalism of the recent past and to produce that cohesion in the government structure which is so necessary in achieving and maintaining the paramount objectives of the National Military Government... national unity.[9]

The same decree unified all the Civil Services in the country. It stated that as "from the appointed day, all officers in the services of the Republic in a civil capacity shall be officers in a single service to be known as the National Public Service..."[10]

The Northern Emirs and Chiefs rejected this decree and told General Ironsi so. In response, the National Military Government, stressed the transitional nature of the new arrangement and made it clear that "it cannot be seriously emphasized (enough) that the Military Government can only run the government as a unified command. It cannot afford to run five separate governments and separate services as if it were a civilian regime".[11]

In practice, the decree hardly changed the structure of the country. But the unification of the civil services threatened the security of the North and the autonomy of the West. In late May 1966 there was 'communal instability' in the North in which the people of the former Eastern Region, mainly Ibos, lost their lives. This was believed to have been ostensibly a reaction to the political events in the country since January 15, 1966.

After five months, Ironsi had opted for greater centralization. It is probably not clear what would have happened if this had been 'well-timed' – that is if it had been introduced before the dust, which followed the coup, had settled. By May, suspicions had become rife with allegations that the January coup was an Ibo attempt to dominate Nigeria.

As the dust settled, the nature of the coup became more suspicious to many Nigerians and General Ironsi's subsequent actions only aggravated it. He took a 'middle of the road' approach. He wanted the loyalty of the North (whose soldiers formed the bulk of the rank and file of the army) and yet he wanted to meet the demands of the South for more radical changes. He was attempting to conciliate the Northern Region, which had lost its leaders (at regional and federal levels) without alienating the Southern support for the "January Coup" as a 'revolutionary' act. He therefore, left the regions to operate the same way as in the civilian regime, except for modifications, which were necessary by virtue of military presence in the political system.

In a way, Ironsi was a *creature* of circumstances – the prisoner of a coup that had been undertaken (largely) by his kinsmen, the Ibo officers under Nzeogwu and Ifeajuna. Unfortunately, the political and military leaders killed during the coup, except for Col. Unegbe, were mainly from the Northern and Western Regions.[12] General Ironsi had called the January coup Majors "mutineers"; but they were mutineers on whose backs he had ridden to power. Moreover, the initial enthusiasm about the coup, particularly in the South, made heroes of the plotters; in the North, the plotters were criminals who should have been punished.

The suspicion continued among various Nigerian groups. Extra-military social cleavages had not only found their way into the military institution since January 1966, but had heightened inter-group insecurity in that institution. In July 1966, the Northern soldiers in the army staged a counter coup, the military had become an institution for articulating societal conflicts. In a sense this coup, like the January coup, was only partially successful. If in January, Major Nzeogwu had established control over only the Northern Region, in July, the

Northern soldiers failed to assert effective control over the Eastern Region.[13] As later events showed, from this point on, the central government was unable to assert its authority over the Eastern Region.

Ironsi's tragedy might have been his vacillation. He missed the opportunity he had to effect changes in January 1966. By May, he had lost his credibility appreciably and existing suspicions had heightened once again. Perhaps, Ironsi should have known that political leadership required the ability to master the environment well, to feel the political temperature of the system and to understand the limits to which decisions can be taken without threatening the basic consensual values which bind the society together. In fact, the fall of the first military regime is illustrative of the relative weakness of the centre in the face of centrifugal pulls in the regions. As regions pulled their strings, instability loomed at the centre, even under military rules.

2. *The Quest for a Model: From Confederation to Military Federalism*

After four days of political confusion, Lt. Col. Yakubu Gowon emerged as the Head of the Federal Military Government and Supreme Commander of the Armed Forces of Nigeria.[14] Lt. Colonel Ojukwu, the Governor of Eastern Nigeria, refused to accept Gowon's authority, who he claimed, was his junior in the army.[15]

Governor Ojukwu's refusal to recognize the authority of the Central Government was a direct challenge to the process of state building. The coup having been partially successful, Gowon could not immediately impose his authority over the Eastern Region. In fact, the Federal Government was advised against the military invasion of the Eastern Region at this point.[16] While the problems of command and control lingered on, military leaders and regional officials agreed that all military personnel be posted to barracks in their regions of origin. The Supreme Commander was to take charge of security in Lagos. Compromising as this was, it gave the Eastern Region greater autonomy than she had.[17] The atmosphere of uncertainty dragged on until the meeting of the *Ad Hoc* Constitutional Conference in Lagos in September 1966.

a) *Ad Hoc Constitutional Conference: The Quest for a Political Stop-Gap*

Gowon as the new Head of the Federal Military Government called representatives (often referred to as 'leaders of thought') of the four regions to meet in Lagos on September 12, 1966, to look into the form of political association among Nigerian groups. Part of the informal function of the *Ad Hoc Constitutional Conference* was to create a framework for restoring mutual confidence among Nigerian groups. As Gowon put it, the conference was to resolve the question – "Where one goes from here."

However, in his address, the Head of State, Gowon, made it clear to members that given Nigeria's heterogeneity and size, a *unitary* form of government was unsuitable.[18] In his broad guidelines of operations given to the conference, Gowon ruled out the option of a "complete break-up", which he said would be "economically and politically suicidal." The alternatives left for the conference were as follows:

1. "a federal system with a weak central government";
2. "a federal system with a strong central government";
3. "confederation";
4. "an entirely new arrangement which will be peculiar to Nigeria and which has not yet found its way into any political dictionary."[19]

After the conference had resolved the issue of the appropriate form of government, they were to consider matters such as:
1. the distribution of powers as between the regional governments and the central government;
2. the territorial divisions of the country; and
3.the system for selecting representatives to the legislatures.

There was no doubt that Gen. Gowon had limited the choice of the committee; the ruling out of secession[20] and a unitary form of government were probably reactions to the earlier experiences of centralization under Ironsi's administration.[21] Clearly Gen. Gowon favoured a federal system with a strong centre.

Gen. Gowon "avoided anything that touched on confederation" because "confederation and secession are one and the same thing in the context of the Nigerian situation... I never accepted and will never accept a confederation."[22] However, he allowed the conference to debate on forms of government, including confederation. Clearly, only two choices were left to the conference: the two forms of federalism mentioned above and possibly a new model.

The conference was left to deliberate on the issues above. The *Northern Region*, in its memorandum, proposed a *confederal system* of government. It suggested that since each region had "managed to preserve some measure of order and sense of unity within its confines, each region should be constituted into an autonomous state, with subjects of common interest to be delegated to a Common Service Commission. Each region or state was to have the right to secede completely and unilaterally from the Union."[23]

Like North, the *Eastern Region* delegation pressed for a *confederation*. It suggested that the right of a region to secede from the union be accepted. Thus far, the position of the Eastern Region with regard to the form of association was very similar to that of the Northern Region. Its spokesman, Eni Njoku, pointed out, "...the sort of association we envisage is therefore one which will be very loose indeed."[24] But going beyond the North's stand, he suggested that each region should have the right to issue its own currency.[25] Thus, Gowon's order that the conference should not discuss secession did not stop conference from doing so.

The *Western Region* delegation agreed that a federal system would be ideal for Nigeria, given its linguistic and ethnic heterogeneity. However, as Awolowo clearly pointed out, the delegation believed that "knowing the attitude of the North, the attitude of the East," federalism would be inappropriate at that point in time. It therefore propose a *confederation* or a "Commonwealth of Nigeria" until such a time as peace returned to Nigeria. As its spokesman, Prof. Oluwasanmi put it, the Western delegation's aim was to "devise a system which is not too loose as to scatter us but is such that it can go with us into a truly federal system."[26]

However, the *Midwestern Region* delegation believed that a *federal system* of government was practicable within the Nigerian context then. Its leader, Chief Anthony Enahoro, pointed out that Midwestern Nigeria's only mandate was for a federal system. The Midwest favoured a federal system with a strong centre within the framework of additional states, given the crisis situation in Nigeria. Chief Enahoro rejected the idea of a confederation because "no confederation has survived." "I would like to open as I would close," he declared,

> ...the Midwestern Nigerian delegation believes that the answer to Nigeria's problem lies in a federation (belief in a Federation of Nigeria) not withstanding the situation which has emerged or which appears to be emerging at this conference in the last few days. We do not abandon that stand. We believe in a federation, and we do not think that because we cannot have a strong federation, we cannot therefore have a federation at all.[27]

Thus, the Northern, Eastern, and Western delegations opted for a confederal system of government as an interim solution to Nigeria's political impasse. For understandable reasons (of the losses of life by Easterners), the Eastern delegation was more rigid in its stand for a loose form of political association. It is interesting that the Midwestern delegation stood firmly on its grounds for a federal system. While the Northern, Eastern and Western Regions could each stand alone in the event of the breakup of the country, the Midwest (comprising numerous minority groups) saw only federalism as its basis for survival. The fear of survival of a small political unit in a confederation led to a change of posture by the Lagos delegation. The leader of the Lagos State delegation, Dr. T. O. Elias, explained this fear succinctly:

> ...we had hoped that we would come here to fashion an acceptable form of government in which it would be possible for us, Lagos, to exist as a State, as one of the States of the Federal Government.
>
> Indeed, there is nothing dearer to the hearts of the people of Lagos than that... I had never thought that...a moment would come when we would be talking of the kind of association that we are putting forward as an alternative to the continuation of a federal Nigeria... And so, we are associating ourselves with the proposal that if the Regions are to have the powers which we had suggested for them, we shall very much loathe to be left as kind of free-for-all territory which is suitable only for a convenient centre of arrangement but which is not really what you would call a Capital Territory of a United Country.[28]

The issue of the creation of additional states featured prominently at the conference despite efforts by some delegates to give it a secondary status.[29]

Ad Hoc Constitutional Conference and the "States" Issue

The three big regions - -the North, West and East - -in their memoranda used the four regions (the North, West, East and Midwest) as the basis for future political association. It was only the Midwestern delegation which, from the beginning, called for the creation of states in a new federal framework with a strong centre. It was willing to compromise on the number of regions for the period of interim government. However, it was unwilling to compromise on the state issue, in general. Thus the three big regions, which had asked for confederation, were unlikely to ask for the creation of additional states. Additional states would mean smaller units, which would be more dependent on the federal government, thus working against a confederal system. Bigger states were more likely to survive outside the association or in a loose form of association than smaller states. On the issue of additional states, all regions had intra-regional problems of consensus. Let us illustrate this point with the case of the Northern delegation.

The Northern Delegation: A Case Study

Contrary to press reports, it was true that the Northern Region declared its support, in principle, for the creation of additional units in Nigeria. In its opening speech, the Northern delegation made its point clear:

> As far back as 1953, when the principle of self-determination was accepted by us all and implemented in respect of Southern Cameroons, we had accepted that finance, economic viability and the wish of the people as expressed through a free election were the basis of self-determination. These principles, which were entrenched in our Constitution, we have always supported. What we have objected to is the habit by which people from outside the North draw up imaginary lines creating new states in the North in order to satisfy a political ambition. If the people in the North want additional states, let them say so. This is their inalienable right. But some people from outside

the North think they have the right to speak for Northerners without conceding the right for Northerners to speak for themselves.[30]

In practice, however, there was also evidence that the Northern delegation did not support the creation of more subnational units (states). In its working paper (among members of the delegation) entitled *Tactical Moves*, the delegation was advised that in case a "confederation" became apparent, the creation of a Lagos State might be supported " in principle," subject to a referendum to determine the wishes of the people. However, if the other regions opted for a "federation," "the political dangers of a Lagos State within such a context are numerous," and the delegation was to insist that there "be no change in the existing Regional boundaries".[31] But the publication of the Northern position in the media as anti-states creation led to the issuance of a press release by the delegation stating its position in the original memorandum, which "in principle" accepted the creation of additional states.

However, there was every evidence that the Northern delegation was under pressure from within and from outside the delegation for the creation of additional states. A memorandum submitted to the Northern delegation, possibly by a member of the delegation, entitled *The Case for the Creation of Additional States in Nigeria,*[32] gives this impression most strongly. The paper noted that there had been persistent demands for the creation of additional states in the North and the East, which had gone unheeded. "The demand must be faced to provide the means of satisfying local aspirations and ending a long-drawn political issue which is certain to continue resulting in disharmony among the people and possible violence." It rejected the argument of viability of states, which it suggested, "should be matched against any weakness and abuses — a centralized administration tends to emphasize and which are greatly reduced in a system where the units of administration are small and contain a greater degree of homogeneity than in larger unit."[33]

With regard to the boundaries of new states, the paper suggested "existing provincial boundaries"— twelve states in the North, and a total of twenty-four states in the whole country.[34] While the writer of this memorandum accepted that the method by which states were to be created could differ from one region to another, he stressed that "the actual creation of the State should be declared simultaneously."[35] This memorandum made two interesting observations, which we shall quote here, in the light of later events:

> Inter-regional jealousies coupled with the fear of domination of one region over the rest arising from either the size of the North with its sheer weight in population or of East with its skilled manpower, and therefore a strong grip on all aspects of our production and administration, are among the root-causes of Nigeria's perennial problem. The creation of additional states and insistence that internal affairs of each state should primarily be the responsibility of its own people would remove most of the causes for the present distrust of one another.[36]

Finally, he warned that "Right now the situation in the country under the military regime is fluid enough to facilitate the creation of states as is being proposed. It is however hardening and any delay over the proposals will have the effect of making its implementation more difficult and unlikely."[37]

We have given these memoranda an elaborate discussion to illustrate some of the pressures from within the Northern delegation. Among pressures from within the delegation for the creation of additional states were those from late Mr. J. S. Tarka, late Alhaji Aminu Kano, His Highness, Late Chief Abraham Ajene Okpabi (Och'Idoma II). Pressures from outside the committee came from military and from various ethnic groups in the North.

Pressures from the military took direct and indirect forms. It was reliably learned from a member of the delegation[38] that after the publication of the Northern delegation's opposition to the creation of states, Lt. Col. Murtala Mohammed[39] met the members of the delegation at their Marina residence later in the evening. He was said to have been angry about the Northern delegation's position and to have insinuated that if the North was not ready to stay within Nigeria, the Northern soldiers should be informed to withdraw to their region before another crisis erupted. This was interpreted by some of the delegates as a deprecation of the Northern delegation's ambivalent position on the creation of states. According to the source, when the

Northern delegation went to see Lt. Col. Gowon at his Ikeja barracks residence later, the latter was said to have confirmed the impression of the delegates earlier in the day. Lt. Col. Gowon was said to have asked them; "What do you think other Nigerians would think of us if we create additional states in the other parts of Nigeria and left North intact?"[40] General Gowon later confirmed this statement to this writer.

From that point, it became clear to the delegates, according to this informant, who was a member of the delegation that the new military rulers in Lagos were in support of the creation of additional states. It was, therefore, not surprising that on returning from the North (after consultations) the Northern delegation openly supported the creation of additional states in Nigeria and a federal system with an "effective central government." It also came out to support the creation of states simultaneously over the country after ascertaining the wishes of the people. However, it opposed the creation of states on a linguistic and ethnic basis. It suggested that the existing regions should be constituted into states with increased powers over their own affairs, "and that in order to allay the fears of domination by sections of the country, the principle of creation of states must be agreed."[41] We do not intend to give the impression that only the pressure from the military was behind the change in the Northern stand, but it was a very crucial factor. Other groups, such as top Northern civil servants also played important roles in convincing the delegation of the disadvantages of confederalism, particularly for the North. Many forces came into the discussion. The result was a Northern change of stand.

Having gone into detail on the Northern case to show some of the forces at work during the *Ad Hoc* Conference, we may now state briefly the position of other regions on the issue of the creation of states.

a) Other Regions and State Issues

It is interesting that the Eastern Region, which had always asked for the creation of additional states elsewhere in the country, should now be opposed to it. But such opposition was plausible. The delegation felt that the creation of states would weaken the already "insecure" position of the Eastern Region in Nigeria—given her verdant memory of the massacres of Ibos only months before.

Hence, Eni Njoku,[42] the leader of the Eastern delegation, announced that his delegation did "not believe that the splitting up of the country into some states at this stage is what we need in order to normalize conditions of life in this country and possible security for its inhabitants." To split the country into states would involve long processes "we cannot afford under the present crisis." Past experiences had shown, Njoku continued, that it was "not in the interest of this country to have a strong central government." Since it was impossible to create states, which would be devoid of minorities, Njoku pointed out that it was the "view of the Eastern Nigeria delegation that this problem can be contained and satisfied within large regional units." While the East accepted the principles of the creation of states, such an exercise "should be the responsibility of the Eastern Regional Government." In conclusion, he continued:

> ...all that we hold at present is that the issue of the creation of new states should be an internal responsibility of the regions. The initiative for the creation must come from the region within which the state is to be created...We recognize that there will be additional states but that for the purpose of what we are engaged in, we do not think that this is an appropriate time for the creation of these states.[43]

Thus, the Eastern delegation opposed the creation of states, even though it recognized the possibility of doing so in the future. By leaving the issue of states to the regions, the Eastern Region was giving the regions more functions than was acceptable to most of the other delegations. It was most unlikely that a region, which believed that the creation of additional states would create a "strong central government" — an idea repugnant to it — would create states on its own. Moreover, it was unlikely that minorities in the East would have had their own state under an Eastern Region, when it was the same delegation, which fought vigorously to exclude memoranda (from minorities in the East) from the official delegation. It can be argued that for the Eastern Region, the experience of the massacres in the months before the conference had made them suspicious of any effort to split the East, because it would dilute its solidarity.

The Western Region delegation accepted the principle of the creation of additional states, which it stressed, should be along linguistic and ethnic lines. But in the context of Nigeria then, the states issue should be shelved until Nigeria was ready to move back into a federal system. However, if the conference adopted a federal system for the country, many additional states should be created, including a Lagos State. The Lagos delegation, of course, favoured the creation of additional states within a federal framework. As T. O. Elias, its leader, maintained: "We, being statists (people who really want a Lagos State), cannot deny the right of other areas of the country having their states..."[44]

The Midwestern delegation had always stood for a federation of many states, with a strong central government. Thus, by the end of the conference, all regions and Lagos accepted the need for the creation of additional states (after a plebiscite to determine the wishes of the people concerned), except the Eastern Region, which reserved its position in view of a conference to be held in that region. We have gone into this elaborate discussion of this conference to show how leading Nigerians felt about the issue of additional sub-regional political units at the Constitutional Conference. The military found itself embroiled in the politics of federalism.

Unfortunately, this conference did not complete its work. Its work was disrupted by further violence in the North,[45] and it was suspended indefinitely. The new killings of Easterners in the North solidified the support for Ojukwu in the East. Pressures for secession of the East had dated as far back as June 1966, when some intellectuals at Ibadan University handed a proposal to that effect to Ojukwu.[46] With the return of many refugees to the East, pressures of various kinds increased for the amelioration of the condition in the other parts of Nigeria. However, if Ojukwu was reluctant about secession in July, the September massacres helped him to make up his mind about it. The political temperature in Nigeria was high. Uncertainty pervaded the whole system. Rumours were rife and the anxiety graph rose steeply.

Meanwhile, on 30 November, 1966, after the suspension of the *Ad Hoc* Committee on Constitutional Proposals, General Gowon made a broadcast to the nation,[47] in which he emphasized that the "idea of a temporary confederation is unworkable", and that each region as a virtually sovereign state can "contract out or refuse to join any common service." To Gowon,

In the stable federation, no region should be large enough to be able to threaten secession or hold the rest of the federation to ransom in times of national crisis. This brings me to major question of the creation of new states. I wish to make it clear to the nation that honestly I personally have no vested interest in the creation of any particular state, but there is no doubt that without a definite commitment on the states question, normalcy and freedom from fear of domination by one region or the other cannot be achieved. [48]

Lt. Col. Gowon then announced the "principles for the creation of new states":

    i) no state should be in a position to dominate or control the central government;

    ii) each state should form one compact geographical area;

    iii) administrative convenience, the facts of history, and the wishes of the people concerned must be taken into account;

    iv) each state should be in a position to discharge effectively the functions allocated to regional governments; and

    v) it is also essential that the new states should be created simultaneously.[49]

"All these criteria have to be applied together. No one principle should be applied to the exclusion of the others." Given Nigeria's "size and distribution of the Nigerian population and resources, the country could be divided into not less than eight and not more than fourteen states." The exact number of states would be "determined through the detailed application of these criteria and will be fully debated in the Constituent Assembly, members of which he had promised to appoint.

Thus, amidst Nigeria's political uncertainty and instability, for the first time, a head of the federal government had committed himself to creating some states in Nigeria. However, the political uncertainties in Nigeria continued until the military leaders, at the behest of Ghana's Head of State, General Ankrah, met at the Peduase Lodge, Aburi, Ghana, in January of 1967.

b) Aburi: The Military and the Politics of Accommodation

At Aburi, Ghana, Gowon and Ojukwu met for the first time since July 1966. At the meeting the leaders agreed that:

1. the army was to be governed by the Supreme Military Council – the Chairman of which was to be Head of the Federal Military Government and Commander-in-Chief of the Armed Forces;
2. a military headquarters in which each region was to be represented, was to be set up under a Chief of Staff;
3. in each region was to be established an Area Command under an Area Commander;
4. the Supreme Military Council (SMC) was to deal with all matters of appointment and promotions of people in executive posts in the Armed Forces and the Police; and
5. military governors for the duration of the Military Government were to have control over Area Commands in their regions for purposes of internal security.[50]

These agreements virtually regionalized the Nigerian Army. The functions of the Defence which used to be within the exclusive legislative list of the Federal Government, was now to be shared by the regions.

The military leaders also agreed that appointments in the public service, into 1) diplomatic and consular posts, 2) senior posts in the Armed Forces and the Police, and 3) super-scale Federal Civil Service and Federal Corporation posts were to be made by the SMC. These and other executive and legislative decisions affecting the whole country must be determined by the SMC, and in the absence of a meeting, be referred to all the Regional Governors for their concurrence and comments.[51] In the final Communiqué, the military leaders agreed that future meetings were to be held in Nigeria in a location to be announced later. All of them expressed regret about the bloodshed and vowed to prevent its reoccurrence.

The Aburi meeting was largely an attempt to resolve some issues of conflict, which had polarized the relationship among the military rulers, with the hope that it would pave the way for the future settlement of Nigeria's political problems. Instead of dampening conflicts between the Federal Government and Eastern regional government, the Aburi resolutions accentuated it. Both Gowon and Ojukwu interpreted these resolutions in various forms. To Ojukwu, it meant extreme decentralization, which should give the Eastern Region full control over its affairs—a-quasi-sovereign state sharing some essential services with other units in the 'federation'.

On the other hand, Gowon saw Aburi decisions differently. To him, Aburi was an agreement for a "return to the constitutional position before January 17, 1966. Thus any powers, which were taken away from the regions after January 17, were restored to them... I emphasize that it was never the intention that any Military Governor should have the power to veto decision taken by the Supreme Military Council."[52] The two leaders must have been viewing Aburi resolutions through two perceptual prisms. Whatever the intensions were, there was greater centrifugal pull to which Gowon had acceded. At Aburi it had been agreed that the regions be more autonomous than they were in January, 1967–an exercise done at the expense of the central government.

By March, 1967, Ojukwu had threatened to take unilateral action if the Aburi decisions were not implemented. But disagreements on details delayed its implementation. Finally, the Decree No. 8, 1967 (which implemented the Aburi decisions) came into effect on March 17, 1967. According to this Decree, Nigeria became more *confederal* than it had ever been. By its terms, a DECREE (which was the sole prerogative of the Federal Military Government, by Decree No. 1, 1966) "was to come into operation only with the concurrence of the Head of the Federal Military Government and all the Military Governors." Both legislative and executive powers of the government of the Federation were vested in the Supreme Military Council. The Federal Executive Council was to discharge only these functions, which "especially delegated to it by the Supreme Military Council."

For the first time, the concurrence of the Head of State and of, at least, three (3) Military Governors, was made essential with respect to certain matters in section 69(b) of the Constitution—for example, trade, commerce, industry, transport, the Armed Forces, the Nigerian Police and higher education. The above provisions made the federal government highly dependent on regional governments. The Federal Government's action on any of the listed items could have been easily paralyzed by the objection of any two regional governors. This was basically a confederal arrangement, in which the "general government is dependent upon the regional governments."[53]

Moreover, each regional governor was to appoint judges of the High Court of his region, while those of the Supreme Court were to be appointed by the Supreme Military Council. Most of the powers given to the HFMG by Decree No. 1, 1966 became vested in the Supreme Military Council. Whereas under Decree No. 1, 1966, the SMC was to advise the HFMG, now it had most of the powers, and the Head of State was a mere Chairman. All appointments in Super-Scale Group 6 and above in the Federal Public Service and posts of Deputy Commissioners of Police and above in the Nigerian Police Force were to be made by the Supreme Military Council. The Supreme Military Council was to make appointments of ambassadors and High Commissioners as well as principal representatives to other countries.

Certainly the decree went very far to meet Ojukwu's demand. The regions became stronger than the federal centre. Ojukwu could have gotten from this decree what he had failed to get at the *Ad Hoc* constitutional conference. As Ojukwu's chief secretary, Chief N. U. Akpan admitted, the Decree No. 8, "in my view faithfully implemented the Aburi decisions."[54] In fact, the decree "for the first time included regional governors as members of the Federal Executive." As Gowon confessed, "the positions of the regional governments have actually been strengthened."[55]

However, Ojukwu rejected this decree and passed edicts seizing federal property in the Eastern Region. Centrifugal pulls had gone to the extent that federal authority was no longer binding on the Eastern Region, in practical terms. With the benefit of hindsight, Nigeria was probably lucky that Ojukwu rejected the decree despite its embedded advantages for him.

The Aburi resolutions were indicative of the military's inability in the politics of compromise and tolerance, which had been typical of Nigeria's political system. Not only did Aburi expose the military's inability to resolve knotty political problems, it showed the military as politically immature. If as General Ankrah had told the inaugural session of the meeting, "Whatever the situation, we are soldiers and soldiers are always statesmen, not politicians,"[56] the military rulers emerged from the meeting as apparent statesmen but not politicians. Later events, which led to secession even, questioned their claims to statesmanship, in view of their roles.

As an exercise by the military elites towards finding solutions to Nigeria's political problems, it was a woeful failure—a masterpiece in contradictions and irresolution, giving rise to a multitude of interpretations. Even the "unaccepted" Decree No. 8 lasted from March 17 to May 27, 1967. It went into the wastepaper basket with less pain than it had emerged as a political memorandum.

Again Nigerian leaders had made an adjustment. They had moved from extreme centralization (under unitarism) back to military-federalism (of January 1966) and then to confederalism. Again, they had failed. As their search for a more conducive form of political association continued, the issue of the creation of additional states became more prominent as an alternative solution to extreme decentralization of Aburi. Ideally, one would have thought that under military rule there would be less preoccupation with forms of government. Nigeria's complex state dictated the pace and even military leaders had to respond. What political adjustments were made from May 1967, and to what extent did these strike equilibrium between centripetal and centrifugal forces in the Nigerian political system? How did such adjustments reflect on the powers of the centre?

c) *The Military and Structural Engineering*

Attempts at bringing about peace in Nigeria and establish better understanding between the Federal Military Government and the Eastern Region government, by various people, had failed. By March 1967, it had become evident that Ojukwu was going to lead the Eastern Region in a secessionist bid. Thus, when, on 26 May, the Consultative Assembly, the Chiefs, and the Elders of Eastern Nigeria were summoned to Enugu, it became very clear that the latent secession of that region was going to be made manifest by a formal declaration.

In the face of this imminent secession, Gowon found himself powerless. If, indeed, force was to be used in defence of the interests of the minorities in the Eastern Nigeria, Gowon would have to declare a State of Emergency. He could not do this without the concurrence of the other military governors, in accordance with the provisions of Decree No. 8. Yet, the pressure on Gowon to take quick action before Ojukwu's declaration of secession mounted. Ojukwu had always been taking the initiative. Now pressures mounted on Gowon to cease the initiative and put Ojukwu on the defensive.

Gowon had promised the nation on November 1966, that much as he would have liked to avoid bloodshed, "if circumstances compel me to preserve the integrity of Nigeria by force, I shall do my duty to my country."[57] That duty to his country could, in the circumstances, only be performed by sidetracking the provisions of a decree to which he had been a party, as Ojukwu could not be expected to agree to the declaration of a State of Emergency. Hence, when (without the concurrence of, at least, three of the military governors of the regions) Gowon declared a State of Emergency over all the country on May 27, 1967, he in effect staged a coup.

In the State of Emergency, Gowon assumed full powers (which had been taken away from him by Decree No. 8, 1967) – "for the short period necessary to carry through measures which are now urgently required."[58] Gowon went on to give an analysis of the political problems of the country and his political prescription.

> The main obstacle to the future stability in this country is the present structural imbalance in the Nigerian federalism. Even Decree No. 8 on Confederation or loose Association will never survive if any one section of the country is in a position to hold others ransom.[59]

Regretting the inability within the circumstances for "consultations and plebiscites", Gowon simultaneously created twelve states out of the four regions.[60]

Thus, after twenty years of demands for the creation of additional states in Nigeria, Gowon had created states by decree, three days before the secession by the former Eastern Region. These new states were six in the North, and six in the South.[61] Why twelve states? The number had no magic twist to it. As Allison Ayida (the Permanent Secretary for Economic Planning in 1967 and later Finance) pointed out "The number twelve is of no strategic value."[62] However, Lt. Col. Gowon had intimated the nation in his November 30 broadcast that he would create no less than eight, but no more than fourteen states. As Ayida noted, it was clear that "the most sensitive potential threat to the stability of the Nigerian Federation was... a North-South confrontation, and it was of strategic importance that the number of "Northern" parts of the country should be seen to be equal to the number of "Southern" states (this was an important consideration which could not be explicit in the days of the "gathering storm" in early 1967)..."[63]

In a swift process of structural engineering, Gowon had created a new Federation with smaller *subnational* units. This move, Gowon said, was designed "to correct the imbalance in the administrative structure of the country" and to "minimize future political friction and ensure a stable federation."[64] Within the framework of smaller states it was unlikely that *subnational* units would "consider themselves self-sufficient and almost entirely independent", as the former regions had done. It was hoped that with the creation of smaller *subnational* units, the federal government would be more able to assert itself as the "real government of Nigeria".

In a way, the military was compartmentalizing areas of conflict in federal–subnational states relations. It was hoped that by limiting the areas of conflict through geopolitical compartmentalization, the intensity and nature of conflict would be correspondingly minimized.

To what extent was the federal government able to assert its authority after May 27, 1967? What was the nature of the relationship between the new states and the Federal Government? What factors are responsible for this relationship? These questions will be treated in the next chapter.

Notes and references

1.   The Federal Military Government, "Constitution (Suspension and Modification) Decree (1966, No. 1)" in *Laws of the Federal Republic of Nigeria, 1966.* (Lagos: Government Printer, 1966), pp. A3 – A11, 17th January, 1966.

2.   *ibid.,* p. A 3.

3.   *ibid.,*

4.   *The Members of the Supreme Military Council.*

a) The Head of the Federal Military Government (President of the Council); b) Head of the Nigerian Army; c) Head of the Nigerian Air Force; d) The Chief of Staff, Armed Forces; e) as from March 1966, the Military Governors of the regions: North, East, West, and the Midwest, see Dudley (1973), *op. cit.,* p. 118; f) the Attorney-General of the

Federation—by Decree No. 20, 1966 1 April, 1, section 4 "shall attend the meetings of the Supreme Military Council and of the Federal Executive Council in an advisory capacity." Laws of Nigeria, *op. cit.,* 1966, p. A99. Dudley claims that the Supreme Military Council "Rather than being a deliberative decision-making body... was in fact, little more than ratification organ." Dudley, 1973, *op. cit.,* p. 128.

The Members of the Federal Executive Council

a) The Head of the Federal Military Government (Chairman); b) The Head of the Nigerian Army; c) The Head of the Nigerian Navy; d) The Head of the Air Force; e) The Chief of Staff, Armed Forces; f) The Chief of Staff, Nigerian Army; g) The Attorney-General of the Federation; and h) The Inspector-General of Police and Deputy Inspector-General of Police.

5. Decree No. 20, 1996, Schedule 2, Section 97, in the *Laws of Federal Republic of Nigeria*, 1966, *op. cit.,* p. 99, of the Federal Executive Council, Dudley observed that:

"Contrary to what might have been expected, they (the Federal Executive Council) provided no guide or leadership to regions, and in embroiling themselves with the problem of administration may be said to have established a pattern which the regions were to follow."

Dudley (1973), *op. cit.,* p. 117.

6. Address by H.E. Major General Aguiyi-Ironsi, Head of the Federal Military Government and Supreme Commander of the Armed Forces of Nigeria, at the Inaugural Meeting of the "Constitutional Review Study Group" in Lagos, March 24, 1966. Also see Billy Dudley, *Instability and Political Order: Politics and Crisis in Nigeria* (Ibadan: University Press, 1973), pp. 117-125.

7.Mr. Nwokedi was made a "Sole Commissioner" in an exercise in which Ironsi would have been wiser to have appointed regional representatives as members, especially since regional services were involved in the unification exercise. The provision that Mr. Nwokedi (an Ibo reputedly very close to Ironsi) should sit with two representatives in every region he visited was not enough. The representatives had no imput in the report write-up (because they were not members of the Commission) and were reported not to have been sent copies of the report submitted to Ironsi.

8. The Federal Republic of Nigeria, "Constitution (Suspension and Modification) (no. 5) Decree No. 34, 1966" in *Laws of the Federal Republic of Nigeria,* 1966, *op., cit.,* p. A153.

9. Republic of Nigeria, *Broadcast to the Nation,* by H.E. Major-General J. T. U. Aguiyi-Ironsi, Head of National Military Government and Supreme Commander of the Armed Forces, May 24, 1966, (Lagos: Ministry of Information, 1966), p. 3.

10. Decree No. 34, 1966, *op., cit.,* p. A155.

11. Republic of Nigeria, *Press Release,* No. 686/1966 (Lagos). Also, Document 31, "Statement issued by the Supreme Military Council on 8 June, 1966" in H.M.A Kirk-Greene, *Crisis and Conflict in Nigeria Vol. 1,* (Ibadan: Oxford University Press, 1971), pp. 184-185.

12. Among the politicians killed were the Prime Minister, Tafawa Balewa (North), Federal Minister of Finance, Chief Festus Okotie-Eboh (Midwest); the Premier of the Northern Region, Sir Ahmadu Bello (North); the Premier of the Western Region, Samuel Akintola (in political alliance with the NPC). The Military officers were Brigadier Zachariah Maimalari (North); Col. Abogo Largema (North); Col. Yakubu Pam (North); Col. Kur Mohammed (North); Brig. Samuel Ademulegun (West); Col. Shodeinde (West); and Lt. Col. Unegebe (East) – the Quarter-Master General shot dead after his refusal to hand over the key to the armoury. These killings and subsequent events created suspicions about the intentions of the coup. It was not the coup itself, but how it was executed which created suspicions about the ethnic tinge to the coup.

13. Robin Luckham, *The Nigerian Military: A Sociological Analysis of Authority and Revolt: 1960 – 67* (London: Cambridge University Press, 1971).

14. Major-General J. T. U. Aguiyi Ironsi had been killed in the July coup together with the Military Governor of the Western Region, Lt. Col. Adekunle Fajuyi.

15. Col. Ojukwu told Gowon at Aburi:

How can you ride above people's heads and sit in Lagos purely because you are the head of the group who have their fingers poised on the trigger?

Ironically, that was how Ojukwu ascended to political power as Governor. The coup-makers in January 1966 had "their fingers poised on the trigger." Federal Republic of Nigeria, *Meeting of the Military*

Leaders: held at Peduase Lodge, Aburi, Ghana, 4 and 5 January, 1967 (Lagos: Federal Ministry of Information), p. 10. But as Commodore Wey told the Military Officers:

> I want to repeat, if we did not have the opportunity of having Jack (Gowon) to accept, God knows we would have all been finished... I do think people can appreciate the difficulty we were in... (ibid., p. 13).

16. R. Luckham, *op. cit.,* pp. 304-305.

17. N. U. Akpan, *The Struggle for Secession in Nigeria, 1966-1970: A Personal Account of the Nigerian Civil War* (London: Frank Cass, 1971). He explained in this book the dynamics of autonomy and regional self-determination in the former Eastern Region at this point in time.

18. In reacting to the Northern opposition to the Unitary Decree, The Supreme Military Council in its statement of June 8, 1966 had made it clear that:

> It cannot be seriously emphasized that the Military Government while in office can only run the government as a Unified Command. It cannot afford to run five separate governments and separate services as if it were a civilian regime.

Thus the SMC was accepting that Military rule was incompatible with federalism. Yet it had operated in the context of federal pretences for five months. Gowon did return to the operation of military *federal* system thereafter.

19. Federal Republic of Nigeria. *Ad Hoc Constitutional Proposals: Verbatim Report* (National Hall, Lagos: 12 September, 1966), p. 3.

20. It is interesting that both the Northern and Eastern delegations wanted the right to secession by regions written into the interim constitutions.

21. The Northern Delegation, "The Form of Association for Nigeria", *Ad Hoc* Constitutional Conference. The delegation observed that:

> We have had two attempts at a unitary form of government. The first attempt proved unsatisfactory, the second proved a disaster. We have also had two attempts at federal system. The first attempt ended in chaos and we are again presented with an opportunity to look dispassionately at our future association. (mimeograph), p.3.

Similarly, Prof. Oluwasanmi of the Western delegation declared the stand of the West: "We think that a unitary system of government is wrong constitutional medicine for the ill which besets this country". *Verbatim Report*, September 1966 (mimeograph).

22. *Drum* Magazine (March, 1968).

23. Northern Delegation, "Form of Association for Nigeria," *loc. cit.,* (mimeograph).

24. *Verbatim Report,* September 16, 1966.

25. Dudley, 1973, *op. cit.,* pp. 153-154.

26. *Verbatim Report,* September 6, 1966.

27. *Verbatim Report,* September 4, 1966.

28. *ibid.,*

29. In response to Dr. Elias' suggestion that the conference set up a machinery for the creation of states, Prof. Oluwasanmi of the Western Region, while supporting the idea, pointed out that the "immediate question before us" is "how to get the country on its feet again." *Verbatim Report*, mimeograph, September 1966.

30. Northern Delegation, "Opening Speech," *Ad Hoc* Constitutional Conference (unpublished), mimeograph, (National Hall, Lagos)

31. Northern Delegation, *Tactical Moves* (unpublished), mimeograph, sections B and C. Most likely a working paper for the Northern delegation came out clearly against the creation of a Lagos State.

32. "The Case for the Creation of Additional states in Nigeria" is a paper found in the file of one of the Northern delegates to the conference. It has no name appended to it, but from the tone of the memo, it is likely to be a memo from someone within the delegation. It is also very elaborate in its analysis of the Northern situation, and one has the impression that it was also presented orally. (unpublished).

33. *ibid.,* paragraph 1 and 2; p.7.

34. *ibid.,*

35. *ibid.,* paragraph 8; paragraph 15.

36. *ibid.,*

37. *ibid.,*

38. Interview with a highly reliable source directly involved in the proceedings.

39. Lt. Col. Murtala Mohammed, as the Head of the Army Signal Corps, was actively involved in the July coup of 1966.

40. The words in quotes were the words recollected by the informant to have been said by Gowon. He believed the content of Gowon's statement was essentially the same as above, and a confirmation of Murtala's position.

41. *Verbatim Report,* September 20, 1966, mimeograph.

42. *Verbatim Report,* September 16, 1966, mimeograph.

43. *ibid.,*

44. *ibid.,*

45. There were reports over *Radio Dahomey* about the massacre of Northerners in the East. This was relayed by Radio-Television, Kaduna. These were in response to a series of massacres in the North... of the Ibos. The Eastern delegation, ostensibly fearing for their security in Lagos, withdrew their presence from the renewed conference of October 23, 1966. For a discussion of the massacres, see Kirk-Greene, *op. cit.,* Vol. 1, 1971, pp. 62-69.

46. *Insight,* October 1968, 22, p.7. In an interview with this journal, Mr. Ukpabi Asika, the Administrator of the East Central State, claimed that as far back as April/May 1966, his colleagues at the University of Ibadan:

> ...who were Ibos began meeting regularly on Sundays. Some of their meetings resulted in a memorandum, which was given to me on 26 June 1966 for comments. The memorandum argued and the arguments have since been published –they are part of the **Crisis 1966** series for division of the Eastern Nigerian government; that Nigerian unity was non-existent; there was no real basis for it, and ended with declaration "Long Live the East! We have a new nation!"
> See also Dudley, *op. cit.,* p. 148.

47. Broadcast by H. E. Lt. Col. Yakubu Gowon, the Head of the Federal Military Government and Supreme Commander of the Armed Forces of Nigeria, (November 30, 1966).

49. *ibid.,* p. 309. It is interesting that Gowon committed himself to creating not more than fourteen states. It is interesting to see that

Nigeria has 36 states today and yet there are still demands for additional states.

50. For a more detailed discussion of this, see J. Isawa Elaigwu. *Gowon: The Biography of a Soldier-Statesman* (Ibadan: West Books, 1986), Chapter 8.

51. Federal Republic of Nigeria. *Meeting of the Military Leaders, op. cit.,* Annex C, p. 68.

52. Lt. Col. Gowon in his address to Heads of Diplomatic Missions in Lagos, March 1, 1967.

53. K. C. Wheare, *Federal Government,* (New York: Oxford University press, 1964), p. 32.

54. N. U. Akpan, *op. cit.,* pp. 56-62.

55. Lt. Col. Yakubu Gowon, Address to Heads of Diplomatic Missions in Lagos, April 24, 1967.

56. *Meeting of the Nigerian Military Leaders, op. cit.,* p. 2.

57. Gowon's Broadcast to the Nation, (November 30, 1966).

58. *Sunday Times* (Lagos), May 28, 1967, p. 1; *Sunday Post* May 28, 1967, pp. 8-9.

59. *Sunday Times* (Lagos), May 28, 1967, p. 2.

60. It is interesting that one of the criteria for the creation of states, as announced by Gowon on May 30, 1967 was that;

no one state should be in a position to dominate or control the Central Government.

61. In the North—Benue–Plateau, Kano, North-Western, North-Eastern, North-Central, and Kwara states. In the South—Eastern, Rivers, Midwestern, Western, East Central and Lagos States; Decree No. 14, 1967 "States (Creation and Transitional Provisions) Decree 1967."

62.A. A. Ayida, *The Nigerian Revolution—1966 - 1967* (Ibadan: Ibadan University Press August 1973), p 6. Ayida was in an excellent position to know what was "really" going on.

63.*ibid.,* pp. 6-7.

64.Major-General Gowon, *Broadcast to the Nation,* May 26, 1968.

5

MILITARY RULE AND FEDERALISM IN NIGERIA: FEDERAL - STATE RELATIONS UNDER MILITARY ADMINISTRATION

Introduction: Federal Governance under Military Rule

Under military rule, except for the brief periods mentioned earlier, Nigeria had always practised some form of federalism. By the terms of the *Constitution (Suspension and Modification) Decree No.1, 17 January 1966,* the federal government was given the 'power to make laws for the peace, order, and good government of Nigeria or any part thereof with respect to any matter whatsoever'. All military administrations in Nigeria have maintained this provision, except for the brief period under the Constitution (Suspension and Modification) Decree No. 8, 1967. The Buhari military Administration maintained these exact words in the Constitution (Suspension and Modification) Decree No.1, 1984. The Babangida and Abacha's regime did exactly the same. Technically, this provision made the FMG the sole repository of power in the State. This violated the federal principle of non-centralization of power among component federal units. Legally, Nigeria was unitary under military rule. One expects, therefore, that in this context, the FMG would merely delegate or devolve its powers to *subnational* units. However, these decrees also stated that the Governor of a region or state could not make laws with regard to all matters in the exclusive legislative list, and was precluded from making any laws with regard to the concurrent legislative list without the consent of the FMG. But the Governor of a region or state could "make laws for the peace, order, and good government" of that region or state. There was a deference to federal principles here. The federal military government had dual roles under these decrees. FMG could make laws for the whole country and had specific responsibility for the running of the federal government. This would become clearer when we deal with the structures. State governments were restricted to the residual list. In essence, Nigeria@s military government never suspended the Constitutions of 1963 and 1 979. Only sections of these Constitutions were suspended and/or amended. The Abacha regime suspended the 1989 Constitution, which was only partially in operation before November 17, 1993. Interestingly both Decrees No.1 of 1966, Section 6, and Decree No.1 of 1984, Section 5, stated clearly that no question as to the validity of this or any other Decree or of any Edict would be entertained by any court of law in Nigeria. In a way, this negates a cardinal federal principle of the role of courts.

The structure of government and of decision- making was also provided for by the decrees. Military regimes increased the political visibility and power of the executive branch as well as those of the bureaucrats. The actors in the executive branch had both executive and legislative powers. Under Decree No.1 of 1966, the Governors of the Regions were members of the country@s supreme legislative organ, the Supreme Military Council (SMC). The SMC made legislation for the whole country and considered administrative issues which involved both federal and state governments. It was usually chaired by the HFMG[1]and Commander-in-Chief of the armed forces.

The Federal Executive Council (FEC) exercised general 'direction and control@ over the affairs of the federal government as contained in the Exclusive Legislative list.[2] While General lronsi did not appoint political executives to head the various ministries, General Gowon did so in 1967. This changed the composition of the FEC.[3] Every military regime since 1967 had appointed civilians to the Federal Executive Council and to the State Executive Council (SEC) to serve as federal ministers or state commissioners.

The judiciary was left to operate in so far as it did not treat existing decrees with levity. The Nigerian military administration never blatantly tampered with the judiciary, except on a few occasions. An illustration of these occasions was federal government reaction to a decision of the court on the confiscation of property of an ex-politician. By the Federal Military Government (*Supremacy and Enforcement of Powers*) *Decree No. 28* of May 9, 1970, the FMG reminded Nigerians that the government had no mandate from anyone and that the judiciary and all unabrogated parts of the Constitution were by her grace. It then stated that for 'the efficacy and stability of government',

> ...any decision whether made before or after the commencement of this Decree, by any court of law in the exercise or purported exercise of any powers under the constitution of any enactment or law of the Federation or any state which has purported to declare or shall hereafter purport to declare the invalidity of any Decree or of any Edict (insofar as the provisions of the Edict are not inconsistent with the provisions of a Decree) or the incompetence of any of the governments in the federation to make the same is or shall be null and void and of no effect whatsoever as from the date of the making thereof.

This position was reinforced in 1984 after some ex-politicians (i.e., Governors) went to court to seek court orders to prevent their having to face military tribunals.

It must be stated, however, that except where courts are constrained by decrees (some of which are retroactive), the Nigerian judiciary seems to have had some greater measure of freedom under military regimes than under civilian regimes in the execution of their functions. The rate at which pressures were brought to bear on the judiciary in the First and Second Republics, and under the Obasanjo Administration (from May 1999) by politicians rendered the judiciary incapable of protecting the downtrodden, even under a seemingly democratic federal system. Members of the bench succumbed to the temptations of status and money. This is not to say that military administrations have not flouted some orders of courts or that the judiciary has a very free hand under the military. There are many cases of military governments ignoring or deliberately refusing to respect court orders.

With respect to federal-state relations under military federalism, two conspicuous features must be identified. The first is the military superstructure: a military regime in which institutions of popular participation were suspended. In the military hierarchy of authority, the HFMG and Commander-in-Chief of the Armed Forces appointed all military governors, and they were responsible to him.[4] This negates the traditional principle of federalism and fits into Apter⊕s model of mobilization with a hierarchical chain of command and 'minimum accountability® to the people.

Unlike the civilian Governor of a state who was elected or ousted from office through the ballot box, the military governor was appointed from the centre and was only removable by HFMG or the SMC. This is typical of the hierarchical nature of military rule. One negative impact of this under military administration was that the lapses of the governors, unlike under civilian rule, reflected on the HFMG or the federal government. The experience of General Gowon, whose governors eroded his credibility, is still very fresh in the minds of many Nigerians. On the other hand, these governors were relatively autonomous in the running of the affairs of the state. They were not prefects. They had substantive powers over the affairs of their states. The degree of supervision of these governors depended partly on the personality of the HFMG. While Gowon gave the states much autonomy and the governors had much latitude in the performance of their duties, General Murtala Mohammed was more centralizing in his administrative technique. It was partly to cut the governors down to size that the Murtala/Obasanjo regime established the National Council of States (NCS). This removed the military Governors from the SMC and contained their exuberance within framework of the NCS, which was under the supervision of the SMC through the office of the Chief of Staff, Supreme Headquarters. The Council brought together all state governors, the HFMG, and selected military officers for deliberation over state issues. This body dealt with 'policy guidelines on financial and economic matters' as they affected the state, national development plans, such as constitutional matters as concerned states, and any other matter assigned to it by the SMC. The NCS under military rule was part of a functioning government structure and not a mere advisory body as was the case under the 1979 Constitution for a democratic Nigeria. It is pertinent to note that there were few changes in the names of these military political structures under the Babangida administration. The HFMG was called the President; the SMC was renamed the Armed Forces Ruling Council (AFRC); the FEC was called the Council of Ministers (COM); and the National Council of States (NCS) remained the same. General Abacha called the highest ruling body the Provisional Ruling Council (PRC) while the Council of Ministers was renamed the Federal Executive Council.

Besides all of the above, other institutions of federalism existed which were mainly civilian in terms of their incumbents. These included the federal and state bureaucracies and local government structures, the federal and state judicial institutions, and federal and state corporations—which retained relative autonomy in their respective spheres of operation, as contained in the Constitution. Even the membership of the federal and state executive councils was predominantly civilian. The above fitted into Apter⊚s reconciliation model, especially when one takes cognizance of the autonomy of the governors under the Gowon administration. It was a reflection of Nigeria⊚s past experiences, a recognition that there are 'social limits to politically-induced change⊚ from the centre,[5] and that penetration and control of subnational units carried forward with disregard for local integrity, amount to no more than experiments in violence.[6]

Military Rule and Centralisation in the Federation

In discussing the impact of military rule on federalism, a number of variables inter-play. These variables are all linked to the military, their mode of legislation and their conception of the role of the centre. The most notable of these variables are:

- the military and its mode of legislation, and the civil war which enabled certain adjustment in powers of component units many of which became apparently irreversible;
- the creation of additional states;
-fiscal relations among component units of federation and the impact of petro-naira; and
-the powers of treaty-making of the federal centre.

More than any other elite group, the military has been most central to the emergence of some unitary trends in the Nigerian federation.

The Military: Constitutional and Administrative Changes
Many actions taken by the military centralized political authority in the Nigerian federation. The situation in federal-state relations in

2005 is a far cry from what existed between 1960 and 1965 when the federal centre was so weak that the *regional tails* were said to have wagged the *federal dog*. The very nature of military legislation contributed to the increase of the federal government's authority at the expense of the states. Unlike their predecessors (civilian politicians), the military legislated by having the Supreme Military Council (AFRC or PRC) pass a decree. Constitutional amendments were carried out with far less problems than under the civilian regime (with its checks and balances). On May 27, 1967 the Military issued the Constitutional (Repeal and Restoration) Decree 1967, (Decree No. 13) which repealed Decree No. 8, 1967. Essentially, Nigeria returned to the situation under Decree No.1, 1966 in which the federal government had the "power to make laws for the peace, order and good government of Nigeria or any part thereof, with respect to any matter whatsoever,"[7] In similar fashion, the Military created states by decree.[8] The Decree No. 14, 1967 which created states provided that the states should inherit the powers of the former Regions. But subsequent legislation by the federal government made inroads into states constitutional powers. By Decree No. 27, 1967, the federal government announced that the "legislative and executive powers of the twelve newly created states in Nigeria are limited for the time being to residual matters". For the exercise of matters in the Concurrent Legislative List, "specific consent of the Federal Military Government is required", the statement continued. It used to be the prerogative of both regional and federal governments to deal with matters in the Concurrent Legislative List. The above decree no doubt placed limitations on the powers of the new states.

Some of the federal violations of state powers were directly the result of the civil war and the creation of additional states. Once taken, these constitutional actions could hardly be reversed—thus adding to the constitutional functions of the federal government. Examples of such federal decrees abound. The Decree No. 17, 1967, *(Newspapers Prohibition of Circulation)* gave the HFMG the power to "prohibit the circulation in the federation or in any state thereof, as the case may require, of any newspaper."[9] This was aimed at preventing the *Nigerian Outlook* (later called the *Biafran Sun*) from circulating in other parts of Nigeria. Under the Republican Constitution 1963 of the prohibition of circulation of newspapers in a region was a regional affair. Similarly, the FMG went further to extend the spheres of its powers consequent upon the situation created by the new states structure. By Decree No. 18, 1967, *Administrative Councils Decree, 1967*, Administrative Councils were created for the former Northern and Eastern Nigeria. According to this decree, the Council was to share the assets and liabilities of these former regions among the new states in the regions, to establish "government institutions where necessary in the states", deploying staff to the new states and considering "matters which from time were included in any directive of the Head of the Federal Military Government addressed to the council".[10] The Head of State was to appoint the Chairman of this Council. In the Constitution, the setting up of administration at *subnational* levels (regions) was the function of such units. However, as Olajide Aluko correctly remarked, the Federal Government was "extending its power by setting up interim administration to fill the vacuum left following the creation of states in the North[11] In the same manner, the *Investigation of Assets (Public Officers and other Persons)* Decree, No. 37, 29 July of 1968, gave the Federal Government the power to inquire into the assets of those politicians who held public offices in the civilian regime throughout the federation. Such an expansion of federal authority was an encroachment on the powers held by the former regions whose duty was to probe their public officers.[12] The legislation above illustrate that the Federal Government, operating within the new institutional framework, was expanding its constitutional authority at the expense of the states.

In other cases, the Federal Government took over the direct administration of certain functions, which were legally under the jurisdiction of the regions, since May 1967. The *Marketing Board Reforms* between 1967 and 1973 illustrates such absorption of state functions. In 1968, the Northern States had requested the Nigerian Produce Marketing Company (NPMC), the overseas sales agent of marketing boards in Nigeria, to suspend overseas sales of their groundnut.[13] In the past, regional governments could suspend sales of their export produce. But in 1968, engaged in a civil war, the federal government was anxious about accumulating foreign exchange earnings in order to purchase equipments from overseas countries. The action of the Northern States Marketing Board was therefore, seen as negative in its effects on Nigeria's foreign exchange reserves. Hence, the Federal Government issued a decree in 1968 which made it obligatory for the NPMC to take directives only from the Federal Ministry of Trade about the sale of export commodities. This decree thus, gave the Federal Ministry of Trade the sole prerogative of taking decisions regarding export commodities to be suspended from overseas sales. The new states could no longer issue order to the NPMC to that effect.

The Federal Government took further measures, which made inroads into the autonomy of the states. Decree No. 50 of 18 September 1968 (*the Central Bank of Nigeria Act Amendment No. 3, 1968 Decree*) asserted the supremacy of the Federal Government with regard to marketing boards. The Central Bank was the only bank to grant advances and loans to state marketing boards. Hitherto, these states could borrow from commercial or private banks. It also gave the upper ceiling of the loan, which a state marketing board would need for its operation at the beginning of each season. Finally, it provided that the marketing boards could fix prices only after consultations with the Central Bank.[14] These measures virtually made the state marketing boards financially dependent on the federal government through its institution, the Central Bank. In addition, this legislation tried to impose federal supervision on the system of price-fixing. The federal government was therefore, eroding most of the powers of state marketing boards.

While the Dina Commission Report had been rejected in 1968, most of its items were adopted through the back door. This Report had suggested the co-ordination of 'pricing and financial policies of boards throughout the country.'[15] On April 1, 1973, the Federal Government abolished export duties on marketing board produce. To offset losses by affected state governments, the Federal Government made available to the states x34 million in 1973/74 fiscal year.[16] The HFMG took over the price-fixing authority of the state marketing boards. Thus, in 1974/75 fiscal years, the HFMG fixed producer prices for marketing board commodities.[17] The NPMC was reorganised to serve as the 'new central sales organisation', though state marketing boards were to continue to organise local purchases for export produce as hitherto.[18] In the 1974/75 fiscal year, the FMG abolished producer sales tax. Export duties on rubber (the only remaining dutiable export commodity) were also abolished.[19] These measures centralised the activities of the state marketing boards. Thus, many functions performed by state marketing boards were taken over by the Federal Government, particularly the authority to fix produce prices, which increased from 10% to 50% between 1973 and 1975.[20] Only a military government at the federal centre could have carried out these constitutional amendments with little or no opposition from the states.

Similarly, constitutional measures were taken when the FMG announced that it had decided to transfer secondary and primary education, from the Residual List to the Concurrent List. The intention was to give the Federal Government more control over the direction of primary and secondary education, though in practice, the states exercised maximum control in this sphere. At the same time, university education was transferred from the Concurrent to the Exclusive Legislative List, "in the best interest of an orderly and well-coordinated development in Nigeria."[21] This policy was aimed at curbing the proliferation of state universities. New state universities were prohibited, although the existing ones could continue to operate.

The introduction of Uniform Income Tax also illustrates federal absorption of certain constitutional functions of the states. In the 1963 Constitution, the former regions (and therefore, the new states) had the power of taxation within their areas of jurisdiction. In 1974, the Supreme Military Council announced that it was going to introduce "a uniform system of personal income tax throughout the country." It was to provide similar personal reliefs and allowances for taxpayers 'wherever they may be'. It was hoped that 'this would facilitate the mobility of high level manpower and is another step towards social and economic integration'.[22]

On April 1, 1975, the Federal Government announced that it was going to abolish that age-old cattle tax, *Jangali* in order to bring relief to the cattle owner on his capital and encourage him to keep his cattle within the country. This tax had never been a federal tax. The states affected most by this decree were the Northern States, which had derived local revenue from the *Jangali*.

On balance, the illustrations above show the federal government growing steadily in its constitutional and administrative powers at the expense of the states. There is no doubt that the presence of the military accounted for the relative ease with which constitutional amendments were made through decrees. Under a democratic setting, long procedural hurdles through regional/states and federal legislatures were required for such constitutional amendments.

These centralizing trends did not end with the Gowon Administration. On assumption of office, Brigadier (later General) Muhammed removed military governors from the SMC to underline the determination of the administration to effectively supervise state administration and centralize political authority. Governors were now to operate in the National Council of States (NCS). Orders came down from Lagos (the former capital) to the states, giving general guidelines and deadlines of particular projects to be carried out, such as the retirement of public officers 'in public interest®. By Decree Nos. 20, 22 and 23[23] of 1975, the Universities of Benin, Ife and Ahmadu Bello were taken over by the Federal government. All universities in the country were to be federal universities.

In an attempt to create a conducive basis for national integration, the *Interim Common Services Agency* for the Northern States was abolished. The Federal Government went further to take over the *New Nigerian* Newspaper (formerly owned by the Six Northern States) and acquired majority shares in the *Daily Times*. In November 1975, the Federal Government announced the 'takeover® of all radio and television networks in the country. These measures, no doubt, added to the federal leverage over the states. The centre was now very strong in relation to the states, and the Supreme Military Council was quite active in decision-making.

In an attempt aimed at curbing the symbolic autonomy of the states, the Murtala administration abolished all states® coats-of-arms. States were only permitted to use the federal coat-of-arms, with the name of the state appearing on or under it. This drive towards uniformity among states was carried further to include more empirical issues. Thus, in their 1976 Local Government Reforms, not only were local governments given the same functions, the same guidelines were given for effecting the reforms.[24]

As A.D. Yahaya observed: "The Nigerian local government systems, for the first time in Post-Colonial Nigeria exhibits some common features throughout the country. Prior to this reorganization

111

the structure of local government system in the country differed considerably from state to state".[25] It was the federal government rather than the state governments which reorganised the local governments. Before then local governments were, throughout the country, essentially state matters. By imposing uniformity, the military regime was further centralising authority. All the states were handed a model edict by the Federal Government for adoption in their various States, as they implemented their reforms. What implication did these attempts at uniformity across *subnational* state boundaries have for the federal system? It was obviously part of the centralising trends under the military's hierarchical structure, incongruously imposed upon Nigeria's supposedly federal system.

After the assassination of General Murtala Mohammed on February 13, 1976, his successor, General Olusegun Obasanjo, continued with the process of centralization of authority. The Obasanjo administration promulgated the *Nigerian Television Authority Decree No. 24 of 1977*. This decree established the Nigerian Television Authority as the only body charged with exclusive responsibility for television broadcast in Nigeria. Thus, as mentioned above, the federal government took over all state-owned television broadcasting stations in the country, without compensating the states.

The *Constitution (Amendment) Decree No. 46 of 1977*, which amended the Schedule of the Constitution of the Federal Republic of Nigeria relating to education, conferred exclusive responsibility on the Federal Government in matters relating to universities and higher education generally. The trend in centralization was severely questioned under the democratic regime of Shehu Shagari. Many state governors felt that the trend in centralisation had exceeded the demands of what was necessary to avoid a repeat of the civil war. Many governors, therefore, took the federal government to court on some issues and challenged the authority of the centre on other matters.[26]

On the return of the military in December 1983, Brigadier (later Major-General) Muhammadu Buhari became the Head of the Federal Military Government. General Buhari, like his predecessors, suspended part of the Constitution and ruled by decrees. Perhaps the most salient aspect of General Buhari's twenty-month administration was that he closely supervised the military administration of the states, thus superimposing and enforcing the hierarchical military superstructure over Nigeria©s polity. The administration abolished the numerous local government councils created by the civilian administration. Many of these local governments had, of course, been created for political reasons.

General lbrahim Babangida took over power from General Buhari on August 27, 1985. While he was less strict over the supervision of military Governors, the constant changes of the Governors made it clear to all where the authority base was. General Babangida continued with the trend in centralisation, which had been pursued by his military predecessors. His Decree No. 16 of 1985 conferred the responsibility for the establishment of standards in all schools on the Federal Ministry of Education.[27] The FMG changed the school calendar from September-June to January-December. It was later reversed by the same administration. In addition, the federal government changed the policy of transmitting local governments© share of statutory allocation through the state governments[28] to one in which their funds were sent directly to the beneficiaries. This robbed state governments one of the last areas of fiscal control over the local governments. Furthermore, the Babangida administration created new local governments in 1987 and in 1991.[29] This was a violation of the powers of state governments which had the responsibility for local governments in the 1979 Constitution. Many institutions were established by the administration, which tended towards centralisation and direct supervision. Among these were the Commission for Primary Schools;[30] the Commission for Colleges of Education,[31] the Commission for Adult and Mass Literacy,[32] and the Commission on Nomadic Education[33]. These Commissions not only established policy guidelines, but also had supervisory role over state and federal institutions.

In a paradoxical fashion, as Babangida implemented aspects of his transition programme, additional powers and funds were given to the local governments which he believed were the most basic grassroot units for democracy and development. Thus, the payment of the salaries of primary school teachers, which had been transferred to the federal government, was transferred back to the states. Similarly, primary health care was transferred to the local government level. To empower local governments, their share of federal revenues was increased from 10% to 15% and later to 20%. This was at the expense of states.

As a constitutionally guaranteed third-tier of government, the democratically elected local governments operated autonomously, to the chagrin of many of the democratically elected state governors between 1992 and 1993. The Local Government chairmen saw themselves as chief executives and 'mini-governors' of their local government areas, and exhibited these traits in their relations with the state governors. The state governors saw their resource bases eroded, while local governments benefitted from these losses. They complained that local governments had far more money than they knew what to do with them. On the other hand, local government chairmen countered with allegations of authoritarian tendencies on the part of state governors in an effort to control them.[34]

In other ways, the Babangida administration did enhance intergovernmental relations. This is exemplified by two cases involving the creation of the Directorate of Foods, Roads and Rural Infrastructure (DFRRI) and the National Directorate of Employment (NDE). Aware that rural development was essentially a state and local government affair; the Babangida administration did not transfer this function to the federal government. But it intervened in the area of rural development by creating DFRRI and giving it some funds for rural water supply, roads and power. DFRRI operated through grants to states and local governments to carry out these projects, which were then closely monitored and supervised. States and Local Governments were expected to make contributions to this fund. Similarly, in reaction to the unemployment problem, particularly among the youths, the government set up the NDE, which had offices at state levels. This outfit gave loans to young graduates to take off on their own in life. They were expected to repay their loans overtime. In essence, these cooperative intergovernmental relations enabled the centre to intervene effectively in areas of subnational preservation, which, it did not want to take over because these units were better placed to implement associated projects.

The Abacha administration also followed its predecessors in aspects of constitutional suspension and modification. It suspended the 1989 and the Interim National Government Constitutions, and returned to a modified 1979 Constitution. One of its most glaring acts of centralisation was the re-establishment of the Primary Education Commission, which was abolished when primary school matters, including payment of teachers' salaries, were transferred to the local governments. This Commission was again given the function of paying the salaries of primary schools throughout the federation.

It is, therefore, clear that the nature of legislation under the military (i.e. by decrees), the hierarchical nature of the military and the 1967-1970 civil war, had given opportunities for such great centralisation of powers which has not been easily reversible. While there are current attempts at reviewing these powers, it is doubtful if the centre will ever be as weak as it was during the First Republic.

The Creation of States

The quest for the structural reorganisation of the Nigerian state dates back to the early 1940s.[35] By the time the military emerged as a political force in the Nigerian polity, problems arising from the structural imbalance in Nigeria©s federal system had already taken its toll on the polity.

Of the Nigeria situation, General Gowon had also observed that the most important principle to ensure the success of a federation is that not a single state or region should be so large and powerful as to be in a position to dominate the rest of the units or hold them to ransom. Under the old Constitution, the regions were so large and powerful as to consider themselves self-sufficient and almost entirely independent".

Given the old threat of secession within the federal framework of four large regions, let us do a political analysis of the creation of states in 1967 under the military. Undoubtedly, the political geography of the creation of states did contribute to the strength of the federal centre. The former Eastern Region accounted for 65.4% of the output of oil in 1967, and the Midwestern Region, 34.6%. The creation of twelve states altered the situation. The former Eastern Nigeria was split into three new states and, therefore, also split were the areas of oil production.

After the creation of states in 1967, the output of the oil-producing states was in the following order: Rivers State, 57.1 %; Midwest, 34.6%; East Central, 2.8%; Rivers/East Central States, 5.5%. The Rivers State, which was, according to the above figures by far the greatest oil producer, had a population of 1.5 millions (2.8% of Nigeria⊚s total population) and occupied only 2% of Nigeria⊚s total area. It did not border with any foreign country, as did the former Eastern Region, with Cameroon. It can, therefore, be argued that a Rivers State outside Nigeria was unlikely to survive. Similarly, the Midwestern States accounted for 4.5% of the country⊚s population and 4.2% of the total area. Like the Rivers States, it was unlikely to survive outside Nigeria. Both Rivers and Midwestern States were eyewitnesses to the effective federal blockade of the coastal ports during Nigeria⊚s civil war.

By removing some of the elements of suspicion, which created friction, such as the domination of other regions and the federal government, the centre had been strengthened. Individually, the states were most unlikely to challenge the authority of the federal government. They were more likely to combine as they actually did between 1980 and 1983, in order to put more pressure on the federal government to allocate funds to them, than to challenge the latter⊚s authority in the form of secession. No single state was in a position to relegate the federal government to the background anymore. They were neither geographically and demographically large enough, nor were they financially strong enough to secede. The guidelines for their creation were clearly stated in 1967.[37]

The creation of twelve states made it necessary for the federal government to take over certain services, which had been previously financed by the regions. The abolition of the former Northern and Eastern Regions made it necessary for the federal Government to take over the payment of scholarships offered by these governments. Similarly, the Federal Government took over the payment of pensions for expatriates previously paid by the former Northern and Eastern Regional governments, following the creation of states. Administrative problems in servicing certain projects in the former Northern Region, necessitated the assumption of these functions, after the creation of states. Among such functions taken over and institutions financed by the Federal Government were the Ahmadu Bello University; hides

116

skins and leather project; laboratory investigation service; locust control; meat inspection (other than inspection of meat for consumption in Nigeria); motor licensing (other than in respect to Benue–Plateau State); Quelea birds control; soil conservation projects (other than local soil conservation schemes), and vehicle inspection (other than in respect to Benue-Plateau State).[38] These are clear examples where administrative and financial difficulties consequent upon the creation of states had led to federal absorption of the services of the former regions. In some other cases, the Federal Government had to absorb state functions at the request of the states. The federal government's takeover of the University of Nigeria and the University of Benin is a good example.[39]

The creation of new states also fuelled the demands for additional states. One of the political rashes or side effects of creating new states has been the emergence of *new majorities* and *new minorities*. The number of demands for additional states spurred General Mohammed to set up the Irikefe Panel on States creation. As the Irikefe Panel stated in its report, "The creation of states should seek to establish institutional framework which would ensure rapid economic development among all the ethnic groups, increase participatory democracy as an insurance against political instability, promote and institutionalize a balanced and stable federation, and finally, remove the fears of domination of the minorities which had tended to slow down economic and political development of the country."[40] Quite obviously, states creation cannot, by itself, remove the fears of the minorities. It was a structural prescription for a structural ailment and not a political *elixir* to cure all political ills. The spirit of fairness, justice and participation developed and exhibited by leaders is just as important.

However, in response to popular demands, General Murtala Mohammed created 7 new states, thus bringing the total number of states to 19. General Babangida found the pressures for creation of states so overwhelming that he had to create two additional states in 1987. This brought the total number of states to 21. Again in response to the pressures by Nigerians, General Babangida created 9 additional states in 1991. This brought the total number of states in Nigeria to 30. The Abacha administration created 36 states in 1996. The history of the creation of states has been such that it has always been easier for the military to create them. Except for the creation of the Midwest Region in 1963, no other attempts by the civilian democratic government have succeeded in Nigeria. Attempts by the National Assembly to create states in 1983 failed, even with the demands for over fifty additional states.

The paradox of Nigerian federalism is that many Nigerians believe that federalism is still the most conducive and appropriate form of government, given the compromises it provides in inter-group relations. They ask for additional states in order to have their own autonomy. Unfortunately, they may have their states, but without expected autonomy. The new states have narrower and weaker resource bases, which detract from their autonomy. In addition, the more additional states are created, the stronger the centre. Paradoxically, the agitations for additional states go on at the same time as calls for the devolution of the power of the centre and for more legislative functions to be passed on to the component units in the federation. One of the greatest impetus to the unitary streaks in Nigeria◉s federation certainly came from the creation of additional states by the military.

Financial/Fiscal Relations

The creation of states in 1967 coincided with the emergence of petro-naira (i.e. naira from sales of petroleum). By 1973 the federal government had become more financially powerful than it was in 1967. The soaring revenues largely from profit tax on petroleum, had given the federal government a greater financial leverage over the states before 1967. The contribution of the oil sector to Nigeria◉s total foreign exchange rose from 19.9% in 1967 to 89.9% in 1974. This was an increase of 451 .7% over a period of eight years.[41] By 2002 the dependence on the oil sector had been reduced only minimally to about 80%.

Petro-naira became quite important in statutory allocations and in grants from the Federal Government to the states. The states came to be heavily dependent on federally derived revenues (statutory allocations) for their yearly budgeting. As one of the key actors correctly put it in an interview:

...the major source of petroleum revenue is the Profit Tax that goes to the federal government, and has been growing very fast. Whereas in the former civilian government the two major sources of revenue were export duties and royalties from petroleum–and these went mainly to the regions—with petroleum tax change, the federal revenue has grown much more than state revenue. It means the federal government has more resources to give the states. That is the basic difference.[42]

In fact, the issue of the centre's financial power generated much political heat even under the military in 1974-75. The states started to complain in 1974. Ex-Governor Abba Kyari of the North-Central State had stressed that "State governments should not be treated as mere beneficiaries of federal bounties but as entities entitled to receive legitimate shares. This is the essence of federalism"[43]. In a similar manner, ex-Governor Mobolaji Johnson appealed to Nigeria's Commissioners of Finance Conference in Lagos in 1974 to resolve the difficult problem of revenue-sharing between the federal and state governments so that "States may not suffer from a feeling of financial cramp in the discharge of their normal activities and in achievement of their legitimate aspirations."[44] By 1994, statutory allocation from the Federation Account (FA) accounted for between 46% and 95% of the annual budgets of the states. Only Lagos and Kano states could generate for their annual budgets about 45% of their revenue from internal sources.

One interesting aspect of federal-state relations under military rule was the regular constant grants from the Commander-in-Chief to his military Governor or Administrator at state level. While such grants usually solved urgent problems of development in some cases, this 'father Christmas' attitude to fiscal federalism created a sense of complacency at state level, especially with regard to revenue generation efforts. The gradual fiscal empowerment of the centre under the military is also illustrated by the way the revenue allocation formula was amended over time by the military. If the principles of derivation were paramount in mineral rents and royalties, these were reduced to a bare minimum by 1992. By 1992, the AFRC approved an allocation formula of 50% from the Federation Account for the federal government; 30% for state governments and 15% for local governments.[45] Later that year, the Babangida administration increased the share of Local government to 20% by reducing the shares of the states to 25% as discussed above. By May 1999 when the military handed over power to elected civilian leaders, the revenue sharing formula was – federal government. 48.5%; states 24%; local governments 20% and special funds, 7.5%. The derivation principle was raised to 13% under the Abacha regime and was so included in the 1999 Constitution.

Some of the most virulent complaints came from the state governments who believed that their tax bases had been drastically reduced and that they had become political paupers. But that was not the only dimension of conflict. Oil producing areas on the horizontal level also complained very loudly that they had been robbed by the rest of the country. As Ken Saro-Wiwa angrily pointed out: "You have taken away all these (oil) from the Ogoni people. You build dams in Hausaland; in Fulani country, you have provided for agriculture. What have you given the Ogoni people? without oil, they will not have the dams that are making agriculture in the North possible."[46] The tempestuous Ken Saro-wiwa also threatened secession, if these grievances were not adequately addressed. Given the incredible powers of the centre, there were many Nigerians who felt that the Northerners who controlled the powers of allocation would also continue to control the pattern of distribution of resources in favour of the North. It is, therefore, not surprising that all efforts were made either to reduce the powers of the centre or introduce a rotational Presidency at the 1994/1995 National Constitutional Conference.

Related to these financial issues, is the *uniformity, which* years of military rule have imposed on Nigerian Federalism. This became more glaring during the wages strike in 1992-93. As local and state governments were democratized under the 1989 constitution, the federal military government negotiated with its workers and increased their wages by 45%. It then asked state governments to go ahead and negotiate with their workers. Of course, state and local government bureaucrats who had been used to uniform salary scales between federal and subnational government officials could not imagine their not benefitting from the 45% federal largesse. To them, it was not important that these states and local governments did not have the resources to pay for these salary increases. The States and Local

120

Governments were then; faced with the realities of democratic governance. The veneer of military uniformity of laws and administrative practices could no longer hold the test of variety in a democratic federal polity. Nor could the state governments easily get the 'father christmas' donations from the centre anymore. The centre had become financially a 'titan' and the states could only survive if they generated more revenues from internal sources and/or successfully pressed for the review of their allocations from the Federation Account. Most states seemed to have chosen the latter.

Treaty Making Powers

Among the factors, which increased the powers of the central government, like in most modern federations, were the national government⊚s powers of treaty-making and foreign trade. All foreign loans by state governments had to be guaranteed by the federal government, with its accompanying guidelines and controls. Moreover, the globalization process made the central government even more visible and relevant in global affairs.

In addition, the necessity for uniform policies in certain matters, which transcend state boundaries, gave the centre additional leverage over subnational units.

Conclusion

Our argument in this chapter is that federalism and militarism are not necessarily incompatible bedfellows. We also explained that the major differences in the operations of federalism under civilian and military regimes in Nigeria are to be found in the style and structures of administration. We showed how military rule has contributed in no small measure to the unitary trends in the Nigerian federation. It must, however, be remembered that, except for Belgium, the powers of the centre have increased at the expense of subnational units in most countries of the world. A number of factors have led to the great strength of the central government. One of the greatest impacts of military rule on federalism was the transformation of Nigeria from a federal system with a very loose centre to a federal system with a very strong centre. Infact, about thirty years of military rule not only imposed its hierarchical structure over Nigeria'ss federal political structure with its attendant uniformity of policies, but also created strong unitary steaks in Nigerian federalism.

Another important issue in the military's centralisation drive is related to, and flows, from the experience of the civil war. As of 1994, many of those who fought in the war to keep Nigeria one, were still in government. The memories of the agonies of war kept haunting them. They believed that only a very strong central government could hold Nigeria together. They believed that a weaker centre might lead to a repeat of the old secessionist tunes among politicians and that Nigeria might not survive it. The civil war itself had provided an excuse for taking over some powers, which belonged to subnational states. Some of these actions have proved to be irreversible over the years.

Similarly, the creation of additional states also provided a further conducive situational context within which centralising actions had taken place. The narrower resource base of the constituent states also helped to give the centre some leverage, a leverage assisted by the advent of *petronaira*. The new financial/fiscal powers of the centre made it a political and financial *titan*, while the states played the *lilliputians*. It is no wonder, therefore, that there were angry demands by many groups for not only a review of the legislative lists but also of the revenue-sharing formula.

Perhaps future threats to Nigerian federalism derive, in part, from the solution Nigerians provided for the role of the military in politics.[47] Could a military which had ruled Nigeria for about thirty years retreat to its original position as an apolitical professional institution? Or was the solution to be found in a transitional power-sharing formula, even if only peripherally, with the military? The future threats to Nigeria©s federation derived also from the solution to the horizontal relations among Nigerians as the centre became increasingly a big political prize to win. This was more glaring as the crisis of allocation of scarce but allocatable resources increased in tempo and aggressiveness.

The military, more than any single factor had the greatest impact on the evolution of Nigerian federalism in the last thirty years. From disintegration, it had built a federal system with a strong centre in which the component subnational states complain of political suffocation under its centralizing grips. What is the way forward? How can non-centralisation take place without necessarily recalling the ghost of the civil war from the political arena? To what extent can development and democracy take place without subnational state autonomy in a complex multinational state such as Nigeria?

Arguably, many of the answers to the above questions can be found in the human domain. Leaders need to be seen to be fair, just and tolerant. Perhaps only then will mutual trust among groups develop and allow a new, balanced and stable federation to be established and operated.

By May 1999, the centre had become very strong and there were complaints by many Nigerians about the unsatisfactory nature of the federation. They called for national conferences to discuss the nature of association within the federation. Many groups called for the devolution of powers in the polity. Centrifugal forces have been banging loud on the polity, not because Nigeria had a federation with a loose centre as in the period between 1960 and 1966, but because the centre had become too powerful and subnational units are protesting against its suffocating grip while searching for a collective liberating formula.

Notes and references

1. By this decree, members of the Council included the HFMG; the Head of the Nigerian Army; the Head of the Nigerian Navy; the Head of the Nigerian Air Force; the Chief of Staff of the Armed Forces; the Chief of Staff of the Nigerian Army; and the Military governors of Northern, Eastern, Western and Midwestern Nigeria. After the creation of twelve states by General Gowon, the state governors became members of the SMC.

2. Note that as the military administration centralised power between 1967 and 1975, many items, such as revenue allocation and university education, came under the Exclusive Legislative List.

3.Originally the FEC comprised; HFMG; the Head of the Nigerian Navy; the Head of the Nigerian Army; the Head of the Air Force; the Chief of Staff of the Armed Forces; the Chief of Staff of the Nigerian Army; the Attorney-General; and the Inspector-General and Deputy Inspector-General of the Nigerian Police. The Federal Commissioners appointed in June 1967 became members of this body. See *Constitution (Suspension and Modification) Decree No. 1, 1984,* Section 7, for the composition of the SMC and FEC.

4.Note under Section 9 of Decree No. 1 of 1984, appointment of HFMG and governors became the responsibilities of the Supreme Military Council. Under the administration of General Abacha, the powers where those of within the Provincial Ruling Council (PRC).

5.J. Lewis, "The Social Limits of Political Induced Change", in C. Morse *et. al.* (eds.) *Modernisation by Design.* (lthaca, N.Y.: Cornell University Press, 1969), p. 24.

6.S. Harrison, *India: The Most Dangerous Decades.* (Princeton, N.J.: Princeton University Press, 1960), p. 11.

7.Federal Republic of Nigeria, "Constitutional Repeal and Restoration Decree 1967", Decree No. 13 in *Laws of the Federal Republic of Nigeria Index,* 1990.

8.Under the 1960 Constitution, the formula for creating states was clearly stated. See, *The Nigeria (Constitution) Order-in-Council,* 1960, Chapter 1, Section 4, 51.

9.Federal Republic of Nigeria, *"Newspapers (Prohibition of Circulation) Decree, 1967"*, *Laws of the Federal Republic of Nigeria, op. cit.,* p. Al11.

10.This Council was not established in Eastern Region because of the civil war in this area.

11. Federal Republic of Nigeria, *Laws of the Federal Republic of Nigeria, op. cit.,* pp. 967, Al13.

12. Olajide Aluko, "Federal-State Relationship", *Quarterly Journal of Administration,* Vol. III, No. 4, July 1969, pp. 289-290.

13. *ibid.,* p. 290.

14. *ibid.,* p. 290-291, *West Africa,* 27 April 1968, p. 502.

15. Aluko, *loc. cit.,* p. 291.

16. Federal Republic of Nigeria, *Report of the Interim Revenue Allocation Committee,* (Lagos: Ministry of Information, 1968) quoted in A. Ayida, *The Nigerian Revolution, 1966-76,* (lbadan: University Press, 1973), p. 8.

17. Federal Republic of Nigeria, "Budget Broadcast" by General Gowon in *Recurrent and Capital Estimate of the Government of the Federal Republic of Nigeria 1973-74.* (Lagos: Ministry of Information, 1973), p. 14.

18. General Gowon⊚s 1974/75 Budget Broadcast. The Head of State fixed producer prices for export commodities, such as 142.13 per ton for Palm Kernel, 141.65 for copra etc. See Federal Republic of Nigeria, *A Better Life for the People; 1974/75, Federal Budget Broadcast*, (Lagos: Federal Ministry of Information, 1 974), p. 7.

19. Federal Republic of Nigeria, 1973/74, "Budget Broadcast, *loc. cit.*, p. 14.

20. Federal Republic of Nigeria, *A Better Life for the People, op. cit.*, p. 7. Export duties on the other items had been abolished in 1973/74 fiscal years.

21. Federal Republic of Nigeria, "Budget Broadcast, 1975/76", (Mimeograph released by Nigeria⊚s Mission to the United Nations, New York, USA), p. 15.

22. 1973/74 "Budget Broadcast", *loc. cit.*, p. XIX. The Income Tax Management (Uniform Taxation Provisions...) Decree of February 1975 introduced this tax system.

23. Federal Republic of Nigeria, "Budget Broadcast to the Nation, 1974/75", *op. cit.*,p. 6.

24. Federal Republic of Nigeria, *Supplement of Official Gazette Extraordinary*, No. 62, Vol. 42, 28 August 1975; Paul Beckett, "Developments in Nigerian Federalism, 1966 to Present: A Summary," Mimeograph, Department of Government, Ahmadu Bello University, Zaria, December 1975.

25. The aims of the Local Government reforms were to:

- make appropriate services and development activities responsive to local wishes and initiations by developing or delegating them to local representative bodies;
- facilitate the exercise of democratic self-government close to local level of our society, and to encourage initiatives and leadership potentials;
- mobilize human and material resources through the involvement of members of the public in their local development; and
- provide a two-way channel of communication between local communities and government (both state and federal).

26. See an elaborate discussion in J. Isawa Elaigwu, *Nigeria's Federal Balance: Conflicts and Compromises in the Political System.* (Monograph) University of Jos Postgraduate Open Lecture Series, Vol.

I, No. 4, January 1984; and J. Isawa Elaigwu and Victor Olorunsola, "Federalism and the Politics of Compromise in Nigeria", in Donald Rothchild and V. Olorunsola, (eds.) *State versus Ethnic claims: African Policy Dilemma.* (Boulder: Westview, 1982).

27. Federal Republic of Nigeria, *Laws of the Federation of Nigeria,* Vol. VII "Education (National Minimum Standards and Establishment of Institutions)" Decree No. 16, 1985. pp. 4662-4663.

28. Federal Republic of Nigeria, *Official Gazette Extraordinary*, No. 1, Vol. 78, January 1, 1991. "Local Government (Basic Constitutional and Transitional Provisions) (Amendments)" (No. 3) Decree No. 23, 1991, pp. Al.

29. Federal Republic of Nigeria, *Laws of the Federation of Nigeria,* Vol. XXII "State (Creation and Transitional Provisions), No. 1, Decree No. 24, 1987, p. 14468 and Federal Republic of Nigeria, *Official Gazette Extraordinary*, Vol. 78; No. 53 October 2, 1991 "States (Creation and Transitional Provisions), No. 2, Decree No. 41, 1991, p. A287.

30. Federal Republic of Nigeria, *Official Gazette Extraordinary*, Vol.75; No. 53, August 17, 1989 "The National Primary Education Commission etc." Decree No. 31, 1988, pp. A707-A717.

31. Federal Republic of Nigeria, *Official Gazette Extraordinary*, Vol.76 No. 4, January 17, 1989 "National Commission for Colleges of Education" Decree No. 3, 1989, pp. A29-A36.

32. Federal Republic of Nigeria, *Official Gazette* "National Commission for Mass Literacy, Adult Education and Non-formal Education Decree" Decree No. 17, 1990.

33. Federal Republic of Nigeria, *Laws of the Federation,* Vol. XV "National Commission for Nomadic Education" Decree No. 41, 1989, p. 10234.

34. J. lsawa Elaigwu, *Autonomy of the Commune: Federalism and Local Governance in Nigeria.* Abuja: (Abuja: National Council on Intergovernmental Relations, 1994).

35. Please see further discussion in J. Isawa Elaigwu, "Subnational Units and the Future of Federalism in Nigeria, *"The Nigerian Journal of Political Economy,* Vol. 1; No. 2, October, 1983, pp. 1-26. Also see, Nnamdi Azikiwe, *Political Blueprint for Nigeria.* (Lagos: 1945); and Obafemi Awolowo, *Path to Nigerian Freedom.* (London: Faber and Faber, 1947); Federal Republic of Nigeria, *Report of the Commission Appointed to*

Enquire into the Fears of Minorities and The Means of Allaying Them. (London: HMSO, Cmd 505, 1958).

36. General Gowon, "Broadcast to the Nation," on 26th May, 1968.

37. The guidelines for the creation of States in 1967 were as follows:

1. no state should be in position to dominate or control the central government;

2. each state should form one compact geographical area;

3. administrative convenience, the facts of history, and wishes of the people concerned must be taken into account;

4. each state should be in a position to discharge effectively the functions allocated to regional governments; and

5. it is also essential that new states should be created simultaneously.

38. Federal Republic of Nigeria, Decree No. 12, "Interim Common Services Agency Decree, 1968", *Laws of the Federal Republic of Nigeria, op. cit.,* Schedule 6, Section 4.

39. *West Africa,* November 5, 1971, p. 1288.

40. See original reference of the Irikefe Panel on Creation of States.

41. Central Bank of Nigeria, *Annual Reports and Statement of Accounts.* (Lagos: Central Bank, 1974) and also S. A. Madujibeya, "Impact of Oil on Nigeria©s Economy (2)," *New Nigerian,* Kaduna, June 21, 1975, p. 5.

42. Interview with Mr. Allison A. Ayida, Federal Permanent Secretary, Ministry of Finance, Lagos, January 21, 1 974.

43. North Central Government, *New Nigerian,* Interviews His Excellency Colonel Abba Kyari, Kaduna: Ministry of Information, 1970, p.7.

44. *Daily Times.* Lagos, May 23, 1974, p. 13.

45. T. Y. Danjuma, "Revenue Sharing and the Political Economy of Federalism," in J. Isawa Elaigwu, P. Chunun Logams, and S. Habu Galadima (eds.), *Federalism and Nation-Building: The Challenges of the Twenty-First Century.* (Abuja: National Council on Intergovernmental Relations, 1994), pp. 87 - 115.

46. *TSM: The Sunday Magazine,* Vol. 9, No. 12, March 12, 1994, p.19.

47. On the role of the military, see J. Isawa Elaigwu, *Nigerian: A Rebirth for the Twenty-First Century* (Jos: Aha Publishing House, 2000).

6

THE POLITICS OF FEDERAL-STATE RELATIONS AND THE DYNAMICS OF NIGERIA'S PRESIDENTIAL FEDERALISM: 1979-1983

Introduction

The nature of federal-state relations changed appreciably under the Second Republic. In the first place, Nigeria operated 19 states instead of the four regions we had up to 1967. Secondly, Nigeria operated a presidential system of government. Unlike the parliamentary system, the president, governors and chairmen of Local Governments were all directly elected by the populace.

Under the military administration, the military structure imposed on Nigeria's federalism since 1966 tied State military governors to their Commander-in-Chief who was also the head of the Federal Military Government. This meant that the central government could take actions to which the states could not object. Under an elected civilian government the political game changed. Elected officials were now in power, and after subnational chief executives found themselves engaged in serious efforts to buttress their autonomy within the federal polity.

However, in federal-state relations under the Second Republic, a few issues may be noted:

i) the nature of political parties and the states they controlled affected federal-state relations;

ii) Federal 'might' established under the military was still on the political scene as the centre waxed stronger under the presidential system;

iii) the political style bequeathed to Nigerian politicians by the military was very much responsible for the relationship of confrontation between the states and the centre;

iv) either the Nigerian Constitution had not been read carefully by many politicians, or some Nigerians were being dishonest in their interpretation of the Constitution, in the light of some controversies generated in the polity; and

v) despite the aggressive declaration of state autonomy and commitment to federalism by many politicians, it may be argued that the more states created, the less the autonomy of states.

Dynamics of Federal - State Relations

With the return to civilian government under the 1979 Constitution many state governments came under different political parties.[1] Since the governing party in the state was, at times, different from the party in power at the centre, Nigeria witnessed aggressive state nationalism. The demands for state autonomy escalated under the Second Republic – an attempt to avoid being swamped by the party in control of the Federal Government. This was very clear in the relations between the President and the Governors of some states. The appointment of Presidential Liaison Officers[2] raised much concern among many Nigerians. To many state government officials, while the President's right to appoint officers under section 5(a-b) of the Constitution was legal, there was no provision for the appointment of Presidential Liaison Officers (PLO) who are not members of the public service.

Many non-NPN state governments rejected the PLOs. Part of the objection was tied to the belief that these PLO jobs were patronages for loyal party men. In addition, some states genuinely believed that the PLOs would erode the autonomy of states. Many Governors did not hide their antipathy to the implication that their governments could only deal with Lagos through these PLOs. The issue of the PLOs was directly traceable to the problem of a communication gap between the President and the Governors in the states.

Another example of actions taken by the Federal Government that took on political colouring was the deportation of Shugaba.[3] Here the President seemed to have been misadvised. Many years later, President Shagari claimed not to have given that order. The Borno State Governor, as the Chief Security Officer of the State, was not informed about Shugaba's deportation. The hurried clandestine operation in the deportation of Shugaba gave political tint to an action the President was entitled to take, but which had become politically stigmatized because of the crudity in implementation. The president however, did not have the power to deport a Nigerian. The Great Nigeria Peoples' Party (GNPP) and even Shugaba himself accused the National Party of Nigeria (NPN) of having masterminded the deportation order. Furthermore it raised the issue of citizenship in Nigeria as allegation that Richard Akinjide, Paul Unongo and Alexander Fom were not Nigerians, seemed to confirm. Yet in politics, stumbles of this nature were not easily ameliorated without loss of credibility.

In their relations with the centre, many State Governors admirably reasserted federally desirable autonomy of states. However, it seemed that many of them found it hard to shed some political traits bequeathed to them by the military. The militarization of political culture in thirteen years of military rule had entailed the militarization of political style and language of most Nigerians. The reference often made to *old brigade* and the *new brigade* in Nigerian politics was a sign of the militarization of political language.

The civilian governors and politicians in the states, having schooled for thirteen years under the military had problems in making a smooth transition from military regime to a democratic civilian regime. The ultimata and threats they issued were the psychological legacies of military governors, which had become hard to shed.

The Governments of Plateau, Oyo and Kwara States threatened a takeover of federal television stations in their States. Most of these television stations were owned by the states before the federal takeover exercise in 1975/76. The States had not been paid any compensation. The States correctly complained that they had no control over the programmes their people watch and that state government activities are often blacked out, especially in states whose government belonged to a political part different from those at the centre. Allegations of the federal government jamming Lagos State TV even went to court.

State Governments had a case. The manner they went about it however, had been one of confrontation rather than discussion and compromise. Clearly, there was the need for greater decentralization of Federal institutions. For example, National Television (N.T.V.—now Nigerian Television Authority) could be so decentralized that while they were still federally owned, the States could control recruitment and programmes, to help reflect the interests of the local people who watched the Nigerian Television programmes.[4]

The Federal Government could co-ordinate activities of the various stations in Lagos. After all, suppose the U.P.N.- controlled states decided to "black out" a Presidential Address, there was little that could be constitutionally done since the TV stations were state-controlled. Yet a Governor of a state from any part today could become the President tomorrow. As Pierre Trudeau, the former Canadian Prime Minister put it:

> The principle of self-determination, which makes federalism necessary, makes it rather unstable. If the heavy paste of nationalism is relied upon to keep a unitary nation-state together much more nationalism would appear to be required in the case of a federal nation-state.[5]

While it is necessary to maintain state autonomy, our past experiences showed that a very weak centre could be very disastrous. True enough, there was the need for separate identity of states, but there was also the greater need for the unity of Nigeria, which is greater than any of its parts.

As the issue of educational institutions took greater saliency, threats to federal institutions also increased in incidence. The Bauchi State government was so angry with officials of Federal Polytechnic, Bauchi, for not being sensitive to the need of the state, that it gave them a quit order from the facilities the state had made available to them as temporary site. In Plateau State, Governor Lar threatened to take over the University of Jos if the University did not show greater response to the urgent needs of its catchment area.[6] No State could take over federal institutions unless the laws, which established them, were repealed. The governors should have known this.

In other cases, some states made ridiculous threats to the Federal Government. Benue State, frustrated after an expected opening of the airstrip in Makurdi, threatened to launch an airline if the Federal Government did not react quickly to the opening of the airport in Makurdi. Under the Constitution, "Aviation, including airports, safety of aircraft and carriage of passengers and goods by air" were in the exclusive legislative list of the Federal Government.[7] Yet Benue State had, like the Federal centre, an NPN government. The states were so conscious of their autonomy that at times, it looked like their officials had not read the Constitution properly.

This was very clear in the case of Ondo State which had indicated its intention to establish a Ministry of Petroleum Resources.[8] Again, item 36 of the Second Schedule of the Nigerian Constitution stated that "Mines and Minerals, including oil fields, oil mining, geological surveys and natural gas" were in the exclusive legislative list.[9] This was an interesting case of abrasive tickling of the Federal Government even when the Constitution was very clear on the issues involved. Perhaps, the states were testing the new constitution to see how far they could go.

There were other cases in federal-state relations where differences in party programmes had created policy problems. In Lagos State, Governor Jakande's UPN programme included free education and government take-over of all Primary and Secondary educational institutions. As far as Shagari's NPN government was concerned, "qualitative" education envisaged in the party's manifesto permitted the existence of private schools. While Bishop Okogie took the Lagos government to court, it seemed that such conflicts were inevitable in federal system. The National Assembly could make a law with respect to private ownership of schools. Once made, any state laws, which violate federal laws, would become null and void. The UPN would have also had the opportunity, just like NPN, of convincing National Assembly members of the worth of their standpoints.

Another interesting aspect of federal-state relations was the attitude of the incumbents themselves. At the federal centre, President Shagari exhibited a humility and moderation in politics. He took up duties slowly but surely. It was gigantic task and he was not in a haste to take off on speed. One could see the executive president like a big jet plane having difficulties in taking off because of technical problems with its wing, or some other parts. Passengers might get frustrated while waiting at the lounge. But when it finally took off, it easily attained high speed and height. People seemed to have been initially frustrated by Shagari's care and slow speed at the take-off stage of the presidential system. This caution was necessary. The Presidency was a big and powerful bird and must be flown with caution at the take-off stage of the Presidential system.

However, Shagari showed his political subtlety on a number of occasions. While state governors basked in the prestige of prefixes such as *His Excellency,* the President's office announced that the incumbent was now to be known as *Mr. President.* He drew the carpet from beneath the feet of governors, many of whom did not realize this. On the symbolic political dimension, Shagari engaged in political capital accumulation for the institution he held and for himself personally. Again, this was vividly demonstrated in his public rejection of the ₦50,000 salary proposed for the President by a committee of the National Assembly. While the members of the Assembly were furious with him and even accused him of turning the country against the National Assembly, Shagari came out of the rumpus with huge political goodwill, stocked in his reservoir, for the future.

Many Nigerians were, however, worried that there was too much of a mixture of Tafawa Balewa's meekness and Gowon's over-consideration of the feelings of others in Shagari's character, for decisive presidential action in policy-making and implementation. But perhaps, the greater fear was of some members of the political entourage in his presidential bandwagon who were believed to be more interested in acquisition for the self than in service for the nation. President Shagari did explain later the difficulties he had in his administration. With a narrow majority in the National Assembly, he had to act cautiously to carry the National Assembly with him. He believed that the legislature virtually immobilized him on many occasions.[10]

On the other hand, apart from *residual militarism* in their style, state governors seemed to have had difficulties in adapting to their new political roles. A good politician is one who is capable of adapting to the role of the politician and the statesman as situations demanded. Many Governors found it difficult to change from their role of a *soap-box politician* (during the election campaign) to that of *statesmen* in Government House. As a successful politician in election, a governor automatically becomes the 'father' of all in his state, whether they were his party *bed fellows* or not. The political blunder committed by Governor Ambrose Alli of Bendel during President Shagari's visit to that state illustrated the above point. Governor Alli had not properly welcomed President Shagari to his State. In a way Governor Lar of Plateau State did make amends on Alli's behaviour (in state-federal relations) by his display of statesmanship during Shagari's visit to Jos in March 1980.

Part of the problems of federal-state relations was related to the hawkish stance of some federal government political executives and officials. In many cases they seemed to interpret the Constitution in such a way as to favour the Federal Government. Two cases illustrate this point.

In reaction to the notorious power cuts by National Electric Power Authority (NEPA),[11] Governor Lar of Plateau State and the House of Assembly of Plateau State considered the possibility of switching to the National Electricity Supply Company (NESCO) which had been supplying part of Jos and its environs with power. In response, the Federal Minister for Mines and Power contended that no state had any powers to generate electricity. Governor Lar came out to challenge the constitutional legality of the Minister's position. While one recognizes that constitutional provisions subject to interpretations, the Constitution was clear on this.

The Second Schedule, Part II, the Concurrent Legislative list, Item F-13 (a-e) recognized the powers of the Federal Government to generate and transmit electricity throughout the federation, and between one state and the other. Thus the Minister was correct to assert federal authority in this area. But Item F-14 (a-e) of the same Schedule stipulated that the House of Assembly of a State "may make laws for

a) electricity and the establishment in that state of electric power stations;
b) the generation, transmission and distribution of electricity within that State;"

Unless it could be proved that state laws on such generation and distribution of electricity as suggested by Plateau State-

i) contradicted federal laws (which by themselves were assumed to be unrepealable or unamendable); and
ii) violated the Constitution, the state did have a case here.

The second illustration was the case of creation of additional local government areas in Nigeria. Some federal sources in the Executive and in the National Assembly, at various times, had publicly contended that State governments had no right to create additional local governments. The main argument of these officials was that First Schedule, Part I which described the states of the Federation, mentioned specific Local Government Areas. Unless these aspects in the Constitution were amended, they argued, state government could create additional Local Government Council. Section 7 (1) of the Constitution states:

> The system of Local government by democratically elected local government councils is under this constitution guaranteed; and accordingly, the **Government of every State shall ensure their existence under a Law, which provides for the establishment structure, composition, finance and functions of such councils.**[12]
> [Emphasis, mine]

It may be argued that the creation of additional local government councils came under the functions of the state government with regard to the "establishment, structure, composition, finance and functions of such council." The argument that the schedule, which described the States of the Federation, referred to existing Local Government Areas, which could not be altered without constitutional amendment, seemed hollow. That Schedule did not refer to local government areas. It merely enumerated areas, which comprise a State.

In the case of Kaduna State, for example, Saminaka was one of the areas mentioned. Two local governments created out of that area would not alter Saminaka as a component area of the State. Similarly, while the areas mentioned might have coincided with local government council areas, there was nowhere in the Constitution where reference to these areas was interpreted as "local government council areas." In fact, Section 3(2) of that Constitution reads:

> Each state of Nigeria named in the first column of part 1 of the First Schedule to this Constitution shall consist of the area shown opposite thereto in the second column of that schedule.[13]

It is, therefore, clear that the power to create local governments belonged to states. If for one reason or the other the second column of that schedule had posed a bottleneck in policy-making, the National Assembly should have amended the Constitution and removed that part. It is pretentious to claim that any other level of authority beyond the State could deal with issues of local governments in Nigeria.

The Federal Civil Service should not be over-bearing in relation to states. The circular by the Head of Federal Civil Service that all public officers who had taken up political positions should resign their posts in state services, was not in order. The state service was autonomous of federal centre. The tradition of centralization under the military seemed to have hardly changed for some Federal officials. If the centre wanted this directive adopted by the state it should have sent it as a bill to the National Assembly and a law can be passed to that effect by the Assembly.

Finally, a ticklish and on-going problem in Federal-State relations was finance. Since the creation of twelve states in 1967, states had become financially heavily dependent on the federal centre. This dependence differed from one state to the other, between 40% in some states to 90% in other states – for their annual budgetary needs.[14] The Okigbo revenue allocation commission therefore had a welter of demands by state governments for additional funds to be allocated to states. The 1981 Revenue Allocation Act, shared revenues among tiers of government, viz: Federal Government, 55%; State Government, 30.5% Local Government, 10%. Frustrated, a number of states went to court but could not reverse the situation.

The problem of state autonomy was compounded by the inability of states to generate revenues from internal sources. In some states, there was little or no effort made to do this beyond community tax and personal income tax. In some others, the creation of additional states had reduced their resource bases and rendered them hopelessly dependent on federally derived sources of revenue. In addition, while oil revenue was very helpful, it increased enormously the powers of the purse of the federal centre at the expense of states – again a legacy of Lagos-centric actions of the military regime. This obviously had its merits and demerits. The oil boom of early 1970s also created a dangerous sense of complacency and false sense of security, which we seemed unable to overcome.

As additional states are created in Nigeria, the tendency towards greater authority at the centre would become more glaring. The experience showed that the more the number of states, the weaker the new states, in their resource bases (no matter what was allocated to them by the Okigbo Commission) and therefore, the greater the power of the federal centre. Finance is an important aspect of federal autonomy. In addition, the nature of modern government worked against the traditional concepts of the autonomy of *subnational* units. In most federal systems the power of the centre grows because of the demands for uniformity of action and complexity of modern government. This has been the case in the United States, Germany and (despite its peculiar problems) Canada. Nigeria is no exception.

Thus, in a paradoxical fashion, while most Nigerians tended to be very much attached to federal principles of state autonomy, they were most vocal about the creation of additional states with its implication of erosion of state autonomy.

In this chapter we observed a number of problems in Nigeria's operation of presidential federalism in terms of federal-state relations. The Federal Government had grown so strong that it had relatively eroded state autonomy. Perhaps Nigerians were reacting to their history. Like the Germans who reacted in similar fashion to the flaws of the *Weimar Constitution*, Nigerians reacted to a checkered history of federalism with a weak centre. Finally, the military centralized political power to the point that Nigerians are now asking for more devolution of powers to states and local governments.

The Federal Government was likely to get more powerful, given the demands of complex modern government, the demands in federal systems for uniformity and the little resource bases of states. As additional states were created, the states were likely to be weaker. Beyond a thresh-hold, the creation of additional states would bring out strongly the undercurrent unitary traits in our federal system.

A number of lessons come out of the experiences of the Second Republic. It may be suggested that for future relations between the centre and the states, federal officials should stop displaying federal arrogance in an over-bearing manner while relating to states. Leaders and officials of state government must stop pecking childishly at the federal centre for every problem. There are many ways of discussing and solving problems without resorting to confrontations on the soap box and in front of television cameras. In this regard the advice of the governors of Imo and Oyo to their colleagues to abandon the technique of confrontation as a mechanism of extracting resources from the centre,[15] was very useful.

The President should have established an informal administrative forum for comparing notes with Governors in order to minimize communication gaps between Federal and State governments. The National Council of State and the National Economic council could not serve such informal purposes.

In addition, the Governors should have demilitarized their political style as fast as possible to allow for the politics of compromise, tolerance and participation. Governors, as statesmen, should not make certain statements; their Party officials and Commissioners should make such statements. In addition, they should stop threatening the centre. Nigeria cannot afford a repeat performance of 1960-67 years.

The issue of the *creation of additional states* continued to pester the Presidential system. Like all medicinal prescriptions, the creation of states, which had helped to resolve the problem of structural imbalance, had its own side effects and some political rashes. These political rashes include the emergence of *new majorities* and *new minorities*. The fear of domination became more salient as groups sought avoidance mechanisms to project their interests. The creation of additional state would lead to greater dependence on the centre. Federal-state power watchdogs should watch this. Given the numerous demands for new states and the procedure for creating additional states, it might be difficult for any civilian regime to create states in the future. The calls for additional states really were attempts to question the nature of association in the federation.

The Dynamics of Presidential Federalism

It is not enough to limit our discussion of the period to the relations between national and state governments. It is also important to have an insight into dynamics of presidential federalism within the period. The

138

very dynamics of the political process indicated that there were many echoes of the past, heard within the polity even if within new and at times, different structures.

The North-South bogey, which hung like a cloud over the First Republic, had not vanished, inspite of the creation of states. Occasionally, the *North-South dichotomy* simmers to the surface in the creation of additional states, revenue allocation, etc. Similarly, the ethnoregional aspects of the old political parties became more apparent after 1979 when the political parties emerged.

The *Nigerian Peoples' Party* (NPP) was very often referred to as the reincarnation of the old National Council for Nigerian Citizens (NCNC) – with its base in Iboland. The *National Party of Nigeria* (NPN) was very much a replica of an enlarged Northern Peoples' Congress (NPC), with strong Hausa-Fulani base. In the same vein, the *Unity Party of Nigeria* (UPN) was seen by many Nigerians as the rejuvenation of the old Action Group (AG), grafted into its Yoruba base. Of course, the *Peoples' Redemption Party* (PRP), despite its internal fissures, was seen as the Northern Elements Progressive Union (NEPU), updated and enlarged, and having more luck this time than it had in the First Republic; the PRP controlled two state governments.[16] Perhaps the only really new political party was the *Great Nigerian Peoples' Party* (GNPP), formed by a splinter group from the NPP. It was very much a protest party in the Northern states – against the Hausa-Fulani establishment. Each of these parties had members from other ethnic groups to satisfy the provisions of the constitution, but each created certain impressions, which were reminiscent of the past.

Given this situation of the parties and the open declarations of 'decamping' by members of one party to the other (usually more propitiously placed in Nigeria's calculus of the "starvation politics),[17] many Nigerians began to wonder if we were not going to have a repeat performance of the politics of intolerance, impatience, and opportunism of the First Republic. The old cliché of "cross-carpeting" in the legislatures had been barred, but non-legislators certainly did cross-carpet, with Machiavellian calculus of convenience.

In addition, the minority-majority ethnic group cleavages of old were still very much around in many political parties. At the NPN National Convention in June 1980 in Kaduna, the issue of the election of candidates to national offices brought minority-majority group conflicts to the surface. Governor Okilo of Rivers State championed the cause of the minority states.[18] He accused members of his party of playing "selfish and sectional politics" and declared that some Nigerians were not yet rising above their "selfish and tribal outlook." He challenged his partymen: "We talk of federal character, why are you afraid of equality of states? Come forward now and accept federal character and equality of states."[19]

On another occasion, the fear that the minority groups might gang up against the majority groups sparred Mallam Adamu Ciroma, the Minister of Industries, to issue a warning. Ciroma warned that any gang-up by minorities would elicit drastic reactions from majority groups. While there was no evidence of such a gang-up by minority groups, even if it were possible, it was not clear that unity among majority groups could be easily attained to counteract the activities of minorities, given their intrinsically diverse and conflicting interests. More often, each majority group had found it easier to ally with some minority groups against other majority groups. Cases of this type of alliance abound in Nigeria's political history especially in the ethnoregional politics of 1960-65. Perhaps, more important was the fact that these fears were expressed at all. It showed very clearly that a potent source of conflict still lingered on: even if pushed under the carpet within the new structures, it occasionally came up to the surface.

As Ivor Duchacek once put the dilemma of majority-minority in federal balance:

> The problem for most ethnic minorities is that they are permanent minorities and the ruling group a permanent majority. In interethnic relations, therefore, the convenient democratic game of numbers – majoritarian decision-making in the framework of a broad consensus – does not work since the unalterable power symmetry between formation of a consensual community. The quota system satisfactorily guarantees jobs, educational opportunities, and presence in decision-making bodies; but no quota system can be really generous as to transform a minority into a majority. No quota system can, therefore, fully protect a minority against tyranny by the majority in a legislative body unless it is coupled with a veto power over central issues. Then,

however, as the history of Cyprus shows, government may become impossible.[20]

The issue defies balancing in a federal system, yet a federal system provides for more compromise than a unitary system in this situation. The problem was not only at the national level. At the level of subnational states, minority-majority issues were also calling for answers. Perhaps only a sense of fairness learned and practised over time can assuage the fears and suspicions, which this political issue creates. The creation of additional states only created *new majorities* and *new minorities*, even though it lessened the intensity of conflicts at the national level.

The differential pattern in the acquisition of Western education (now a passport to social mobility) had always been a source of fear in the old republic. It was very much present in the Nigerian political arena in the Second Republic. The crises over the admission of students into universities led the military government in 1977 to establish a central body – the *Joint Admission and Matriculation Board* (JAMB). Yet by 1979, there were widespread protests in parts of the country against the pattern of admissions into universities under this agency. The widespread demands for the abolition of this body led to the president's bill for the establishment of a University Entrance Examinations Agency. The bill sought to return admission of students to the universities again. The bill was never passed before the regime was over thrown. The demands for a more equitable admission formula still go on. This issue, by its nature, defies balancing.

Revenue allocation was a real bone of contention in the First Republic. It was still very much a problem in the Second Republic. As mentioned earlier, the President had signed a revenue bill, which gave the federal government 55 percent, 30.5 percent for state governments, and 10 percent for local governments. As in 1964, states reacted with anger to this formula, arguing that it gave the federal government too much money at their expense. In fact, two legislators and twelve governors took the President to court. The court nullified the Okigbo Report, but the adjustment made after that, became the Revenue Act of 1981/82. These governors understandably, were not NPN governors.[21] The problem of revenue allocation was an echo of the past that still bugged the Nigerian political system. But it is also a problem of all federations.

There is no doubt that states were heavily dependent on the federally collected funds for their finances. While a case could be made for more funds accruing to states, most states seemed very frivolous in their expenditure and hardly attempted to raise revenue from internal sources. Moreover, many Nigerians wanted to see a strong federal centre in the light of Nigeria's historical past, which was still very green in people's memories. However, they did not want to see a centre, which suffocated the states.

Finally, generational conflicts between "older" and "younger" politicians simmered to the surface very often. The PRP crisis between the Aminu Kano/S.G. Ikoku group on the one hand, and the Governors Abubakar Rimi and Balarabe Musa group on the other, were partly related to this issue. While the PRP was the most ideological of all Nigerian political parties, the extent of its radicalism as represented by Rimi and Musa went counter to the grain of the elders of the party such as Aminu Kano and Ikoku (both seasoned politicians). While Aminu and Ikoku saw relations with the UPN and GNPP as antiparty activities and as posing a threat to their leadership, Rimi and Musa could not imagine themselves functionally interacting with the NPN. While there were more reasons for the PRP crises of leadership, the generational issue was very cogent. Similarly, the NPP caucus in the Senate found itself embroiled in a crisis of leadership and a member of the "old Brigade," Senator Jaja Wachukwu, lost his leadership position to a member of the "new brigade," Senator Obi Wali. The NPN had similar problems with its Kaduna-based caucus, usually referred to as the "Kaduna Mafia" – generally younger and very active members of that party.

Generally, these issues were all echoes of the past, which still pestered the Nigerian body politic. Solutions to them were not easy. Some of these issues defied any attempts at balancing within Nigeria's political equation.

Federalism is "about cooperation, that is the terms and condition under which conflict is limited.[23] It is, therefore, a mechanism for effecting compromise. The art of compromise involves delicate balancing of conflicting claims. While some of the issues mentioned above are part and parcel of Nigeria's attempt to balance imbalance, some issues by their nature defy balancing and pose real challenges to decision-makers. These issues create political dilemmas, which are often difficult to solve. Let us take a few examples.

The differential pattern of the spread of education had been identified as a very potent source of fears and suspicions among Nigerian groups. Yet one could not balance the situation by holding static the educationally advanced areas until the less advanced areas catch up. Quota systems would keep out some of the most brilliant Nigerians from educationally advanced areas while offering no absolute guarantee for closing the gap. Yet a widening gap between these two areas in one country would only create a reservoir of problems for greater crises later. The general argument was that more money should be spent in the less educationally advanced areas to enable them to correct the imbalance. But as theorists of change know, a head start in education can hardly be slowed down. This issue defies balancing, and yet it is closest to the hearts of Nigerians, for understandable reasons. Perhaps Nigerians may set a minimum level of educational standard for everyone and hope that, with the encouragement of disadvantaged areas, the gap would be appreciably narrowed – narrowed to a point where disparities in educational acquisitions no longer pose grave threat to the nation.

Related to this is the attempt to ensure that the composition of public institutions reflects "federal character" as outlined in section 14, subsection 3 of the 1979 Constitution. There is no doubt that representation creates a sense of belonging to the nation. Yet, laudable as it is, Nigerians have not yet been able to define appropriately the mechanism for effecting 'federal character'. Does it mean that every state must be represented? Even some minority groups may never get represented in federal or state institutions. If all states and local governments have to be represented, what happens to efficiency? What happens when there are fewer vacancies than the number of states? If "federal character" does not mean equal representation of states but an attempt to ensure that one or two groups do not dominate a particular public institution, to what extent can one balance the situation without alienating others and inserting seeds of frustration into the institution? Yet "federal character" is problematic because it is linked to Western education, which had become a passport for entry into the modern sector, such as the public service.

Another issue, which defies balancing, is the federal structure. As mentioned earlier, the minority-majority issue is contextual and situational. A minority group of yesterday becomes a majority group today, in the context of a newer and smaller state. Often the new majorities are even more vicious than the old majorities. This problem is likely to go on tickling the federal system. But perhaps even more dangerous is the calculus of state creation in the background of the old North-South line. Can Nigeria really have as many states in the North as in the South? Will the creation of additional state not tilt the balance in federal-state relations much more in favour of the centre, and possibly lead to the unitary system?

The issue of federal balance is not always structural – that is, among component governments. There are certain forms of imbalance in the federal system, which can be corrected, in relative terms to permit the system to operate above certain levels of efficiency. On the other hand, certain issues, by their very nature, defy "balancing" in the short term. Too much pressure for balancing may break down the system. The demand for the creation of additional states, with its implication for the erosion of state autonomy, was probably a case of too much pressure for balancing. The creation of states within the federal structure was a device to reduce the perceived overcentralizing predisposition of the federal government. Unfortunately, Nigerian states found themselves in the throes of a dependence paradox. There was inadequate understanding that there was a point of diminishing return in the utility curve of the creation of additional states. Indeed, the creation of additional states had reduced the resource bases of many states and rendered them exceedingly dependent on the federal government. Thus, federal government's actions of the past were unwittingly encouraged by tactics and strategies calculated to bring about an acceptable equilibrium between state coherence and ethnic self-determination.

While the Second Republic had established a network for effecting checks and balances, the titanic central government created by military regimes still remained politically and fiscally very strong. Attempts were made to effect compromises in the federal polity, even though some issues defied any immediate solutions. The Second Republic was having a learning experience in presidential federalism. To what extent did the politicians have opportunities for further learning experience under the same republic?

Thus, in a paradoxical fashion, while most Nigerians tended to be very much attached to federal principles of state autonomy, they were most vocal about the creation of additional states with its implications of the erosion of state autonomy.

The structure of the federal system and the distribution of powers in this structure, posed problems for the new politicians. They learned gradually. The system was new, the political platform was also new, and the political actors were a mixture of the new and old.

We shall now turn to those issues, which created problems for the strategy of federal balance as a result of the dynamics of the presidential federal process.

Notes and references

1.   The *Great Nigeria Peoples Party* (GNPP) controlled Borno and Gongola States; *Nigerian Peoples' Party* (NPP) formed the governments of Plateau, Imo and Anambra States; *National Party of Nigeria* (NPN) was in charge of Cross River, Rivers, Benue, Sokoto, Niger, Bauchi, and Kwara States; the *Peoples' Redemption Party* (PRP) was in power in Kaduna and Kano States; while the *Unity Party of Nigeria* (UPN) effectively controlled Ogun, Lagos, Oyo, Bendel and Ondo States.

2.   These were supposed to be Presidential Liaison with the states to coordinate federal agencies and projects. Some states – Imo, Plateau and Anambra—refused to have anything to do with Federal Housing project if these were handled through PLOs. *New Nigerian,* May 20, 1980, p. 1.

3.   Shugaba was the majority (GNPP) leader of the House of Assembly of Borno State. He was deported by the federal government as an alien and was later brought back into the country by court order.

4.   *New Nigeria,* 29 May, 1980 – carried a report of the federal governments plan to review the issue of NTV. These would still be federally controlled but would be increasingly decentralized.

5.Pierre Trudeau quoted by Shridath Ramphal, Keynote Address, in A.B. Akinyemi, et al, *Readings On federalism, op. cit.* p. xxii.

6. *The Nigeria Standard*, (Jos), Dec. 1980, p. 1.

7. Federal Republic of Nigeria, The *Constitution of the Federal Republic of Nigeria, 1979*, (Lagos: Government Printer, 1978), Second Schedule, item a, p.96.

8. *The National Concord*, (Lagos) May 17, 1980, p. 3.

9. *The Constitution of the Federal Republic of Nigeria, op. cit.*, item 36, p. 98.

10. Shehu Shagari, "The Power and Limitation of The Executive and the Legislature in the Presidential Experience," in J. Isawa Elaigwu, P.C. Logams and H.S. Galadima (eds) *Federalism and Nation-Building in Nigeria: The Challenges of the Twenty-First Century*, (Abuja: NCIR, 1994) pp. 135-144.

11.NEPA had given so many reasons for its constant power cuts. These included, at one time, drought and its effects on River Niger, and at other times, flood in River Niger and others.

12. Emphasis is mine to show the relevant part of the quoted section of the Constitution.

13. *The Constitution of the Federal Republic of Nigeria, 1979* section 3 (2).

14. J. Isawa Elaigwu, "The Military and State-Building" *loc. cit.*, pp. 175-177; also see Rafiu Akindele, "Federal Grants-in-Aid to State Governments: A Note on An Aspect of the Federal Spending Power in Nigeria" in Akinyemi *et. al.* Readings In Federalism, *op. cit*, pp.182-189.

15. *Daily Times*, 21 May, 1980.

16.PRP expelled its only two governors from the party. There were court cases on this expulsion.

17."Starvation politics" is used to refer to a situation in which a party member changes his party with the hope of harvesting some perquisites (contracts, status, etc.) from the new political party he joins.

18.Minority states are those composed of minority groups in the old four regional structures such as Niger, Benue, Plateau, Cross River, Rivers and Bendel states.

19.*The Nigerian Tide*, July 1, 1980, p. 1.

20.Ivor Duchacek, "Antagonistic Cooperation: Territorial and Ethnic Communities," *Publius*, 4 (Fall 1977): 23.

21.See *The Nigerian Standard,* February 4, 1981, p. 1, and *The Punch,* February 8, 1981, p. 16.

22.Aaron Wildavsky, "A Bias Towards Federalism: Confronting the Conventional Wisdom on the Delivery of Governmental Services," *Publius,* 6, 2 (Spring 1976): 95.

THE PARADOX OF AUTONOMY AND CONTROL: THE FUTURE OF SUBNATIONALISM IN NIGERIA

If Nigerians are committed to federalism, how does one maintain a delicate balance between the centre's demand for national self-determination and subnational state's demand for identity and autonomy? To what extent can state autonomy be retained if many additional states are created? Would federalism still serve as a technique for managing conflicts? If federalism would not, has Nigeria transcended the issues, which led to her adoption of federalism? Is there not a paradox in subnational demands for autonomy and protection of identity, which basically erodes this autonomy? Is the creation of additional states a solution to all the political problems of Nigeria? Or is state creation a particular prescription for particular structural ailments? What implication does this have for federalism? In our attempt to answer these questions we suggest that:

i) the creation of subnational states is a particular prescription for particular national ills which have been extended as a cure for all political ills;

ii) state creation exercise has paradoxical implication for the maintenance of subnational self-determination and protection of group identities;

iii) the more new states are created, the greater the trend towards unitarism;

iv) since some of the issues which led to the adoption of federalism have only subsided and have not really been minimized or transcended, unitarism now, would have implications for political stability; and

v) Nigerians should develop conflict resolution mechanisms to cope with inter-group problems rather than opt for an avoidance mechanism as a solution to all societal problems.

Subnational States and Nigerian Federalism

Let us examine our first contention that the creation of subnational states is a particular prescription for particular political ailments in Nigeria's federal structure. The quest for structural reorganization of the Nigerian state dated as far back as the 1940s. The demands were essentially for changes in the size and number of subnational political units in Nigeria.

In 1943, Nnamdi Azikiwe had suggested the division of Nigeria into eight units within a federal framework of government.[1] But the Richard's constitution established three regions, which drew opposition from various nationalists. In 1947, Awolowo suggested the division of Nigeria into 10 units,[2] along ethnic and linguistic lines. The NCNC charter argued for ethnic groups as the basis of federation in 1948.[3]

In the course of constitutional reforms between 1946 and 1954, *subnational* group nationalism escalated as groups tried to protect their interests in the process of decolonization. As we have already discussed in Chapter 2, many groups feared that their interests could hardly be protected by dominant groups, which were likely to inherit political powers in each of the regions. Demands galore for the creation of states filled the Nigerian political atmosphere. Among such demands were – the Midwest, Middle Belt and Calabar-Ogoja-Rivers (COR) States. As we discussed in Chapter two, these demands had led to the establishment of the Willink Commission in 1957 to investigate the fears and suspicions of minority groups and to suggest ways of alleviating them, including the creation of states.

The report of the Commission confirmed that these fears were genuine and made recommendations about how to allay minority fears.[4] On the creation of states, the commission felt that since the regions had acquired enormous powers, it was unlikely that they would forego the powers they already had. Faced with the choice between the delay of independence and the suspension of the creation of additional states, Nigerians opted for independence in 1960, but with a formula for the creation of additional states inserted in the constitution under a Fundamental Human Rights clause. However, by

149

shelving the issue of states creation before independence, Nigerian leaders stored a rich legacy of problems, which cast thick shadows over the political system after independence.

The period 1960-65 witnessed the creation of only one state, the Midwest region in 1963. After taking over power in 1966, it took a while before the military took any positive action on the creation of additional states. On May 27, 1967, General Gowon created twelve states, six in the North, and six in the South,[5] in order to correct the imbalance in Nigeria's federal structure. As Gowon observed, until the creation of states in 1967, "our constitution was a glaring contradiction of the Fundamental Principles of Federation." Gowon's act of structural engineering was to "correct the imbalance in the administrative structure of the country" and to "minimize future political friction and ensure a stable federation."[6] The essence of creating equal number of states in the North and South was to satisfy the various geo-ethnic groups that justice had been done.

The creation of states was essentially a political pill to cope with the problem of structural imbalance in Nigeria. In many ways it was quite effective, given the new medium it provided for the emergence of a strong federal centre during and after the civil war.[7]

But like all medicinal prescriptions the creation of states, which had helped to resolve the problem of structural imbalance, developed its own side effects – some form of *political rashes*. Among such political rashes were the emergence of *new majorities* and new *minorities*. In the framework of new states emerged *new majorities, which* were seen as domineering in their relations with others, while in some other cases, complaints of neglect, discrimination, intolerance and arrogance were leveled against some minority groups in power, usually seen as dominant minorities.

If states were created as pills for correcting Nigeria's structural imbalance in order to establish a framework for relative stability, it soon took on a different meaning and function. For many Nigerians it became an *elixir* for solving all political and economic problems ranging from poverty, drought and flood to the allocation of scarce but allocatable resources. By 1974, it had become clear that Nigerians were no longer ready to resolve issues of inter-group relations through other means. They resorted to avoidance mechanism as a technique for coping with intergroup problems in the subnational state and at the same time as a device for protecting their group/individual interests and identities. The number of demands for new states by 1974, (barely seven years after the twelve states) so overwhelmed General Gowon that he had to advise the nation:

> ... I am aware that there are certain grievances, which have led to the demand for the creation of additional states. Some of these grievances relate to the question of more rapid development projects. Some people also feel that all sections of a state should be fully represented in all organs of the government in the state. We cannot satisfy these grievances by creating additional states since there will be no limit to the number of states. Honestly, we cannot push the principle of creating additional states too far.[8]

Nigerians did not heed this advice. For many Nigerians, the state 'pill' had the capability to cure all political ailments. The number of demands escalated as groups vilified one another, using some of the most obscene epithets.

151

Table 1
The Changing Structure of the Nigerian Federation: 1960-2005

Year	Federal Government	Regions/States	Local Governments
1960	1	3(Regions)*	**
1963	1	4(Regions)	**
1967	1	12	**
1970	1	12	299
1976	1	19	299
1979	1	19	301
1981	1	19	781
1984	1	19	301
1987	1	21	449
1991	1	30	500
1991	1	30	589
1996	1	36	774[#]
2005	1	36	774[#]

* There were actually 4 regions at independence, which included Southern Cameroons. When Southern Cameroons opted to join The Cameroon after the plebiscite of 1961, Nigeria returned to a three-regional federal structure.

** what existed during these periods was called Native Authorities in the North; Local Governments/Divisions in the South - before 1966.

The 36 states were zoned into six — North-Central, North-East, North-West, South-East, South-South and South-West. These geo-political zones were not included in the constitution but they have been used for political purposes.

Source: Culled and amended from Danjuma, T. Y. "Revenue Sharing and the Political Economy of Nigerian Federalism" in Elaigwu, J. I., Logams, P. C. and Galadima, H. S. *Federalism and Nation-Building in Nigeria: The Challenges of the Twenty-First Century* (Abuja: NCIR, 1994), p. 88.

In response to these demands, General Murtala Mohammed created seven additional states on February 3, 1976. In his broadcast General Mohammed warned that Nigerians could not continue to dissipate all their energy on the states issue and that for him that was the end of the road on the creation of subnational units. Nigeria then

152

emerged with a nineteen-state structure (ten in the North and nine in the South).

But Mohammed barely died before Nigerians started making requests for additional states. Of course, Obasanjo refused to be stampeded into taking action on this. In fact, his regime was essentially one of effecting the demilitarization of the polity. He handed over a package of unenviable legacy, of which the states issue was one, to Alhaji Shehu Shagari and the new civilian rulers. There were demands for the creation of about sixty states (some which overlapped) in the Second Republic.

Of course, many of these requests were not devoid of maneuvers by political parties during the civilian era. It is interesting to note that out of the various requests, fifteen (15) were recommended by the conference committee of the National Assembly for referenda.

The Buhari administration did not have the time to entertain the request for additional states creation. However, the administration was quick to abolish the numerous local government areas created during the preceeding civilian administration. The number of local government areas was reversed from 574 to 308 as contained in the 1979 constitution.

The Babangida regime had a softer spot for the demands for additional states. It was the only regime that responded twice to the unending request for creation of additional states. In the national debates under the Political Bureau in 1979, the creation of additional states was one of the hotly debated issues. There were also views, which were opposed to the creation of additional states – such as abolishing, merging or retaining the existing states.

There were many requests for additional states made to the Political Bureau. Below is a list of such requests from the existing states.

Table 2
Summary of Requests for States Creation Submitted to the Political Bureau (1985/86)

EXISTING STATE	REQUESTED STATE
Kaduna	Katsina
Cross River	Akwa Ibom
Bendel	Delta /Anioma
Anambra	Enugu (Wawa)
Kwara-Benue	Kogi
Gongola	Sardauna
Rivers	Port-Harcourt
Bauchi	Gombe
Oyo	Split into 2 or more
Kano	Split into 2 or more
Sokoto	Split into 2 or more
Borno	Split into 2 or more

Source: *Report of the Political Bureau* (March 1987), pp. 179-180.

Based on these requests, the Political Bureau recommended the creation of additional states.

In 1987, the Babangida regime implemented one of the recommendations of the Bureau with creation two additional states – Akwa Ibom and Katsina. The number increased from 19 to 21. The military regime seemed to have heeded the advice that the creation of states was easier under military regimes, for President Babangida increased the number of states from 21 to 30 in 1991. The newly created states were Delta, Enugu, Kogi, Taraba, Osun, Jigawa, Kebbi, Yobe and Abia. Also some of the existing states were renamed, such as, Adamawa (former Gongola) and Edo (former Bendel) – after the creating new states from them.

However, the request for additional state persisted. The Abacha regime was confronted with the same problem. Admittedly, the military government indicated its intention to address this problem. The then Head of State, General Abacha justified the continuous requests for additional states, at the inauguration of 1995 Constitutional Conference:

> It is right in the democratic process that these demands (for creation of states and local governments) should be freely aired and given a fair hearing. But this can only be done against the background of the economic and other implications.[9]

The committee tasked with creation of states made recommendations for creating additional states based on these principles:

i. Viability (verified or potential)
ii. Human resources and population
iii. Terrain, land mass or water mass
iv Willingness and determination of a people
v. Historical antecedents
vi. Homogeneity and compatibility
vii. Compact geographic area
viii. National stability/security.

The committee received thirty-five (35) requests for additional states but recommended the creation of twenty (20). The table below summarizes the recommendations.

Table 3
Summary of Recommended States for Creation in 1995

Existing State	Requested State
Bauchi	Gombe, Katagum
Benue	Apa
Plateau	Nasarawa
Jigawa	Hadejia
Kano	Tiga
Adamawa	Sardauna
Niger-Kebbi	Kainji
Rivers	Bayelsa, Orashi and Rivers East
Delta	Anioma
Ondo	Ekiti
Enugu-Abia	Ebonyi
Oyo	New Oyo
Cross-River	Ogoja
Akwa-Ibom	Itai
Ogun	Ijebu-Remo

Source: *Report of the Constitutional Conference containing The Resolutions and Recommendations, Vol. II,* (1995).

From this long list only six states were eventually created — Gombe, Nasarawa, Zamfara, Bayelsa, Ekiti and Ebonyi. A major factor used as a criterion for this creation was the creation of geopolitical zones. One state was created from each of the six zones. Although these zones were not constitutionally recognized they became useful in the politics of allocation in the federation even after the regime.

Yet like the insatiable thirst of a caravan in the middle of a desert, the issue resurfaced during the 2005 National Political Reform Conference under President Obasanjo. The Committee on "Models and Structure of Government" at the conference received requests for additional states based on viability and boundary adjustments to enable groups to join their kith and kin in states other than where they are presently located. From the several requests the committee however identified seventeen cases as genuine. The proposed states were: Anioma, Ijebu, New Oyo, Ibadan, Savannah, Ndaduma, Oke-

Ogun, South Kaduna, Toru-Ebe, Coast, Northern Sardauna, Kainji, Katagum, Orlu, Efik, Ogoja, and Oil Rivers.[10]

Our point here is that from a position in which the number of states was increased to correct a dangerous imbalance in federal structure, we arrived at a stage in which states became avoidance mechanisms for coping with problems of inter-group relations. It not only became faddish to ask for new states out of one's present state, it became a political card for demonstrating that a politician was concerned with the cultural subnationalism of his people.

If we had political universities,[11] it made sense to some politicians to ask for political states. If states were created to correct the imbalance in federal structure, is Nigeria's Federal structure, still unbalanced? What dangers of such structural imbalance as are still left? Is state creation the only effective mechanism for distributing resources more equitably in the system? Just like the reckless use of antibiotics could be counter-productive, so it is with reckless proliferation of subnational units with pretensions of federally desired autonomy and self-determination. Is there not really a humorous but serious paradox in all these?

Autonomy and Control

The principle of federalism emphasizes the autonomy of component units and the maintenance of coordinate status among these units.[12] This is the essence of legislative lists in federal systems. Legislative lists do not make sense in unitary systems.[13] The demands of two types of self-determinations – national self-determination and subnational self-determination – make it imperative to have clearly defined roles. Thus, in Nigeria, the *Exclusive Legislative list* goes to the federal government, while *Residual functions* (those which are found neither in exclusive nor in *Concurrent*[14] *Legislative list*) accrue to states.

The important point, as K.C. Wheare reminds us, is not which government takes on which legislative list, but that 'whoever has the residue, neither general nor regional government is subordinate to the other in its sphere of operation.[15] National self-determination forces pull towards the centre, while subnational self-determination forces pull away from the centre. The important point is the balance between the two pulls – centripetal and centrifugal forces, at any point in time.

Federalism is a paradoxical *elixir* to be purchased from any political market. It not only provides for the security and survival of a nation (because of the very compromise it is capable of effecting), it also safeguards self-determination of parochial subnational groups.

For many of the states agitators, a state of their own would give them an opportunity to "have ours and do it our way". It will provide new boundaries within which they could have control over their affairs' without necessarily having to interact with those other Nigerian groups they see as operating in such ways that are antithetical to their perceived interests. 'Let us pull away from them so that we can control our own affairs' becomes a rallying cry for these elites. But it is an avoidance mechanism – avoiding the others in the system by 'having our own'. However, this runs counter to the realities of nation-building that groups in these new autonomous domains would still have to interact cooperatively for the nation to be built.

In a way, federalism provides an impetus for the demands for additional states. After all, is one of its principles not the recognition of desires for union without subnational groups losing their identities? To the extent that Nigerians are asking for states to protect their identities and interests in the federal system, their demands are legitimate. These demands are also consonant with principle of subnational self-determination in federal systems. Yet, it is equally a fact that these same demands for subnational self-determination could, in a paradoxical sense, work against subnational self-determination and the same autonomy being sought. Beyond a threshold, the number of states and their capability could undermine this very self-determination and autonomy. If demands for states are demands for subnational autonomy of groups, this same subnational autonomy is also drastically eroded by the dynamics of federalism and complex political processes.

Let us turn to the logic of the agitation for additional states in order to see the above points more clearly. There had been over sixty demands for creation of additional states by December 1983. These included, Taraba, New Benue, Binda, Kogi, New Oyo, Katsina, New

158

Kaduna, Delta, New Cross River, Anioma, Edo, Okura, Ebonyi, New Anambra, the Middle Belt, Nasarawa and myriads of others.

It was interesting to watch the number of delegations, which had undertaken political pilgrimages to the centres of power in Lagos in order to make their cases (on the television). Each delegation was led by some of the most respectable citizens of the country. Each of these delegations created the impression that its own case was unique and urgent. Space constrains our treatment of the reasons put forward by each delegation for the creation of states. The important point is that these reasons were no different from those, which had been advanced for earlier exercises in states creation. These reasons (manifest and latent, or ostensible and real) include broadly – (i) discrimination in the present geopolitical setting: (ii) possible instability if the suggested states were not created, thus amounting almost to a threat; (iii) lack of opportunities for participation and access to scarce but allocatable resources; and (iv) personal ambitions of individual elites which were cloaked by group interests.

We have argued earlier that the echoes of North-South conflict led to the creation of six states in the North and six states in the South. The Gowon number of twelve thus had a strategic significance, as Allison Ayida had observed. Although Nigerians reacted angrily to Ayida's statement, [16] the issue re–emerged later. Many publications in newspapers by states agitators, especially from the Southern states, reacted against the imbalance created by the 19 states structure. Up to 1987, there were 10 states in the North and nine states in the South. General Babangida created two additional states, thereby making Nigerian federalism a twenty-one in 1987. In 1991, additional states were created, bringing the total number to 30. In 1996, Sani Abacha made Nigeria a federation of 36 – states structures. Thus there were 19 states in the North and 17 states in the South. Why would this bother any one?

It bothered some people because of the perception of states by politicians and electorates alike. States served a useful political function. The *logic of federalism* harped on equality of states in the 1979 Constitution. Section 126 (2-6) as well as the Amendment to Section 126 (by Decree No. 104, - *Constitution of the Federal Republic of Nigeria (Amendment)* Decree 1979 made it conditional that a candidate was elected the President only if in addition to the number of votes acquired, he or she 'had not less than one-quarter of the votes cast at the election in each of at least two-thirds of all states in the Federation'. This provision was repeated in Section 132 (1-4) of the 1989 Constitution. The number of states in each geopolitical area thus acquired political salience. Hence many agitators for the creation of states have argued in favour of the creation of states in such a way that it gave the North and South equal number of states. This was much an echo of the past as it is a present political reality. Currently Nigeria has 19 states in the north and 17 states in the south.

Another reason for the demand for additional states is to be seen in an *economic* and *democratic* interpretation of the role of states in the federal system. The economic logic behind the agitation was that if Anambra State, for example was split into two states, additional resources would be allocated to the area. By the revenue distribution formula bequeathed to the politicians by the military as well as the current formula, resources were to be distributed among states from the Federation Account on the basis of 50% on federal equality of states and 50% on population of states.[17] By this logic an Anioma State created out of Anambra State would be entitled to these resources as much as Ogun, Oyo, Ondo, Osun and Ekiti (five SouthWestern States) were entitled.

There was also the *political economy* of states creation, as old rivalries simmered to the surface occasionally, even if in different contexts; for example the Ibo-Yoruba rivalry seemed to have taken a new turn in the demands for resources. The former, Ibo land had two states, while Yoruba land (excluding Kwara) had four states by 1976. In the competitive process of resource acquisition, the Yorubas were seen by the Ibos to have a better deal. Hence K. O. Mbadiwe once called on Ibos in all political parties to rally together on the issue of states creation in order to sort out their differences. There were many other cases similar to the above. The mobilization of ethnic bedfellows for particular political actions still took place, even if within different contexts. The former Speaker of the House of Representatives, Chief Ume Ezeoke, had observed that Imo and Anambra States had not been fairly treated in the states game and that these states should make requests for additional states. Even well after the creation of the two states by General Babangida in 1987, the Ibo representatives at the Constituent Assembly still lobbied for the creation of additional states.

Yet there was the *democratic logic* that additional states would offer opportunities for participation – through representation (in the senate) or through appointments (in the federal public service) of more people and for more groups. Translated into practical terms, this meant that a Katsina State gave the people from the former Kaduna State three more representatives in the Senate. Each state is expected to have three representatives in the Senate.[18]

The content of section 14 of the 1979 and 15(3) of the 1989 Constitutions also made it mandatory for any Presidential incumbent to appoint people from various states in order to meet the requirements of reflecting federal character in appointments. These include ministers, board chairmen and other political offices.

These rationales for additional states were quite understandable. One of the humorous sides of Nigerians is their commitment to subnational autonomy in a federal framework. The assertion of autonomy by states had been clearly demonstrated during the civilian administration of President Shehu Shagari between 1979 and 1983. The relations between the centre and states had been a mixture of confrontation and occasional consensus.[19] In requesting for additional states, did Nigerians really hope to retain states' autonomy as they were in the 1960s? Yes. But the reality is different albeit, to their chagrin. The reality is different because, the creation of additional states lessens the capabilities of the new states and makes them more dependent on the centre, thus paradoxically eroding the same autonomy being sought. This has been the empirical position since 1967.

Additional states lessen the resource bases of subnational states and thus make them less financially solvent. As an illustration, the former Eastern Region accounted for 65.5% of the output of oil by 1967, and the Midwest Region produced 34.6% of the oil. The creation of twelve States altered this after the former Eastern Nigeria was split into three new states. The impact of the creation of States on the resource base of the former Eastern Region was reflected in the new production output in the new States created from that region in 1967 - Rivers

States, 57%; East Central, 2.8%; Rivers/East Central States, 5.5%. We discussed this in chapter 5.

In most of the states, there was hardly any serious effort at raising internal revenue, which would help, assert their federally desired autonomy. Most of the states are heavily dependent on federally derived revenue (mainly statutorily allocated revenues) for their budgets. The states invariably wait for federal budgets to be announced to help them in their budget. This trend started under the military regime and has gotten worse. Over thirteen states had difficulties in paying salaries of their staff in the various services proper and in their educational institutions by 1983. These included states, which had abolished community taxes and increased school fees in astronomical proportions, such as Benue State.

There was financial imprudence almost everywhere in Nigeria – at Federal and State levels. But the states are becoming basically financially unviable as the financial recklessness of their leaders (military and civilian) worsens their already bad situation. Yet, financial autonomy is one of the bedrocks of federalism. A state that depends on federally allocated resources for over fifty percent of its financial resources (as most of the states are) is dependent on the centre, and this works counter to the grain of *subnational* self-determination. A state needs to set its priorities and such dependence is most likely to skew these.

Similarly, a state that cannot pay its workers has strung the base-strings of its autonomy. Since such states are supposed to carry out development programmes, it would be a pity if they cannot. In fact, the cost of running such governments, with sprawling civil services, a sybaritic class of exploitative legislators and other autonomous state institutions and incumbents, only diverts funds from developmental projects. Actually, a state's fiscal dependence on the centre can only lead to greater control. For if the federal government pays the piper, (especially through grants) it will be unusual for it not to call the tune – at least in terms of monitoring the utilization of its resources. The situation is desperate and yet there are requests for additional states – all in the context of an overly–looted treasury and fragile economy. It is not surprising that there are numerous requests for extra-arbitrary allocations under the military rule as desperate military governors rush to their Commander-in-Chief for assistance. Under civilian democratic rule, this is not so easy.

It seems that the various requests for these states (with pretensions of autonomy) are paradoxical, because, beyond a threshhold, the newly created states would be neither autonomous nor viable. They would be autonomous states in name, but linked to the federal centre by the latter's apron strings. This leads us to our third contention, that the more new states created in Nigeria, the greater the tendency towards unitarism.

Unitary Trends in Nigeria's Federalism

It is clear that the demands for additional states Nigerians are making on their political system would have far-reaching consequences for the political system. The demands for creation of additional states tend to contradict the commitment of Nigerians to the federal formula as a compromise solution to problems emanating from contradictory types of self-determination.

By definition, a unitary system of government is one in which the subnational units are dependent on the centre.[20] In the unitary system, the centre could decentralize authority through the processes of devolution of authority or deconcentration of offices.[21] Unlike this, federalism emphasizes the development of non-centralization of powers by establishing functions and power for component units as centres of power in their own right.

At the moment, the legacy of the military era is very much with us. The power of the purse of the federal government, is formidable.[20] The states, especially as they are reduced in size by proliferation of states are heavily dependent on the centre, except for Lagos and old Kano States. The dependence of the states on the centre now is indicative of unitary traits in the Nigerian political system, which will be further exacerbated by the creation of additional States, among other factors.

The creation of additional states will merely reduce states to provinces which depend on the centre and which are likely to have no more autonomy than possessed by the current local governments. As of 2005, all states have complained of the excessive fiscal strength of the centre, which they claim is suffocating and strangling the states. Thus, more states would have been created but subnational self-determination would not have been achieved in the sense of the desire 'to have our own and do it our way'. The agitators would have had 'their own', but would be unable to 'do it their way!'.

This leads us to our fourth contention – that the issues, which led to the adoption of federalism, have only subsided but have not really been transcended, and the adoption of unitarism would have serious implications for political stability in Nigeria.

Echoes of the Past and the Relevance of Federalism

Many of the factors which had led Nigerians to opt for a federal compromise formula are still very much here with us today. The mutual fears and suspicions of domination which were behind the earlier agitations for states are still here with us; the intolerance of politicians; the love-hate and friction-charged federal-state relations under democratic governments; political victimization; blatant violations of the constitution; mutual fears and suspicions among groups; the rigging of elections; the imbalance in educational spread; squabbles over revenue allocation, and inter-party violent conflicts, with their attendant use of political overkill, are very much here today,[22] even under the Fourth Republic.

It takes a Nigerian to live in another state in which he has to make requests for land and for schools for his children, to show him that subnational identities are still very strong. In essence, in the horizontal relations among Nigerian groups, and in vertical relations between subnational and national governments, the very factors, which led us to adopt a federal compromise, are still glaringly here with us. If this were so, (i.e. if subnational identities are still very strong and are aggressively autonomous) would the emergence of strong unitary trends in Nigeria's political system not be a clarion call to political suicide? Would it not generate political instability to the point of challenging the integrity of the country; the second time?

There is nothing wrong with unitarism. If the factors, which made federalism a political imperative in Nigeria had been appreciably transcended unitarism would have been very useful. Economically it would prune all unnecessary financial expenditure on subnational institutions and incumbents. But things have not changed sufficiently. Unitarism is a victory for national self-determination. Unfortunately, there is no evidence that a delicate balance between centripetal and centrifugal forces have become unnecessary. More than ever, such balance is becoming more desirable, as the federal pendulum swings between the two forces.

Yet, in a paradoxical fashion, while the realities of the Nigerian setting calls for the maintenance of federalism, the demands of groups for protection through the framework of smaller states, erodes federal principles, which guarantee such protection. Sixty additional states created now (assuming they have all met the criteria) would transform states into glorified local governments, tied to the apron strings of the central government. Given the current realities of Nigeria, there would be gross political instability of all forms, especially elite and mass forms of instability.[23] There have been numerous calls by Nigerians for the merger of some of the current 36 states, in order to reduce the number. As part of the debates on the federal structure at the Political Reform Conference of 2005, there were demands for the regionalization of the federation, by merging existing States. The impact of numerous States in relation to a strong federal centre had become evident to some delegates.

Nigerians should develop a conflict resolution mechanism to cope with inter-group problems rather than opt for an avoidance mechanism as solution to all societal problems. Nigerians must learn to live with one another, quarrel and resolve these quarrels. Avoidance through proliferation of states is escapist, for after all the clouds are gone, Nigerians will still be exposed to one another, and interact to make Nigeria work. The creation of additional states is no political *elixir* for curing all ills in the political system.

Conclusion

In this chapter we have argued that states creation was a particular medicinal prescription for particular ills in the Nigerian political system, which has developed its political rashes. Our contention is that Nigerians should not see states creation as a solution to all problems. This becomes even clearer when one finds that the more states created, the less autonomy these states have and the less protection they have for their identities and interests. Further erosion of autonomy is likely to result from greater dependence on the centre and the tilting of the Nigerian federal system in the direction of unitarism.

Since the factors, which led to the adoption of federalism, are still with us, our argument is that unitarism (introduced by default through the reckless creation of states) will store a rich harvest of political instability for Nigeria, at this stage of her development.

Finally, we contend that since states creation cannot provide solutions for all political problems of the country, Nigerians must face their problems squarely. States creation is a medicinal prescription to the structural imbalance in the federal system. It is an attempt to compartmentalize conflicts in order to cope with them. We suggest that such compartmentalization has grave side-effects for Nigeria's federal system, which will be for a long while yet, the most conducive form of government for the country. Federal systems are subject to infinite forms of adjustments. In the world today, the trend is in favour of the federal centre because of the demands for uniformity, security and enormous expansion of federal functions. The reckless proliferation of states can only exacerbate this trend.

Perhaps for once, all Nigerians should settle down to face their problems – how they can develop mechanisms for resolving conflicts in inter-group relations. In the immortal words of some scholars,

> ...for a federation to be able to resist failure, the leaders must feel 'federal' – they must be moved to think of themselves as one people, with one, common self-interest – capable, where necessary, of over-riding most other considerations for small group interest. It is not enough that the units of a potential federation have the same ideal of 'the good' but that 'the good' for any one must be consciously subordinate to or compatible with 'the good for all'. This then is tantamount to an ideological commitment not to federation only as a means – such as for example, a means to gain independence or financial stability, to utilize secondary or tertiary factors – but to federation as an end, as good for its own sake, for the sake of 'answering the summons of history'.[24]

Notes and references

* The original version was published in *Nigerian Journal of Political Economy*, Vol. 1, No. 2 (October, 1983), pp. 80 – 91.

1. Nnamdi Azikiwe, *Daily Times* (Lagos) 19 May, 1975, p. 5; and also Nnamdi Azikiwe, *Political Blueprint for Nigeria* (Lagos: 1945). Zik explained his criteria for additional states in 1943:

> When I proposed that Nigeria should become a federation of eight regions in 1943, I was political, and not sociological in my approach. I did not necessarily overlook the tribal factors but, in my innocence, I minimized it. *(p.5)*

2. O. Awolowo, *Path to Nigeria Freedom op. cit.* Also see Federal Government reaction in 1967;

> *In 1947, Chief Obafemi Awolowo, a Yoruba, in his book, 'Path to Nigerian Freedom', suggested the division of Nigeria into forty states, with cultural and linguistic affinity as the basis of division.*

In Federal Republic of Nigeria, *The Struggle for One Nigeria* (Lagos: Ministry of Information), p. 23.

3. Eme Awa, *Federal Government of Nigeria* (Berkeley: University of California Press, 1964), pp. 61-62.

4. *Willink Commission Report, op. cit*

5. Federal Republic of Nigeria, "Decree No. 14, 1967 "States (Creation and Transitional Provisions) Decree, 1967". Also see, A.A Ayida. *The Nigeria Revolution, 1966-67* (Ibadan: Ibadan University Press, August 1973), p. 6.

6. *Broadcast to the Nation*, 26 May, 1968.

7. J. Isawa Elaigwu, *Gowon: The Biography of a Soldier-Statesman* (Ibadan: West Books, 1986), Chapter 11; J. Isawa Elaigwu, "Military Rule and Federalism in Nigeria" in J. Isawa Elaigwu and R. A Akindele, (eds.) *Foundations of Nigerian Federalism, 1960-1995*, (Jos: IGSR, 2001), pp. 166-193.

8. General Gowon, "Broadcast to the Nation," October 1974, *Daily Times*, October 2, 1974, p.6.

9.Federal Republic of Nigeria, *Report of the Constitutional Conference Containing the Resolutions and Recommendations)* Vol. II, (Abuja: Government Printer, 1995) p.8. (Lagos)

10.*The Punch*, May 17, 2005, pp 1 and 2.

11. These are Universities built with the objective of scoring political points, such as the proliferation of Universities of Technology, some of which were merged by the Buhari Administration. Two of these Universities were later transformed into University of Agriculture by the Babangida Administration.

12. See Ronald Watts, *Administration in Federal Systems* (London: Hutchinson Educational, 1970); R. Simon, *Federal Provincial Diplomacy: The Making of Recent Policy in Canada* (Toronto: University of Toronto Press, 1972); and William Anderson, *Federalism and Intergovernmental Relations* (Chicago: 1946).

13. Unitary systems are marked by centralization of power while federal systems are typified by non-centralization of power.

14. The *Concurrent Legislative List* provides for an area of concurrent legislative jurisdiction by both federal and state governments.

15. K. C. Wheare, *op. cit.*, p. 12.

16. A. Ayida, *loc. cit.*, p. 6.

17. The Okigbo Revenue Allocation Commission recognized the logic of federal equality of states. So also did the National Assembly in the revenue sharing formula that was passed into an Act. The revenue formula under the military has been mentioned earlier, but shall be discussed under Resource Distribution.

18. The National Revenue Allocation and Fiscal Mobilization Commission set up by the Babangida Administration also recognized this federal equality of states in revenue sharing. Section 46 of the 1989 Constitution provide for three Senators per State instead of five stipulated in the 1979 Constitution.

19. See a discussion of this in J. Isawa Elaigwu and Victor Olorunsola, "Federalism and The Politics of Compromise", in D. Rothschild and Victor A. Olorunsola (eds) *State Versus Ethnic Claims: African Policy Dilemmas* (Boulder, Colorado; Westview Press, 1983), pp. 281 – 303.

20. K. C. Wheare, *op. cit.*, pp. 23-24, has elaborate discussion of this.

21. Federal Republic of Nigeria, *Ad Hoc Constitution Proposals: Verbatim Report* (National Hall, Lagos: 12 September, 1966), p.2

(Unpublished Mimeograph). The 'May last' incident refers to the May riots of 1966 in the Northern Region, essentially (and ostensibly) against the Unification Decree, No. 34 1966, introduced by General Ironsi.

22. See an account of this in J. Isawa Elaigwu, *Nigeria's Federal Balances: Conflicts and compromises in The Political System.* (Jos: University of Jos, Postgraduate Open Lecture Services) Vol. 1 (No. 4) January 1984.

23.D.G. Morisson and H.M Stevenson, "Integration and Stability: Patterns of African Political Development" *American Political Science Review, LXVI* (September 1972) No. 3, makes an interesting distinction between 'elite' 'communal' and 'mass' instability.

24.Shridath S. Ramphal quoted the work of a Team of Federalism Scholars at the Centre for International Studies at New York University, under Tom Frank, – "Keynote Address" in A.B. Akinyemi et. al. *op. cit.* p.xix.

8

THE SHADOW OF RELIGION ON NIGERIAN FEDERALISM

In recent times, Nigeria's federal system has witnessed a large and dark shadow of religion over the political system. Suddenly, religious issues, which used to be cautiously handled and reduced to low levels of political visibility in inter-group relations, have taken on high visibility and loud bangs on the polity with violent ramifications. If ethnic, geoethnic, ethnoregional, and economic differences had spurred Nigerians into adopting a federal system of government, that very system of government is now undergoing serious strains arising from religious conflicts.

In a multi-cultural state like Nigeria, one expects that issues such as religion would be important in relations among groups. The federal system is supposed to provide a conducive framework for handling these kinds of problems. After all, as mentioned earlier, a federal system of government is a compromise solution in a multinational state between two types of self-determination — the determination to maintain a supra-national framework of government which guarantees security for all in the nation-state on the one hand, and the self-determination of component groups to retain their identities and maintain practices dear to them, on the other.

To what extent has the federal political grid been able to assuage the negative impacts of religious conflicts on the Nigerian polity? How dark is the shadow of religion on Nigeria's federal system? Under what circumstances do these shadows become darker and larger, and what have been the reactions of leaders to these problems arising from religious intolerance among Nigerian groups? Do we have a prospective Lebanon in Nigeria? We suggest that:

i) religion forms an important shadow over the Nigerian polity;

ii) the federal system provides some form of compromise for coping with problems arising from competing religions;

iii) the nature and mode of competition within and among religious groups have implications for the political stability of Nigeria;

iv) the very factors which necessitated the adoption of a federal system in the terminal colonial period are still very much with us even if they tend to surface in different forms; and

v) for a long while in the future, while federalism may not be able to always resolve problems arising from religious intolerance among groups, it may remain a political imperative.

Let us now turn to Nigeria's political history for some insight into the adoption of the federal system and see how religion has hung, like a bogy, over the political horizon—occasionally fading away, while at other times, operating like a heavy cloud over the system, preventing any form of sunrays from reaching the polity. Using the imagery of shadows, the shadow of religion (like the human shadow) has, at times, been many times larger than the actual size of the country (marking relatively high points in the level of religious intolerance in the country) while at other times, it has been many times smaller than the actual size of Nigeria (that is, at relatively low levels of religious intolerance). Usually, however, the size of the shadow oscillates between these two points.

British colonial rule brought together over 400 ethnic and lingo-cultural groups. It also brought together people of different religious beliefs. The major religions among Nigerians are *African Traditional Religion (ATR), Islam and Christianity*. It was this multi-culturalism, which partly goaded Nigerians to adopt a federal system of government in the terminal colonial period. The aggressive subnationalism, which emerged between 1951 and 1954, made federalism a political imperative. As independence became more imminent, so also did aggressive subnationalism escalate as groups sought protective devices for their interests. Many groups had written petitions to the colonial authorities seeking redress before independence was granted. Among the fears expressed by various Nigerian groups included religious intolerance.[1]

The Willink Commission, which investigated the various fears, found out that there were allegations of religious intolerance against majority groups in some regions. In the Northern region, the Commission found that Christian bodies had expressed fears about the future. They had clearly stated:

> ...that they did not wish for political separation, they did express the hope that the new constitution would embody a statement on human rights which would give minorities the freedom which to practise their religion, and which would specifically lay down that there should be no obstacle to a person changing his religion.[2]

The Christians alleged that the government of the North did bring pressures on chiefs to change their religion from Christianity to Islam. In addition, they complained about the propriety of trying non-Muslims in courts and according to Muslim law. To a lesser extent there were also complaints about religious intolerance in the Western Region. In essence, federalism in Nigeria was partly the result of socio - political, economic, and cultural forces at work in Nigeria, as centrifugal forces sought greater self-determination in the terminal colonial period. The human rights clause in the new constitution only temporarily assuaged the fears of religious discrimination among minority religious groups but the matter did not die there.

To what extent was religion an important element in the strengthening or the weakening of the federal system?

Religion and Federalism in the First Republic: 1960-1966

The nature of the Nigerian society dictated the degree of religious tolerance. In the Northern region, the legacy of the Usman Dan Fodio *jihad* still remained. Often the political institutions established by Dan Fodio were strengthened by the colonial authorities. Thus the emirate system was further entrenched and consolidated by the indirect rule in order to achieve their goal of law and order for purposes of control and in exploitation. The traditional rulers were partners in exploitation with the colonial authorities. This is an interesting issue, which, however, we cannot pursue here. The important point, however, was the line between the political and religious head of these emirates was very thin. In fact, the Sultan of Sokoto, is still the religious head of Muslims in Nigeria as well as the traditional political leader of the Sokoto Emirate.

Since there was hardly any distinction between religion and politics in the Islamic Emirates of the Northern Region, any extension of Emirate rule to non-Muslim areas meant that new areas of conflict were being opened up. Thus when the British administration extended the Indirect Rule administration to non-Muslim areas and legitimized the authority of the Emir to appoint traditional rulers (usually faithful Fulani and Muslim aides of Emir) for the so-called "pagan" societies, they were also creating new areas of conflict. The experiences in Gongola, Bauchi, Kaduna and other states of today, illustrate this point.

Meanwhile, Christianity had (especially through the establishment of Western-type schools) begun to make in-roads into the Northern Region, especially in the Middle-belt.[3] As Western education became a visa into the modernizing sectors of the society, these middle-belt people occupied strategic position in the Northern Public Service. With sizeable Christian population in the middle-belt, came the clash in the modern sectors as groups opposed to the system of traditional authority of their areas, which imposed 'aliens' on them as rulers. Moreover, the attempt by some of these rulers to reap some undue privileges of office, ran counter to the religious grain of the growing elite in these middle-belt areas.

Thus, what is often seen as religious conflicts have political foundations, which run deep into history. The ostensibly religious conflict in Kafanchan in 1987 was only the religious face of a political reaction by Southern Kaduna peoples against Fulani rule. Ironically, it is in the former Northern Region that the most violent inter-religious group crises have taken place in Nigeria. Similarly, the most devastating intra-religious group violence has also been geographically located in the former Northern Region. Our contention is that where there is a convenient matrimony between religion and politics, where religion legitimizes politics and vice versa, the conflicts are usually more serious and enduring over time, especially in a multi-religious society.

In the Western Region, the three religions co-exist with only minimum conflict. In fact, religion and politics were not really fused in

173

traditional Yoruba society. If the Alafin of Oyo symbolized political authority, the Ooni of Ife epitomized religion in traditional Yoruba. In the same family, it is not unusual to have each religion represented. It is common to have a Muslim father, a Christian mother, a Muslim daughter, and a son who worships 'Ifa' or 'Oshun' and a Christian daughter. If anything, among the Yorubas it seems that the traditional religion provides a common factor. As many objective observers will confirm, it is not unusual for both Christians and Muslims to visit the 'babalawo' or the priest of traditional religion (at times referred to as 'juju' priest) in the end.

In the Eastern Region, the situation by independence was less complex. The dominant religions were Christianity and Traditional Religion. In fact the conflicts in this region, were not inter-religious but intra-religious. It was often the result of competition among Christian denominations, such as between the Roman Catholic Church and the Anglican Church.

In the First Republic, religious conflicts were reduced to a minimum. The need to recruit and mobilize for politics meant that religious fanaticism was politically disadvantageous to the average politician. Mediatory institutions, such as political parties, blunted the sharp ends of religion as various groups cooperated to win votes.

In the Northern Region, Sir Ahmadu Bello, a descendant of Usman Dan Fodio, had been accused of exhibiting religious intolerance in dealing with aides who adhered to other religions. From all available evidence, the Sardauna was more politically prudent than that. Christian ministers as well as Provincial Commissioners under the late premier, confirmed to this author that the late Premier was very subtle in his evangelism with Christian members of his cabinet. In his entourage on tours of the region, the Sardauna was known to have stopped by the roadside during his regular prayer time, while others waited and carried on thereafter. Of course, he did try to convert many of his lieutenants, chiefs and politicians by using the attractions of the carrot provided from government sources, but if these were persistent in their refusal to change religion, he let them be, without any attempts to marginalize them. Mr. Michael Audu Buba and Mr. Jolly Tanko Yusuf had worked with the Premier at one point or the other.

Perhaps one of the most valid allegations that can be leveled against the Sarduana was that he made little distinctions between government treasury and his personal purse. He did not enrich himself, but he used public treasury to shower gifts on chiefs and some new converts—probably to demonstrate the advantages of belonging to his religious group. He demonstrated a remarkable ability in welding the North together and mobilizing the same to fight any Southern encroachment. More important to Sir Ahmadu Bello was which Northerner was qualified and available to be seconded to the Federal Government to represent Northern interest. It is a fact that most of the Northern civil servants seconded to the federal government were from the middle-belt - such as, Sunday Awoniyi, Dr. Edwin Ogbu and Abdul Aziz Attah. As an old politician from the middle-belt once put it:

> ... the reasons for the current religious tension are rooted in the greed ambition of the self-appointed successors to the Sarduana. While the Sardauna accumulated no wealth, these young pretenders are greedy economic merchants; while the Sardauna wooed people to his religion, these so-called successors cajole; while the Sardauna was a genuine faithful, these pretenders only use religion to maximize the political ends. Tell me, why should I interact with them?[4]

Basically, religion played very little part in the national politics of Nigeria during the First Republic. At local level, of course, religion was important in the calculus of politics. But generally, amidst the many sins of the First Republic, perhaps religious bigotry of groups ranked lowest. The intervening political parties, interest groups and associations, beyond parochial religious groups, often submerged or pushed to lower level, the religious issue.

The Shadow of Religion on Federalism under Military Rule, 1966 -79

When the military intervened in politics for the first time in 1966, the political class had eroded its credibility. As the legitimacy of the politicians sagged, the legitimacy of the military, as an alternative political elite, escalated. Initially there was a sign of relief. Soon, however, the nature of the killings in the January coup began to have new interpretations. With these interpretations also began new

175

dimensions of suspicions among various ethnic and ethnoregional groups. It is interesting that there were no religious meanings read into the pattern of killings because the killings cut across religious lines.

What the killings of January 1966 did in the North was that it consolidated the North into one solid block against the South generally and against the Ibos in particular. Another coup in July 1966, this time by Northern soldiers, further raised the political temperature of the country. The situation climaxed in the use of religion as a campaign strategy. Northern Muslims were said by the Eastern Region to be engaged in a pogrom against Christian *"Biafrans"*. Of course the Federal Military Government was at pains to point out that the Head of that government, General Yakubu Gowon, was not a Muslim but a Christian with very deep religious commitments. Evidences were produced to show that in the Federal cabinet (or the Federal Executive Council - FEC) were eight Christians and six Muslims. This was to show that the federal government was not run by Muslims alone. Beyond the war propaganda on both sides of the civil war, the religious issue hardly surfaced as a serious political issue under administration. Nor did it become a very important issue after the assassination of General Murtala Mohammed in 1976, even though some foreign newspapers did allege that Murtala's death was a Christian reaction to an intolerant Muslim leader, or that Murtala was a Muslim martyr in the hands of Christian villains.[5] With a more important scapegoat in the person of General Gowon provided by the government, the religious undercurrent slowly diminished into significance. Nigerians were asking for Gowon's head rather than searching for the religious villains.[6]

The major manifestation of religious intolerance among Nigerian groups in this period was the *Sharia* debate, which began at the Constitution Drafting Committee stage of Nigeria's transition to democratic rule. This platform provided the elites with the opportunity for expressing some of latent religious grievances, which had been kept below the political surface.

The Muslims had asked that there be established in the Constitution, a *Federal Sharia Court of Appeal* which would cater for matters of Islamic personal law. In the ensuing debate, there were intolerant, provocative and spurious exchanges between Christian and

Muslim members of the drafting committee as well as their fellow religious devotees in the larger society. In fact at a stage, fifty Muslim members of the Constituent Assembly walked out in protest, thus making it impossible for the Assembly to operate. The Military Government of General Obasanjo had to intervene to get them back to work. Ironically, one of those who had walked out of the Assembly then was Alhaji Shehu Shagari who later became the President of the Federal Republic of Nigeria's Second Republic.

In the end, a compromise was found. A *Sharia Court of Appeal* was to be established in any state, which so desired. In addition, appeals from State *Sharia* Courts of Appeal were to go to the Federal Court of Appeal, which was to include three Judges learned in Islamic law. This would have been more difficult to handle in a unitary system.[7] The federal principle of autonomy of *subnational* units provided a line of retreat and compromise for the two parties involved in this hostile debate.

Religion had generated intense political heat among the elite members of Nigeria's Christian and Muslim communities. Of course, the interests of adherents of traditional religion were hardly regarded as important. A gesture was however made to include the establishment of the *State Customary Courts of Appeal* in states, which so desired. After these compromises, the heightened political temperature soon showed signs of dramatic cooling as politicians found that they needed to form political parties under a constitution which had prohibited the registration of political parties on the basis of race, religion or ethnicity.[8] Erstwhile religious protagonists became members of the same political association, and later of the same political party. Thus Alhaji Shehu Shagari (pro-*Sharia*) and Mr. Mvendega Jibo (anti-*Sharia*) became members of the same political party—the National Party of Nigeria (NPN). As political associations and parties emerged as mediating institutions, the religious intolerance of terminal period of transition from the military to civilian rule, declined.

It is pertinent to note that the conflict over the *Sharia* Court marked the first overt religious conflict of national significance in the political terrain after independence. Was this end of the beginning or the beginning of the problem of religious tolerance in Nigeria's religiously plural state? Does Nigeria have the capability for managing an ecumenical society?

Selected Cases of Religious Intolerance, 1980-2005

We argue that the nature and mode of competition within and among religious groups have implications for the political stability of Nigeria. The year 1980 marked a watershed in the history of intra- and inter-religious group harmony in Nigeria. For the first time since independence violent religious riots broke out in unanticipated proportions. Death tolls rose, innocent citizens were rendered homeless, property were recklessly destroyed, sacred places of worship were vandalized and burnt, and security agencies were rendered impotent (at least in short run) by the magnitude of violence unleashed by religious fanatics.

Let us take a brief look at the spate of religious violence since 1980s (see table 4).

Table 4
Nigeria: Religious Violence between 1980 And 2005

Date	Location	Principal Actors
May 1980	Zaria (Kaduna State)	Disturbances in Zaria during which property belonging mainly to Christians were destroyed
December 18-29, 1980	Yan-Awaki Ward in Kano (Kano State)	Riots by *Maitatsine* sect. 4,177 people died. Extensive destruction of property.
October 29-30, 1982	Bullumkutu, Maiduguri (Borno State)	*Kala-Kato* and *Maitatsine* sects. 118 people died. Extensive damage to property.
October 29-30, 1982	Kano (Kano State)	Muslim demonstrators burnt down Churches.
February 27-March 5, 1984	Dobeli Ward, Jimeta-Yola (former Gongola State)	*Maitatsine* sect. 568 people died. Wanton destruction of property.
April 26-28, 1985	Pantami Ward, Gombe (Bauchi State)	*Maitatsine* sect. 105 people died. Extensive destruction of property.
March 1986	Ilorin (Kwara State)	Muslims and Christians clashed during a Christian procession at Easter.
May 1986	Ibadan, University of Ibadan (Oyo State)	Demonstrations by Muslims in which they burnt the figure of the Risen Christ in the Chapel of Resurrection, University of Ibadan.
March 1987	Kafanchan (Kaduna State)	Clashes between Muslims and Christians at the College of Education, Kafanchan. Loss of some lives and the burning of some Mosques by Christians and native Kajes.
March 1987	Katsina, Funtua, Zaria, Gusau and Kaduna and Sokoto (former Kaduna State)	Wave of religious riots in which Muslims burnt down numerous church buildings and damaged property belonging to Christians. Many lives were lost.

179

February 1988	Kaduna, Kaduna Polytechnic (Kaduna State)	Religious riots, ostensibly among students. Foundation walls of the Christian Chapel were destroyed.
April 1991	Katsina (Katsina State)	Religious violence spearheaded by Malam Yahaya Yakubu, leader of the fundamentalist *Shi'ite* sect in Katsina. It was a protest over a blasphemous publication in *Fun Times*. Several lives were lost and property destroyed.
April 1991	Tafawa Balewa (Bauchi State)	Started as a quarrel between a Fulani man and a Sayawa meat seller in Tafawa Balewa. Escalated into full blown violence and later took the colouring of a religious war in Bauchi. Several lives were lost and property valued over hundreds of million Naira was destroyed.
October 1991	Kano (Kano State)	A peaceful procession initiated by the *Izala* sect to halt Rev. Reinhard Bonnke from having a crusade in Kano later degenerated into a very violent and bloody religious confrontation. Thousands of lives were lost and property valued in millions of Naira was destroyed.
May 1992	Zango Kataf, Zaria, Kaduna, Ikara (Kaduna State)	A communal feud between the Katafs and the Hausas later took the dimension of inter-religious war between Muslims and Christians in other major cities of Kaduna State. Several lives were lost and property was destroyed.
January 1993	Funtua (Katsina State)	The *Kalakato* religious sect assaulted the Village Head and burnt down Police vehicles. Lives and property were also lost.
December 1994	Kano (Kano State)	Communal violence triggered off by the beheading of a Christian who had allegedly desecrated the *Qur'an*.
May 1995	Kano (Kano State)	Communal violence triggered off by quarrel between Hausa and Ibo boys led to the burning of houses, churches and shops and killing of innocent people.
May 1995	Abule-Taylor (Lagos State)	A bloody clash between the police and members of the dreaded *Maitatsine* sect.

February 28, 2000	Kaduna (Kaduna State)	Kaduna city exploded in violence as Muslim and Christian extremists and other hoodlums clashed over the proposal to introduce *Sharia.*
February 29, 2000	Aba (Abia State)	The riot which began in Aba as a reprisal to that of Kaduna, later spread to other Eastern states.
September 8, 2000	Kaltungo (Gombe State)	A religious violence that was sparked off by the presence of the state *Sharia* implementation committee.
December 2, 2000	Hadejia (Jigawa State)	A sectarian disturbance that was caused by a debate between Muslims and Christians. There was wanton destruction of worship places.
September 7, 2001	Jos (Plateau State)	A violent ethnic/religious crisis between Muslim/Hausa-Fulani and Christian/indigenes. The subject of discord between the Jasawa Development Association and Plateau Youth Council was originally over a political appointment in Jos North LGC.
September 15, 2001	Onitsha (Anambra State)	A reprisal killing of Northerners in Onitsha following the Jos crisis in which several Igbos were killed.
October 12, 2001	Kano (Kano State)	A peaceful anti-American protest over the bombing of Afghanistan turned violent, taking ethnic and religious tone. It degenerated into uncontrollable violence which claimed lives and damaged property and places of worship.
November 2, 2001	Gwantu Crisis, (Kaduna State)	A clash that started on a political ground (over the relocation of Local Government Headquarters) later took on ethnoreligious dimension. Places of worship were destroyed.
May 2, 2002	Jos Mayhem (Plateau State)	Another mayhem that followed Peoples Democratic Party (PDP) congress, which later took ethnoreligious dimension.

June 2002	Yelwa Shendam Mayhem (Plateau State)	An ethnoreligious fracas between the native people (predominantly Christians) and Hausa settlers (predominantly Muslims)
November 21, 2002	Kaduna (Kaduna State)	A violent protest in Kaduna following a Newspaper editorial on hosting of beauty pageant in Nigeria.
March 2003	Langtang North, Wase and Kanam L.G.C of (Plateau State)	Fresh ethnoreligious conflict in the three neighbouring LGCs.
January 2004	Yobe State	Militant Islamic group operating under the name of *Muhajirun* launched a Taliban-like attack on police. Men of the Nigeria Army killed five and arrested several others.
April 3, 2004	Makarfi, (Kaduna State)	Religious protest in Makarfi town over alleged desecration of the *Qur'an* by a Christian teenager.
April 26, 2004	Bakin Chiyawa (Plateau State)	Renewed hostilities launched by suspected displaced Fulani herdsmen. Conflict was believed to be a spill over of the ethnoreligious crisis that has bedevilled southern Plateau local governments of Langtang South and North, Wase, Kanam and Shendam.
May 1, 2004	Yelwa Shendam, (Plateau State)	An ethnoreligious mayhem that claimed over 500 lives and many women and children were abducted by suspected Taroh militia. This was a revenge killing.
May 12, 2004	Kano (Kano State)	Kano mayhem following the Yelwa-Shendam ethnoreligious crisis in Plateau. Non-Muslims were attacked in reprisal of the Plateau crisis. Over 200 people were feared dead.
June 8, 2004	Numan, (Adamawa State)	Ethnoreligious crisis in Numan over the construction of a mosque's minaret over the Haman Bachama's palace. Over 50 people were killed and the traditional ruler of the area deposed.

182

September 27, 2004	Limankara, (Borno State)	A self-styled *Taliban* group hiding on the Goza hills and Mandara mountains on the north-eastern boarder with Cameroon raided police stations killing officers and stealing ammunition.
January 16, 2005	Ipakodo, (Lagos State)	A religious mayhem between OPC and Muslims over the erection of Ogun Shrine in a Muslim praying ground. Over 50 lives were feared lost.
August 20, 2005	Isale-Eko area of Lagos Island Local Government; Lagos State	No fewer than 30 muslim youths feared dead when cultists and members of the out-lawed Odua Peoples Congress (OPC) attacked muslims.

NOTE:
(a)   There are many cases of religious riots in schools such as Queen Amina College, Kaduna, and many other forms of religious intolerance among Nigerian school children that are not covered here. It is always not clear if these students were acting under the influence of outside forces or whether they picked up the habit of intolerance from the adults.
b)   These figures of casualties given here are official figures.
Sources: From many sources coded 'B' and 'C' from confidential documents and newspapers.

Let us now turn to the first four years of the 1980s, which was essentially under a civilian democratic regime.

Religious Conflicts in the Second Republic: 1980-1983

The Second Republic witnessed the first major religious violence in May 1980 when Muslims in Zaria violently protested against the sale of alcohol in the town. During the disturbances many hotels belonging to Christians were burnt. Personal houses of individual Christians in the town were also reportedly burnt. It reminded many of these victims (mostly from the Southern part of the country) of the dark days of riots in the former Northern Region in 1966. The insecurity, which this created, can best be demonstrated by the fact that many Ibos and Yorubas packed up and left Kano for other parts of Nigeria.

In December 1980 more religious violence were yet to erupt. This was intra-religous. The Muslims fundamentalist group called *Maitatsine* had begun to settle in Yan-Awaki quarters of Kano. Their leader Muhammad Marwa,[9] (alias *Maitatsine*) was a cameroonian by birth, who had been arrested for preaching without permit in 1973 and jailed at Makurdi prison until 1975 when he was released. Marwa or *Maitatsine* returned to Kano were he continued preaching and recruited more followers. The *Maitatsine* brand of preaching was also unique. The *Maitatsine* preached for example, that "any Muslims who reads any book besides the Qur'an or rides bicycle or motor-cycle should be regarded as an infidel..."[10] Between April and October 1980 eleven cases involving the followers of *Maitatsine*, ranging from preaching without permits to assault had been prosecuted by the police.

By December 18, 1980, *Maitatsine* had started encroaching on the property of residents in Yan-Awaki ward, had seized markets stalls, forcibly occupied the abattoir, and had forced two primary schools to close down before their holidays. Passers-bye were attacked with reckless abandon and the safety of individuals and their families in the area could no longer be guaranteed by law enforcement agencies. Was the *Maitatsine* just a religious protest? One is more likely to agree with Mr. Bala Takaya that:

> The Maitatsine unrest is a religious phenomenon; Islamic in nature both from the point of participants and historical trends. Like all other religious uprising, however, it is basically a power struggle employing the mass mobilization potential of Islam in Nigeria for the purpose."[11]

Takaya's point becomes more important when one realizes that the main constituencies of the *Maitatsine* fanatics were the urban ghettoes marked by high level of poverty and alienation from the wealthy, of the followers even if there were wealthy Muslims. Many of the followers "only manage to survive precariously through unsecured and unpredictable earnings from menial labour like truck-pushing, orange-vending, manicure services (finger-nail trimming)..."[12] They were spurred on by the fact that they were made to believe that anyone who died in the course of uprising would have engaged in a righteous act of self-absolution.

Meanwhile, in response to the activities of the *Maitatsine*, the Governor of Kano State, Alhaji Abubakar Rimi had given Marwa and his followers 14 days to quit his enclave. The order expired and the defiant Marwa continued to threaten the security of citizens. In response to the plan of *Maitatsine* to take over the fagge area of Kano and the Central Mosque on Friday, December 18, in order to forcibly impose their Imams, the police launched an attack on their stronghold. The police suffered heavy casualties. The Maitatsine shocked the police with their military combat techniques and the sophistication of their weapons.

Nigeria's federal structure and the uneasy relations between the State Governor and the Federal Police Commissioner (there is no state police or local police in Nigeria) made matters worse. Controlled by opposing political parties, the relationship between federal and Kano State Governments were cool, to say the least.[13]

In the end the military took over the operations, routed the *Maitatsines* and handed the operations back to the police on December 29, 1980. The official death toll was put at 4,177 many were injured and 1,673 people were arrested.[14]

After the trials many members of the *Maitatsine* (the leader of which had been killed in the riot) were jailed. But that was not the end of *Maitatsine* as a religious group. In October 1982, in Bullumkutu, in Maiduguri, the police was confronted with the rampaging activities of another Maitatsine group. In the clash, which followed 118, were officially acknowledged to have died, while 411 people were arrested.[15] Again the police were overwhelmed by the battle-readiness of this group.

Just about the same time, another *Maitatsine* riot had broken out in Kaduna. Between October 29 and 30, 1982, the police had to contend with another *Maitatsine* uprising in Rigasa ward in Kaduna, Kaduna State. In this confrontation with the police, 53 people died and 166 were arrested. So far conflict among Islamic sects had unleashed undesirable harvest of violence and bloodshed, and wanton destruction of property on innocent citizens.

Let us now go back to Kano on October 30, 1982. This time was an inter-religious conflict between Christians and Muslims. The immediate cause of the conflict was the construction of the new Church

185

in place of the old one at Christ Church, in Fagge area of Kano. Some Muslim fundamentalists objected to this as well members of other Churches in the predominantly Muslim areas of Kano city. This time the Police were ahead of the fundamentalists (who were not known to be the members of *Maitatsine*). Frustrated by the police cordon around the Church, the fundamentalists attacked other Church buildings in Kano. Two Churches were completely burnt down, three set on fire, and six others partly damaged.

The burning of Churches raised new issues of the federal association of Nigerians. To the fundamentalist Muslims, by building their worship houses in the predominantly Muslim areas, the Christians were being insensitive to their hosts. To the Christians it was not clear what constituted their rights if they could not have the places of worship where they lived. They further argued that as Nigerian citizens, they had the right to apply for land and legitimately build their places of worship. The Christians felt incensed that in many of the areas in which the atrocities were committed, Churches existed before the Mosques were built in adjacent plots of land. Most well meaning Nigerians of the two religions condemned the riots. It is important to remember that most Churches were built by people who were regarded as non-indigenes, and therefore, 'strangers' in Kano.

Often their economic activities and their operation in the modernized sectors of the society had generated negative feelings against them. Thus when the reaction against building of Churches was extended to shops and market places, it clearly went beyond a religious issue. It also highlighted the issue of citizenship and rights in Nigeria's federal arrangement. While the 1979 constitution treated citizenship as exclusive matter and recognized single citizenship, the aggressive statism among Nigerians had undercut this provision in practice. Should Nigeria, like United States of America, adopt dual citizenship? What would be the implications? The 1989 and 1999 constitutions still provided for single citizenship without any arrangements for resolving the problems, which go with it.

Thus, by the time when Shehu Shagari was overthrown in December 1983, his hands were full with religious problems. Luckily because of the federal system, the governors of the States bore the immediate brunt except where the police could not cope with the situation. It is interesting that even the issue of civil unrest were also subjected to politicking among political parties, thus diluting what would have turned out to be sectarian and religious lines of cleavages in the polity. Before he was toppled on December 31, 1983, Shagari had pardoned those who had been arrested in the *Maitatsine* uprisings. This action of his in October 1983 turned out to be a mistake.

Religion and Federalism under the Military 1984-93

As the *Maitatsine* prisoners were released, they trooped to new areas of residence. Between February 27 and March 5, 1984, another *Maitatsine* uprising erupted in Dobeli ward, Jimeta-Yola, of current Adamawa State. In the carnage, which followed, 568 people were officially declared dead and 980 arrests were made. Nigerians had not learned a lesson on how to handle these religious fanatics. Even under a military regime, the *Maitatsine* dared the military to battle. As General Buhari regime tried to recover from the Jimeta-Yola problem, the *Maitatsine* struck again in the Patmi ward of Gombe in present Gombe State between April 26 and 28 1985. In this case, 105 people died and 295 people were arrested.[16] What was the real problem? Were the *Maitatsine* being incited by some elite groups who had interest in the overthrow of Islamic and Emirate establishment? Or was it the protest of the impoverished who genuinely wanted to establish a new order, and religion merely provided the mobilization vehicle for achieving their purposes?

As Takaya correctly observed,

> Anybody familiar enough with the city of Kano, Maiduguri, Kaduna, Jimeta-Yola and Gombe will immediately recognize the fact these wards... from which each of the cities sparked off are the most depressed part of those cities."[17]

If the politicians, government leaders and security agents enjoyed the serene atmosphere of *Government Reserved Areas* (the new name for *European Quarters*), the Residents of the *Government Rejected Areas* (mostly unskilled rural migrants, unemployed and perhaps unemployable, who become the target of fundamentalist Islamic preachers) shocked them into the awareness of new dangers and new social forces in the system.

One important lesson from the Maitatsine riot was that it made Nigerians to realize the dangers of religious wars. If intra-religious wars could take so many lives and lead to so much suffering for many, how predictable would an inter-religious war be? Keenly aware that a religious war was an ill-wind that blew no one any good, Nigerian political leaders had always try to avoid the Lebanese model being replayed in the country. Generally, while the issue of religion had always been below the surface, it had occasionally simmered to the top briefly, before being submerged again.

This situation changed from 1986. What was responsible for this change in the low visibility of religion in Nigeria's federal discourse? Nigeria had been an observer in the meeting of the Organization of Islamic Conference (OIC) for about 17 years. Given the multi-religious nature of Nigeria, General Gowon, Nigeria's former leader did not go beyond observer status. However, in December 1985, Nigeria responded to the invitation to join as full member. It was even more interesting that the news came from *British Broadcasting Corporation (the BBC)*. The former Chief of General Staff (CGS)[18] Navy Commodore Ebitu Ukiwe, denied any knowledge of government's application to join the OIC. This further worsened the situation because as the political second-in-command, he was expected to know what happened.

In his address to the inaugural meeting of the committee, President Babangida tried to put forward government position. The President traced the history of the OIC, claiming that the advantage of the organization were so obvious that "many of the OIC sister States and neighbours", Chad, Cameroon, Gambia, Gabon, Uganda, Guinea, Guinea-Bissau, Sierra Leone, Mali, and Burkina Faso - as examples of African countries which had joined the OIC. According to the President, despite its name, members of the organization were "distinguished more by their identity as Third World nations than by religious affinities. Its business is strictly international cooperation and the struggle for economic development and self-reliance."[19]

He reaffirmed the determination of his administration to abide by the provision of 1979 constitution, which stipulated, "The Government of the Federation or the State shall not adopt any religion as a State Religion." (Section 10). According to Babangida:

> To do otherwise will not only be unconstitutional; it will also be an invitation to chaos...no government which is rational and anxious to succeed, will deliberately create problems for itself...[20]

The task of the committee, he concluded, was to examine the implication of Nigeria's full membership of the OIC, now "that Nigeria's application for membership has been accepted..."

The reaction of Christians was first against the surreptitious manner in which the exercise had been handled. They referred to the aim of the organization (i.e. the Charter of OIC) and drew attention to three issues. The first was the objective, which sought 'to promote Islamic solidarity among members.' This they felt put them at a disadvantage, given Nigeria's pluralism. The objection of the Christians was the OIC objective which called for the coordination of 'all efforts for the safeguarding of the struggle of Palestine and help them to regain their rights and liberate their land'.[21] This related to the assumption that there was consensus over Nigeria's foreign policy on the Middle Eastern question. The third grievance of the Christians was against the sixth objective of the organization - "to strengthen the struggle of all Muslim peoples with a view to safeguarding their dignity, independence and nation right." This provision, they believed, ran counter to provisions of the Nigerian Constitution. The Christian delegations made a number of recommendations, which we cannot cover here.

The Muslim delegation expressed surprise that Christians would regard membership of the OIC as an indication that the country was being gradually Islamized. They explained the economic benefit, which they argued, would accrue to all Nigerians. In addition, the delegation redefined the concept of secularism. They claimed that Section 10 of the constitution meant that "no state is allowed to cater for one religion only and neglect the other but all religions should be catered for in accordance with its meaning and scope."[22] The Muslim group went to great details to point out many issues in the constitution, which were 'inconsistent with secularism'. They pointed to Nigerian Embassy in the Vatican and wondered why Christians should complain when Nigeria joined the OIC. The delegation expressed the dissatisfaction of the Muslims with the Christian calendar and a number of other symbols, which were being used in public places. The Muslims also made a number of recommendations, which we cannot discuss here because of space constraints.

The Presidential committee deliberated for some days and came up with very general and fluid recommendations: (i) that the multi-religious nature of Nigeria should be maintained as expressed in Section 10 of 1979 Constitution; (ii) that religious leaders should educate and guide their followers about the need for peace stability and unity of this country; and (iii) that a multi-religious consultative group should be established to advise on sensitive religious issues. The function of the committee seemed to have been to reduce the tension in the country to a tolerable level. Government then set up an Advisory Council on Religious Affairs (ACRA) which since remained inactive, except for occasional meetings. (

The importance of our discussion of these OIC issue is to show that from January 1986, every action of the government became suspect to various religious groups. Issues, which never mattered before, took on new saliency. Nigerians had always quarreled over representation in federal institutions. But such conflicts were usually along ethnic, geo-ethnic and state lines of distinction. Suddenly the religious devil added its mark on Nigeria's already complex allocation problems. Membership of the Armed Forces, which used to be seen in state or geo-ethnic terms, became a victim of new religious perceptual prism. If Alhaji Abubakar Gumi had complained about the number of Christians in the Armed Forces and the way they had been deployed in 1987, it was Bishop Olubunmi Okogie who was to complain about the deployment into General Babangida's cabinet in 1989. As the *Newswatch* magazine correctly observed,

...Nigeria's membership of the Organization of Islamic Conference in 1986 has come to represent to many, an extreme case of creeping intrusion of religion into state affairs. In a decade that has witnessed the Maitatsine riots, in a decade that saw the two great religions, Islam and Christianity growing more hostile to one another, the OIC affair

190

only served to upgrade religion to a critical factor in the national question.[23]

The intolerance between the two religious groups was demonstrated by the frequency of clashes between the two groups. In March 1986, Muslims and Christians clashed in Ilorin during a Christian procession on the occasion of Easter celebrations. In May 1986, Muslims students in Ibadan demonstrated over a wooden stature of 'Risen Christ' (at the Protestant Chapel). This Cross had been there for about thirty two years that is well before the Mosque was built on the University's 'holy ground' in December 1985. The Muslims had complained that the Cross was offensive to Muslims who were required by the Qur'an to face the east during prayers. The Cross was to the east of the Mosque. The demonstrators burnt the Cross and this nearly led to the serious religious crisis on the campus and its environs.[24]

In March 1987, a Christian Religious Conference on the College of Education, Kafanchan triggered off another religious crisis. Some Muslim students who were in the audience took exception to certain references made to Prophet Mohammed during the conference. Soon what began as an intra-student squabble spread to the town and took on political colouring. The uneasy relations between Kaje and Fulanis raptured into violence, as the former killed some Fulani and Islamic leaders. Government intervened and soon closed down the college. That government action did not stop the degeneration of relations between members of both religions. What was important about the Kafanchan case was the ease with which what had started as a religious crisis quickly took ethnic and political dimensions.

In the same month, a wave of religious riots started simultaneously, with military precision in Katsina, Zaria, Funtua, Gusau, and Kaduna - all then in former Kaduna State. In these riot Muslims burnt down numerous Church buildings and damaged property belonging to Christians. In Wusasa, General Gowon's father's house was razed to the ground and old St. Bartholomew's Church was burnt down. Many lives were lost and even the government was unsure of the official figures. This crisis showed clearly the insecurity of many Nigerians in some areas of the country. It was clear to many

191

observers that the crisis transcended religion. Interestingly, political and economic reasons were adduced by some scholars to explain what had happened. It was the precision with which the whole exercise took place and the scale of havoc done which prompted Dr. Usman and his colleagues at Ahmadu Bello University, Zaria to publish a statement accusing some sectors of the society for organizing riots.[25] The Bala Usman group included both Muslim and Christian scholars who believed that things were drifting beyond the threshold of rationality.

Again, in 1988, another religious conflict surfaced at the Kaduna Polytechnic in which Muslim students destroyed the foundation of the Christian Chapel. There were also many incidences, young children in secondary schools protested against dressing in school uniforms, which their predecessors had used for over twenty years, ostensibly because these no longer complied with the requirements of their religion. In some cases there were physical clashes among students. In Bauchi State some nurses at the government hospital felt their uniform unduly exposed certain parts of their body, contrary to their religious requirement. New uniforms had to be designed for these nurses only for them to resort to using the old type of designs because of the heat in the area.

All these are manifestations of religious intolerance among Nigerian religious groups especially after 1986. A more glaring repeat of the intolerance of the past was displayed at the Constituent Assembly in Abuja. As if the tape of 1977-78 Constituent Assembly was being replayed in 1988, the *Sharia* issue stalled any work of the Constituent Assembly for days. While the pro-*Sharia* group wanted to expand the parameters of the *Sharia Court* beyond what was stipulated in the 1979 Constitution to include civil proceedings as well as questions of Islamic Law, the *anti-Sharia* group wanted the word 'Sharia' to be expunged from the Constitution. The two sides were ready for showdown before the Federal Government removed the *Sharia* issue from the purview of the Assembly.

Like the situation in 1978, the religious adversaries in the Constituent Assembly re-assembled and sorted out their differences as they cooperated in the new political parties in Nigeria. However, unlike the 1978, the OIC issue had left political scars in the terrain, which were likely to constantly serve as unfortunate reminders to the various constituencies of the hallmarks of religious intolerance among Nigerian groups. The shadow of religion over Nigeria's federal system was large and dark under the Babangida administration. It was hoped that the mediating effects of political parties and the need to mobilize support beyond the confines of religious groups would gradually restore mutual confidence among members of various religious groups.

After a very long holiday, which lasted for two years, a dark shadow of religion appeared and hovered over the bright and sunny city of Tafawa Balewa and extended to Bauchi town and other prominent towns of Bauchi State. These raised the political temperature of the Nigerian Federation.

It all started on April 20 1991, in Tafawa Balewa as a minor skirmish between a young Fulani man and Sayawa meat-seller. The Fulani man bought some meat, which he thought was beef from the Sayawa meat-seller only to be told by his friends after that the meat, which he had just eaten, was pork — regarded in Islam as *haram* (unlawful). As a matter of fact, there had been existing tension between the Hausa-Fulani who are predominantly Muslims and Sayawa who are predominantly Christians, over the use of abattoir for the slaughtering of pigs. When a fight broke out between the Fulani man and the Sayawa meat-seller, the Hausa-Fulani on-lookers felt that this was time to resolve the crises once and for all. A free-for-all fight ensued. What looked like a small confrontation, escalated and subsequently degenerated into killings and arson. Several people were killed and others badly injured. Houses and property were burnt. What used to be Tafawa Balewa was in smoke and a dark cloud hovered over the sky of the town. Ironically, however, even though the Christians (Sayawas) overpowered the Muslims (Hausa-Fulani) and killed many of them, the Mosque was left intact.

News of the holocaust began to filter into the neighbouring villages and Bauchi town. Tension began to mount. The tension found expression when corpses of the victims, of mostly Muslims, arrived at the Bauchi General Hospital with shouts of *ALLAHU AKBAR* (Allah is great). On hearing this and on seeing the corpses, Muslims who had relations in Tafawa Balewa took over the street in search of any Sayawa person to avenge the death of their brothers. This later escalated into attacks on any Christian. Other Muslims thought it was a *Jihad* and decided to join in the religious mission. Incidentally *Igbos,* who are predominantly Christians, became victims as most of them were killed and their property looted or burnt. For over 48 hours there was a total breakdown of law and order in Bauchi town. *Igbos* began to flee the town to neighbouring towns and informing them of the attack on the Igbos. This caused further tension in the country. The military and mobile police force were drafted in rather too late.[26]

The shadow of religion blew across Bauchi to Katsina on April 19, 1991. Mallam Yakubu Yahaya a disciple of *EL-ZAK-ZAKY* (the man who had led the attack on the American consul in Kaduna during the Gulf War), an extreme *Shi'ite* who on several occasions had challenged the government of Col. John Yahaya Madaki in Katsina State, spearheaded the Katsina religious uprising. It was triggered off by December 1990 publication of the *Fun Times, which* was captioned: born-again "would you marry a known prostitute turned born-again Christian?"[27] References were made to Holy Prophet Muhammad and to Jesus Christ. Both prophets are held in high esteem in Islam. Mallam Yahaya and his followers saw this publication as blasphemous. They then decided to attack the *Daily Times* office in Katsina State. This angered the Governor of Katsina State. He called a press conference and threatened Mallam Yahaya and his supporters that if they killed even an ant in Katsina State, he would personally get Yakubu Yahaya tied to a stake at Katsina Polo Ground and shoot him. This drew serious reaction from Yahaya's supporters who saw the threat as a challenge.

The fateful day, a Friday (April 19, 1991) when Muslims usually attended congregational prayers at the central mosques, turned out be a day of violence in Katsina. Mallam Yakubu and his supporters, dressed in uniform, went in large numbers to the Katsina Central Mosque for *juma'at* prayers chanting *Allahu Akbar* (Allah is great) even when they got inside the mosque. This drew a lot of attention and caused a lot of tension. The supporters of Mallam Yahaya Yakubu went opposite the mosque and began shouting that if Col. Madaki was bold enough he should come out and execute Yahaya. On seeing this confrontation and eminent danger, the police who had earlier on surrounded the area, then decided to fire the canisters of tear gas on the supporters of Mallam Yahaya Yakubu. The supporters started by throwing stones and objects at the police. This escalated to the burning down of public vehicles and buildings. There was virtual breakdown of law and order, which lasted for over four hours.

Barely six months after the Katsina incident, the dark shadow of religion moved over to Kano. On Monday October 14, 1991, a group of *Izala* Islamic sect initiated a peaceful procession to the palace of the Emir of Kano, Alhaji Ado Bayero, to plead with him to prevail on the Governor of Kano State, Col. Idris Garba to prevent a German-born evangelist from preaching in Kano under the auspices of Christian Association of Nigeria (CAN). The Reverend claimed to have divine powers to heal the sick, the blind and the crippled. The *Izala sect* not only perceived double standard, as an earlier request to the Governor to permit South African Sheikh Ahmed Deedat to preach in Kano was turned down, but also saw the coming of Reverend Bonnke as a threat to their religious faith.

On reaching the palace they were received by the Emir's spokesman who advised them to return home peacefully and wait patiently since their grievances would be speedily addressed and Rev. Bonnke's crusade would be put off. The *Izala* sect and their supporters dispersed peacefully. However, instead of going straight to their various places, they decided to head straight to the *Eid* prayer ground to observe a prayer. This gesture as a preparatory stage of a *Jihad*, was quickly interpreted by other Muslims as a *Jihad*. As news began to spread around city of Kano, so also did the dark cloud of religion began to gather over the city of Kano. The Fagge area where there was a high concentration of the unemployed, beggers, vagrants and the down-trodden, got to hear of the event taking place in the city. Of course, they interpreted this as part of the *Jihad*. They therefore plunged into the *Izala* protest, and instead of heading to the *Eid* prayer ground, they headed straight to the Sabon Gari area (where non-indigenes have their homes and operate their business activities). Their main targets were initially the *Igbos*, and later all non-indigenes, especially Christians. What followed was catastrophic as properties were looted and several shops were burnt. Several lives were also lost as fire bombs, motolov cocktails, machine guns and grenades were freely used.[28] The Army and Air force had to intervene along with the police to halt the riot. This riot also raised doubts about Nigeria's

Federalism as a major ethnic group continued to be the victim of communal or religious violence. On this occasion, the *Igbos* struck back with reciprocal violence until the military intervened to calm the situation.

Eight months later, another season of religious violence commenced on May 15, 1992 at Zangon Kataf in Kaduna State. The riot, which was well organized and very bloody, spilled over to Zaria, Kaduna and Ikara. The Kataf people (predominantly Christians) had, for long time, resented Hausa domination. The Katafs claimed that the Hausas (predominantly Muslims) were settlers and such should vacate their farmlands. The confrontation, which followed afterward, was very bloody. The whole area was virtually destroyed. The surprising thing here was that though the conflict was basically ethnic, it soon acquired the colouring of religion, and was perceived and interpreted as a war between the Muslims and Christians and as such people acted accordingly. This colouring gave rise to violent religious clashes in Zaria, Kaduna and Ikara where people were publicly slaughtered.[29]

Another wave of religious violence broke out in Funtua in Katsina State between 19-21 January 1993 when what started as a fight between some children culminated into an assault on the village head by fanatics of a religious sect called *Kalakato* — a sub-sect of *Maitatsine* sect. The police were invited. The fanatics chased away the police and burnt down their vehicles. The police then went back for reinforcement from Kano and Jigawa States before they could restore law and order. Meanwhile, many lives and property had been lost in the mayhem.[30]

Religious Conflicts: 1994-2005

By December 1994, the dark shadow of religion over Kano had become darker and more menacing. Another wave of religious crisis began when some Muslim passers-by, noticed that a page of the Qur'an had been desecrated and used as a toilet paper. Incidentally, it was traced to the house where Gideon Akaluka, an *Igbo* Christian trader lived. An argument ensued between Akaluka and the Muslim passers-by. The attention of the Police was drawn to the diatribe and upon investigation, it was traced to a female co-tenant who used the pages to clean up her baby. However, Gideon Akaluka was arrested and kept under preventive custody so as to calm down the religious temperature, which had risen high. He was kept at the Bompai prison in Kano. Unknown to the Police, some Muslim fundamentalists broke into the prison on December 26, 1994 and killed Gideon Akaluka, cut off his head, hoisted it on a spike and paraded it around the town.[31] This angered the *Igbo* community, who in the absence of any reaction from the government, poured into the streets and began to chant war songs.

The tension generated by Akaluka's murder never evaporated even by May 1995. On May 30, 1995, it found expression (in Kano) when what started as a small fight between a Hausa and *Igbo* boy, escalated into an inter-ethnic violence exuding through religious pores. *Igbo* shops, houses and churches became targets as they were attacked and burnt. The *Igbos*, who had been very ready, responded by attacking houses, shops and mosques belonging to Muslims. The dark shadow of religion was undoubtedly becoming dangerously darker in Kano.

In Oyo State, religious crisis loomed large on the horizon and began to cast a menacing shadow on the politically volatile State. The Muslim community accused the State administrator of marginalising Muslims in the state in political appointments, and made allegations against Christian principals for the evangelisation of schools in the state. They pointed out that out of the 10 commissioners in the state, only three were Muslims.

In May 1998, there was a bloody clash between the police and members of the dreaded *Maitatsine* sect at Abule-Taylor, in Lagos. Kaduna in Kaduna State was the next seat of religious violence on February 28, 2000. The riot was in reaction to the news of the introduction of the *Sharia* by the State government. Kaduna exploded into violence of devastating proportions, as Christians and Muslims clashed. It reportedly took on ethnic colouring and was said to have led to the redefinition of settlement patterns along religious lines in Kaduna.

In reaction to the Kaduna violence, February 29, 2000 saw the killing of Northerners in Aba and Owerri and other parts of the South Eastern States. Yet on September 8, 2000, violence erupted in Kaltungo, in Gombe state, apparently sparked off by the presence of the State's *Sharia* Implementation Committee in the area. Hadeija in Jigawa state was the seat of the next religious violence, on December 2, 2000. Muslims and Christians clashed violently and there was wanton destruction of worship places.

In Jos, Plateau State, what originally started as an opposition by the indigenes of Jos to the appointment of a Hausa-Fulani man into a political office in Jos North blew up as evident ethnoreligious conflicts. Initially, the conflict over appointment was between the *Jasawa Development Association* and the *Plateau Youth Council.* It soon took on a religious dimension, when some Muslims alleged that a Christian girl was indecently dressed when passing by the Mosque during a prayer session. They regarded this as provocative. The Christians denied the allegation. The violence, which erupted, engulfed Jos for over one week, and soldiers had to be drafted to restore law and order. It was estimated that over 1000 lives were lost and millions of Naira worth of property were destroyed. Jos, "the home of peace and tourism" had lost its innocence.

On September 15, 2001, there were reprisal killings of Northerners in Onitsha, Anambra State – in reaction to the Jos crises in which many *Igbos* lost their lives and property. Again in Kano, on October 12, 2001, an apparently peaceful anti–American protest over the bombing of Afghanistan turned violent, taking ethnic and religious tone. It degenerated into uncontrollable violence, which claimed many lives, and damaged property and places of worship.

On November 2, 2001, a clash among the inhabitants of Gwantu, in Kaduna State over the relocation of Local Government Headquarters was transformed into an ethnoreligious crises in which property were destroyed and places of worship were burnt. In May 2002, Jos, Plateau State, witnessed another mayhem following the Peoples Democratic Party Congress, which later took ethnoreligious dimension. In June 2002, a violent ethnoreligious crisis erupted in Yelwa/Shendam areas of Plateau state. The crisis was between the natives (predominantly Christians) and Hausa-Fulani settlers (predominantly Muslims). Again many lives and property were lost.

Kaduna town witnessed a violent protest on November 21, 2002 against the holding of a beauty pageant, which had been condemned by some Muslim groups. Langtang North, Wase and Kanam Local Governments of Plateau State experienced fresh violent ethnoreligious conflicts in March 2003. In January 2004, a militant Islamic group operating under the name of *Muhajirun,* locally known as the *Taliban,* launched an attack on the police in Yobe State. Five of their members were killed by the members of the Nigerian Army while several were arrested.

The peace of Makarfi town of Kaduna State, was shattered on April 3, 2004 by a violent religious protest by Muslims who alleged that a Christian teenager had desecrated the Qur'an. On April 26, 2004, in Bakin Chiyawa, Plateau State, there were renewed hostilities launched by Fulani herdsmen. The conflict believed to be a spill-over of the ethnoreligious crisis in Southern Plateau Local Governments of Langtang North and South, Wase, Kanam and Shendam, again raised the political temperature in Plateau State.

On May 1, 2004 there was a revenge religious onslaught on Fulanis and Muslims in Yelwa-Shendam town of Plateau State, which reportedly led to the loss of about 500 lives. The Taroh militia was alleged to have been responsible for this. As a result of these series of violent events, a state of emergency was declared in Plateau State for six months on May 18, 2004. On May 12, 2004, there was mayhem in Kano following the Yelwa-Shendam ethnoreligious crisis in Plateau. Many non-Muslims were Killed, with an official toll of over 200 lives lost.

There were still more cases of violence. On June 8, 2004, in Numan, Adamawa State, ethnoreligious violence erupted. The immediate reason for this violence was the construction of a Mosque's minaret over looking the Hama Bachama's Palace. Over fifty people were reportedly killed, and the traditional ruler of the area was deposed. In Limankara, Borno State, a self-styled *Taliban* group hiding in the Goza hills and Mandara mountains (on the Northern-eastern border with the Cameroons) raided police stations killing officers and stealing ammunitions. While they called themselves the *Talibans* (like the Yobe group) the religious content of their mission was unclear. Many members of this group were later killed by a security patrol comprising the Nigeria Police Force and the Nigeria Army.

On January 16, 2005, at Ipakodo, Lagos State, there was a violent religious conflict between the OPC and Muslims over the erection of *Ogun* Shrine on a Muslim praying ground. Over 50 people lost their lives. These are all illustrations of religious and ethnoreligious conflicts in Nigeria, which cast shadow on the Nigerian federation at different points in time.

Conclusion

In this chapter, we have argued that religion forms an important shadow over the Nigerian federation. At different points, in time, the shadow had shortened or enlarges as a symbol of the level of religious tolerance or intolerance respectively. We have also argued that federal system provides some forms of compromise and a medium for managing problems arising from competing religions. In other cases, the federal grid could hardly help. The basic issue of human ability to accommodate other human beings, to have respect for the other people's beliefs, and the willingness to share *the sweet and the bitter* in the common experiences of political community, cannot be provided by any system of government. These are values, which must be imbibed over time.

While intra-religious and inter-religious crises had taken place under democratic civilian regimes in Nigeria, the shadow of religion on Nigeria's federalism tend to be larger and darker under military regimes than under civilian regimes. This may not be unrelated to the absence of intervening or mediating political institutions under the military rule.

Even though the federal system may not be able to soothe certain religious conflicts in the Nigerian polity, it is likely to continue to serve as a useful compromise in Nigeria — a strategy for managing Nigeria's complexity and pluralism. Essentially the factors, which necessitated the adoption of the federal system in the terminal colonial period, are very much around today, even if they tend to surface in different forms and within different contexts such as religion. Yet, on balance, it is most unlikely that Nigeria will become Africa's Lebanon. For if Nigerians had learnt anything from their past history, in a hard way, it is acquisition of some skills in compromise — at times to the shock of despairing observers.

Notes and references

1.	*Report of the Commission Appointed to Enquire into the Fear of Minorities and the Means of Allaying Them,* CMNd.. 505 (1958).

2.	*ibid.,* p. A6.

3.	The concept of the Middle-Belt used here to refer to the various minority groups in the middle of Nigeria. Currently they are identifiable in Benue, Plateau, Bauchi, Adamawa, Niger, Kaduna, Kogi, Borno, Taraba, Kebbi and Kwara States. This term is broader than the geopolitical category of North Central zone.

4.	Interview with an old politician from Middle-Belt who had worked with Sir Ahmadu Bello (September, 1983)

5.	Bala Usman, *The Manipulation of Religion in Nigeria: 1977 -1987,* (Kaduna: Vanguard Publishers, 1987), p. 12.

6.	See J. Isawa Elaigwu, *Gowon: The Biography of a Soldier – Statesman* (Ibadan: West Books Publishers, 1986), chapter 15 for an account of this period in Nigeria's political history.

7.	Federal Republic of Nigeria, *Constitution of the Federal Republic of Nigeria, 1979* (Lagos: Government Printer, 1979) section 242 (1).

8.	*ibid., sections* 201-209.

9.Muhammad Marwa had been deported from Nigeria to Cameroon under Emirship of Alhaji Sanussi. He only came back to Kano after the Emir had been sent on exile.

10.	Extracted from a confidential and reliable source.

11.	Bala Takaya, "The Foundations of Religious Intolerance in Nigeria: Backgrounds for Understanding the Maitatsine Phenomenon." Paper presented at the conference on "Religion and Peace in Multifaith Nigeria", Obafemi Awolowo University, Ile-Ife, Nigeria, December 4-8, 1989; *mimeograph,* p.3.

12.	*ibid.,* p. 6.

13.	See J. Isawa Elaigwu and Victor Olorunsola, "Federalism and the Politics of Compromise" in Donald Rothchild and Victor Olorunsola (eds.) *State Versus Ethnic Claims: African Policy Dilemmas* (Boulder, Colorado: Westview Press, 1993) pp. 281-303, for a discussion of the relations between federal and state governments in this period.

14.	*Report of Kano Maitatsine Disturbances Tribunal of Inquiry* (Kano: Government Printer 1981).

15. Takaya, *loc. cit;* p.4 and many documents on the crisis code-named 'C' and 'CO', for purposes of confidentiality.

16. *Report of the Judicial Commission of Inquiry into the Gombe Disturbances - Main Report* (Bauchi: Government Printer, June, 1985).

17. Takaya, *loc. cit.*, p.5.

18. The Chief of General Staff was the equivalent of a French Prime Minister under the Military regime, without a democratic base. He was the political No.2 man in Nigeria. The controversy surrounding this position led to the ouster of incumbent in 1986.

19. Federal Republic of Nigeria, *Annexes to the Report of the Presidential Committee on Nigeria's Membership of the Organization of the Islamic Conference* (Lagos: Government Printer, March 1986), Annex A, p.4.

20. *ibid.*, p.6.

21. OIC Report Annex C; p.3.

22. *ibid.*, Annex Ell, p.3.

23. *Newswatch* (Lagos), Nigeria, October 8, 1990.

24. Rotimi Suberu, "Religion and Politics in the Transition" paper presented at the Conference on Nigeria's Transition to Civil Rule and the Structural Adjustment Programme, the Hoover Institution, Stanford University, California, USA, August 26-30, 1990.

25. Bala Usman and others, "The Violent Politics of Religion and Survival of Nigeria" in *The New Nigeria (Kaduna, Nigeria),* March 25, 1987.

26. *African Concord,* (Lagos), October 28, 1991.

27. See *African Concord,* (Lagos), May 6, 1991.

28. *Citizen Magazine,* (Kaduna), February 8-14, 1993, p. 34.

29. *Today Magazine,* February 16 - 22; and May 24-30, 1992, p. 3-4.

30.*Newswatch* (Lagos) February 6, 1995, p. 25.

9

THE POLITICS OF RESOURCE DISTRIBUTION

The next threat to the continued existence of Nigeria will not come from the East. The next crisis is most likely to have its origins in basic economic issues and social conflict–the equitable allocation and proper management of the increased disposable resources of the federation and the familiar conflict between the haves and have-nots.[1]

1. Introduction: Distribution and Equity

For Joseph LaPalombara, "all problems of governance may be considered distribution problems that may or may not reach crisis proportions..."[2] According to David Easton, "a political system deals with authoritative allocation of values."[3] Authoritative allocations "distribute things in one of these ways. An allocation may deprive a person of a valued thing already processed, it may obstruct the attainment of value which would otherwise have been attained or it may give some persons access to values and deny them to others".[4] To Harold Lasswell, politics deals with "who gets what, when and how."[5]

The allocation or distribution of resources among component units of a federation can extract high levels of emotional reactions from contending parties. This becomes even more apparent in the perception of equity and fairness by leaders of the component units. As Dankwart Rustow correctly observed, the problem is that "Equality is the most widely proclaimed political ideal of the modern age; but it is one of the most imperfectly achieved."

Distribution, for our purpose deals with the degree to which scarce but allocatable resources are relatively equitably distributed among all members and groups of a State. It also concerns the equitable location of programmes/projects in different parts of the State, recruitment into the public services; and the provision of essential and basic services in the constituent *subnational* units. Distribution is, therefore, governmental decision taken on how, where, when and who gets what. Conflict inevitably results from unequal distribution of resources and desirables such as power, prestige, and others. Individuals (and groups) compete to maximize their shares of scarce but allocatable resources. Such conflicts that emanate from the distributive process may even threaten the stability of the state.

Often, participants in the political arena forget that there are two aspects to the issue of equity in distribution – i) the increase in the production of allocatable resources; and ii) the nature or basis of the distribution of these resources among groups. In Nigeria, there is more emphasis on the distribution of scarce but allocatable resources (called the 'national cake') than there is concern about the increase in the production of resources (the 'national cake') to be shared.

The problem of distribution lies in its effects on the pattern of development among subnational units. "The process of uneven development tends to continue according to its own logic and dynamic unless counterveiling influences such as egalitarian political resources not only ensure regional equality, but also 'level up' the less developed areas."[6] Herein lies the dilemma of political leaders. Dispersion of resources among subnational groups to meet an egalitarian ideal may under-cut capacity – the development of the country as a whole. Yet the concentration of resources in few "poles of growth" or "centres of strength" as some economists argue, in order to maximize short-run capacity,[7] may create gross inequalities which may endanger the survival of the political system.[8]

Rustow was probably correct when he observed that modern life "creates strong pressures for equalization along with pressures of organization just as strong that threaten and thwart equality."[9] The conflict between *capacity* and *equality*, for a federation may be seen as the overall development of a country on the one hand and even development among subnational units of a federation for purposes of political stability. A balance has to be struck between these two ideals at each point in time. For, as mentioned earlier, there have to be some resources before effective distribution can be undertaken.

In many modern federations, there are fiscal imbalances because component units of a federation hardly have enough resources to meet their desirable expenditure. Fiscal equilibrium is often not easy to attain. Paul Boothe explains the situation even more succinctly when he wrote:

> It is a fact of life in modern federation that the division of expenditure and revenue responsibilities is never such that both orders of government are fully self-financing... when one order of government collects more revenue than it needs for its own expenditure responsibilities, a vertical imbalance is said to exist. Fiscal transfer from one order of government to another is used to deal with vertical imbalances. In some federations, specific transfers are designed to deal with both vertical imbalances and imbalances between provinces, i.e. horizontal imbalances.[10]

The examples of Canada and Australia come to mind. We shall return to this later.

Historically, the issue of distribution "has overtaxed elite capability and sometimes led to revolution and destruction of existing regimes."[11] In Nigeria, complaints by various groups about inequalities in the distribution of resources dated back to colonial times. In the year 2005 the National Political Reform Conference called by President Olusegun Obasanjo, became so emotion-laden over the issue of resource distribution that it contributed in no small measure to the abortion of that conference.

In all federations there are two important issues, which underlie the association – equality and diversity. Diversity is usually the reason for a federation while equality nourishes the association. As the one-time Chairman of the Australian Commonwealth Grants Commission observed:

> In a federal system, equality and diversity are two important objectives. Equality requires that any state should be able, if it wishes, to provide services to its citizens at the same standard as other states without imposing higher taxes and charges. Diversity, on the other hand, means that each state should be free to choose the standard and range of services to be provided to its citizens, and the level and

pattern of its taxes and charges, independently of what is done in other states of the federation.[12]

One of the greatest difficulties in the distribution[13] of resources among *subnational* units in Nigeria is to be found in the various definitions of equity/equality. The way these terms are perceived usually characterizes the nature and dimension of the politics of resource distribution among the various interest groups. In many cases, equality is defined within the context of the expressed interests of those concerned.

Fiscal adjustment in a federation is necessitated by at least four factors as pointed out by Adebayo Adedeji.[14] These factors are: 1) "the problem of resolving the imbalances of resources and needs between the federal and regional governments," 2) "the problem of harmonizing income with needs in different regions" (or *subnational* units as states), 3) "the need to ensure that 'economic equilibrium' is achieved for the federation as a whole," and 4) "the need to 'level up' so that the poorer regions are raised and the level of services provided in different regions is equalized" (or relatively equalized).

In the history of resource distribution in Nigeria, four major principles have been utilized over time, with relative consistency. The first is the principle of derivation, which emphasizes that federally, collected revenue on resources from land or water of a particular state should be returned to them wholly or substantially. Here the quarrel is over how much of the collected revenue should be returned to the states from where these resources were derived.

The second is the principle of need. Need is often difficult to operationalize as revenue capacity and expenditure profiles are reconciled. In Nigeria, population has been used as an index of need. Essentially, however, the principle of need emphasizes the need to meet expenditure demands of subnational units, in order to carry out desirable devices.

The third principle is equality or the logic of federalism. The logic of federalism presupposes the equality and autonomy of all subnational units of the federations. Not only should they receive equal shares of federally derived revenues (irrespective of population and contribution to the account of the federation), they should have their independent sources of tax or revenues. As a sole criterion of distribution, the argument has been made that the logic of political equality of subnational units, which ignores population, is likely to create inequality of development in the country. There is also a fourth principle – national interest. The principle of national interest emphasizes the need to raise the living standard of those people in poorer subnational units, above the minimum national standard as fixed by the country's leaders.

The problem with these broad principles of revenue distribution is that they are in potential conflict with one another in the course of fiscal adjustments in a federal system. Thus, the principle of derivation works at cross-purposes with the principle of need. If each state gets back resources in proportion to its contribution to the account of the federation derivable from resources in the state, many states which need the resources to cater for larger population and/or more socially mobilized states (such as those with higher number of children of school-going age) may find themselves in a more financially precarious position. Derivation also works against 1) the necessity to "harmonize income with needs" of states in a federation; and 2) the need to 'level up' so that gaps between poorer and richer states may be, at the very least, narrowed to some minimum level.

Most federations have the problem of maintaining fiscal equilibrium among the subnational units. Subnational units usually vary in levels of economic development, resources, population, and size. Yet, in a federal system, there is the necessity to maintain at least a "marginal equilibrium" among subnational units in order to keep the system together. In order to maintain this relative "economic equilibrium",

> Not only should the federal government have constitutional authority to impose direct and indirect taxes, but it should also be given constitutional powers to transfer resources from the relatively more developed parts of the country to the relatively less developed parts by means of grants-in-aid. Indeed, poverty anywhere in a federation is a limitation to prosperity everywhere.[15]

The history of revenue sharing in Nigeria has been one of inter-regional or inter-state conflicts. It shows a gradual movement from the derivation principle to a mix of principles for distribution purposes. While revenue sharing has vertical dimension (i.e. allocation among tiers of government), there will be a greater discussion here of the politics of horizontal allocation (i.e. among component units of the federation). Let us take an overview of revenue sharing from 1948– 2005.

2. Resources Distribution in Historical Perspective

a) Unitarism to Quasi-Federalism: 1948-1953

The Richards Constitution of 1946 was a unitary constitution, which gave the Regional Councils no powers to raise or appropriate revenue for regional expenditure. In order to establish some fiscal arrangement for the regions under the Richards Constitution, **Sir Sydney Phillipson**, the Financial Secretary to the government, was appointed to undertake a review of fiscal systems in Nigeria.[16]

Phillipson suggested two principles as the basis for regional shares of "non-declared" revenue (export duties, import duties, excise duties and companies' tax), collected by the central government. The first was the principle of derivation, by which each region was to get as much share of "non-declared" revenue as it contributed to the country's revenue. The other was the principle of "even progress", which he found could not be adequately implemented because of lack of statistical data and because of the need to encourage regional fiscal responsibility. Phillipson opted for derivation as the principle for sharing customs and excise duties. Although, he expressed his personal preference for allocation according to population, which he claimed was the "best available measure of human needs," he did not adopt the principle. The formula was in operation between 1948 and 1952. This formula became contentious and was an important issue of discussion at the 1950 Constitutional Conference. Misunderstandings arose, as feelings grew among Northerners that the Eastern Region was being developed at the expense of the Northern Region.[17]

Thus, at the 1950 Constitutional Conference, the Northern delegation pressed for a review of this revenue allocation system. The Northern sense of deprivation was so strong that the Conference found it necessary to appoint a committee to inquire into "the division of revenue over a period of five years between the three Regions and the central Nigerian services..."[18] In its terms of reference, the conference urged the committee to find out if any region had been unfairly treated, in which case that region would be entitled to a block grant. This was basically the term of reference for The Revenue Allocation Commission headed by **J.R. Hicks.**

The Commission presented its report (here after known as the **Hicks-Phillipson Report**) in 1950.[19] The commission saw revenue allocation as predicated upon four basic criteria: "Liberty, Justice, Fraternity and Efficiency". It found that revenue allocation based solely on derivation principle was inadequate and recommended four principles of revenue sharing. These were: 1) the principle of independent revenue (the power of regional government to impose taxes in certain matters); 2) the principle of derivation; 3) the principle of need (based on population and sparsity or density of population, as in Northern and Eastern Regions respectively), and 4) the principle of national interest (grants by Central Government to the regions for specific services to the nation as a form of horizontal equalization). The last criterion, national interest, was fluid in definition. The commission accepted its difficulty and confusion with regard to the appropriate principle of inter-regional shares of central resources. However, on the argument that derivation should not be the only principle of revenue allocation, the commission used "per capita revenue effort and relative under-capitalization of regions to determine the principle of needs".[20] Interesting enough, the commission suggested that a uniform income tax be introduced throughout the country. This was never implemented throughout the period of its operation. It took a military regime to introduce a uniform tax in 1975, (after the Udoji Commission Report) given centrifugal forces in the Nigerian Federation.

It is interesting that each region pressed for the principle, which favoured it most. The Western Region wanted derivation, the Northern Region wanted need, and the Eastern Region wanted national interest. Thus, derivation and need seemed to have been taken into account, while the proviso for grants from central government to regions for purposes of education and police were on the basis of national interest. The Commission confessed that it did not find a principle of distribution, which suited the Eastern Region – which had neither resources nor population. In a little over a decade, the Western Region was to inherit the unenviable position of the Eastern Region, after cocoa prices slumped in the world market and petroleum (in the East) emerged as an important revenue earner.

b) Quasi-Federalism under Colonial Rule, 1954-60

With the constitutional conference of 1953 and the demands for greater autonomy under the subsequent Lyttleton Constitution, a new fiscal arrangement became a political imperative. The Western Region was dissatisfied with the limited emphasis on *derivation* by the Hicks-Phillipson Commission Report. During constitutional conference of 1953, there were therefore pressures for a review of the Hicks-Phillipson Commission formula. Politically, the central government was still supreme in the 1951-53 quasi-federal structure. It was the Lyttleton Constitution of 1954, which gave greater autonomy to the regions, and therefore the need for a review of the fiscal system.

The **Louis Chick Commission** of 1953 was set up to "assess the effect on the public expenditure of Nigeria as a whole of the re-allocation of functions between the centre and the regions..."[21] Among other things, the commission was asked to give weight to the "need to provide to the regions and the centre an adequate measure of fiscal autonomy within their own sphere of government," and further to ensure that the total revenue available to Nigeria are allocated in such a way that the principle of derivation is followed to the fullest degree compatible with meeting the reasonable needs of the centre and each of the regions."[22]

Thus the Chick Commission was given specific instruction to emphasize the derivation principle in revenue sharing, and it did exactly that. One of the glaring effects of the Chick Commission Report was to accentuate disparity among the regions. As Adebayo Adedeji lucidly pointed out, the

> ...new fiscal arrangement accentuated regional disparity; 1) by making available to the regions part of the proceeds of export tax on the derivation principle; 2) by transferring the control of market boards to the regional governments; and 3) by giving the regions the revenue from import duties on all goods other than tobacco and

210

motor spirit, the whole of the proceeds from import and excise duties on tobacco, and import duties on motor spirit.[23]

The Northern and Eastern governments' positions remained unchanged, while the Western Region recorded a substantial increase because of its favourable position under the derivation principle. The emphasis on derivation meant that the Northern and Eastern Regions were worse off than the Western Region, but it made the Western Region more dependent on the export sector. A summary of the Chick Commission Report is in Table 3.

Table 5
The Louis Chick Formula for Revenue Allocation:
1954-59 (A Summary)

	Items (Duties)	Federal	Regions By Derivation	Remarks
A. IMPORTS				
1	Tobacco	25%	50% on basis of Consumption	General imports duties shared among states.
2	Motor Spirit & Diesel Oil	–	100% on basis of Consumption	
3	General (excluding tobacco, motor spirit & skin)	50%	50% on basis of Consumption	South Cameroon 1%
B.	**EXPORTS**			
1	Produce, Hides & Skin	50%	50% on basis of Production	
C.	**EXCISE**			
1	Tobacco	50%	50% Consumption	
D.	**MINING RENTS & ROYALTIES**			
	(Tin and Columbite)	–	100%	
E.	**SPECIAL GRANTS FROM FEDERAL GOVERNMENT**			
			North: £3 m; West: £2m; East: £2m	as contribution to their increased responsibilities

Source: *summarized from the Louis Chick Commission Report.*

212

The Chick formula of revenue allocation virtually disregarded the principle of need and the ability of regions to raise enough revenue to meet their functions. It was therefore not surprising that regional fiscal imbalance drew strong protest from the Northern and Eastern Regions, which then pressed for the review of the formula and for compensatory allocations to them.

In essence, between 1952 and 1954, Nigeria moved from a multiplicity of principles of revenue allocation to a single principle of revenue sharing – **derivation**. However, the formula was only in operation till 1958.

Dissatisfaction with the Chick revenue formula led to the setting up of the **Sir Jeremy Raisman Commission**[24] by the Constitutional Conference of 1957. The terms of reference of this commission was broader than those given to the Chick Commission.

The commission was to "examine the present division of powers to levy taxation in the Federation of Nigeria and the present system of allocation of the revenue thereby derived in the light of: 1) "experience of the system to date"; 2) "the allocation of functions between the governments in the federation as agreed at the present conference"; 3) "the desirability of securing that the maximum possible proportion of the income of regional governments should be within exclusive power of those governments to levy and collect, taking into account consideration of national and inter-regional policy"; 4) in connection with (3), the "special problems in the field of indirect taxation as a result of the positions of Lagos as federal territory"; and 5) "insofar as the independent revenues that can be secured for the various governments are insufficient to provide not only for their immediate needs but also for a reasonable degree of expansion, and bearing in mind the federal government's own further needs, the desirability of allocating further federal revenue in accordance with such arrangements as will best serve the overall interests of the federation as a whole.[25]

The commission tried to grapple with some of the defects of the Chick formula: 1) the limited range of independent revenue under regional control; 2) inter-regional imbalance created by the emphasis on derivation principle and the difficulty of applying it effectively to regional shares of import duties other than motor spirit and tobacco;

and 3) the neglect of the relationship between particular needs of a region and its ability to raise revenues within its boundaries.[26]

In their presentations to the Raisman Commission, the Northern and Western Governments "advocated maximum decentralization and the exercise of regional fiscal jurisdiction within regional areas." On the other hand, the poorer Eastern Government argued for a federal levy and collection of revenues enough to enable it to support specific national services and to give discretionary grants to the regions to harmonize the standard of the social services of the various regions.

In an attempt to cope with the problems created by excessive dependence on derivation principle, the commission recommended the establishment of a new organ, the Distributable Pool Account (DPA). The DPA was to be a common pool for the regions into which some federally derived revenue and grants to be shared among the regions were to be deposited. The funds in the DPA comprised: 1) 30% of all revenue derived from general import duties[27] (i.e. including duties on tobacco, motor spirit, diesel oil, and liquor); and 2) 30% of all mining rents and royalties.

The content of the DPA was to be shared among the regions according to a formula worked out by the Commission. Unlike the Chick Commission, the Raisman Commission tried to strike a compromise between the principles of need and of derivation. Hence, it used the four factors as the basis of its formula for allocating the funds in the DPA among the three regions. These factors were: 1) Population as an index of need; 2) the basic or minimum responsibilities of each regional government; 3) The necessity to preserve continuity in government services; and 4) The need to ensure balanced development throughout the federation.

Other recommendations by the commission for sharing customs and excise duties and mining royalties are summarized in Table 4.

Table 6
The Raisman Formula for Revenue Allocation: 1959-65
(A Summary)

Items (Duties)	Federal	To Regions By Derivation	DPA*	Remarks
A. IMPORTS				
Tobacco	–	100% Consumption	–	
Motor Spirits & Diesel Oil	–	100% Consumption	–	The DPA is a new factor in revenue sharing. The method of distribution of DPA funds among states is in the text.
Beverages (beer, wine & spirits)	100%	–	–	
General Imports (other than tobacco, m/spirits, diesel oil)	70%	–	30%	
B. EXPORT				
Produce, Hides & skin	–	100% Production	–	
C. EXCISE				
Tobacco	–	100% Consumption	–	
Beer	100%	–	–	
D. MINING RENTS & ROYALTIES				
Tin & Columbite Petroleum Oil	20%	50 %	30%	

* 2 items only in the Distribution Pool Account. **Source:** *The Raisman Commission Report.*

A comment is necessary at this point regarding rents and royalties from mining. Up to this point, only tin and columbite (from the North) enjoyed rents and royalties. Under the Chick formula, revenues from mining rents and royalties had been allocated on the basis of derivation. But by 1957, with test production for petroleum in the Eastern Region, it became necessary to review the Chick formula for the purposes of relatively balanced development in the federation. Hence, the commission recommended that any government

> ...in whose region oil royalties originate should clearly have a significant share in them. Secondly, the federal government ought also to have a share...in the interests of balanced development between the regions, we consider it to be essential that, whatever oil royalties may arise, all the regions should have some share.[28]

Therefore, mining rents and royalties were to be allocated 50% to the region of the origin of the mineral, 20% to the federal government, and 30% to the DPA. Under the Chick formula, all revenues from mining rents and royalties went to the regions in which the mineral was derived.

The fiscal powers of the regions were increased. They could collect revenues from a number of sources, including personal income tax on people within their region (African and non-African); taxes on clubs, trusts, and other incorporated associations; license fees; revenues from Regional Departments; and sales tax on produce (other than tobacco, motor fuel, hides and skins).

The Raisman Commission went a long way to rectify some of the deficiencies of the Chick formula. Like the Hicks-Phillipson formula, it saw a federation as based on mutual assistance among its component units. The DPA was a new fiscal organ in Nigeria's revenue-sharing which was to assume greater importance over time. The formula was in operation between 1959-64, and within that period the revenues of the regions increased rapidly. The Western Region lagged behind the Northern and Eastern Regions in total financial increase within the period. In this period, cocoa prices slumped in the world market and mineral oil was becoming an important factor in Nigeria's economy.

To the extent that the Raisman formula moved away from derivation and considered other issues such as need and balanced development, it could be said to have moved in the direction of greater equity than earlier formulae in the distribution of resources. The establishment of the DPA, which appreciably lessened the degree of dependence on the principle of derivation, was a novelty in Nigeria's fiscal system. Its importance was yet to grow. This formula was operated for six years – longer than any other revenue-sharing formula since 1948. That it proved inadequate with time was seen in the clamour for its review in 1964, four years after independence.

c) Fiscal Adjustments in Independent Nigeria, 1960-May 1967

In 1963, the Midwest Region was created, making Nigeria a federation of four regions. This made the review of the Raisman formula for revenue sharing necessary. In addition, the regions were already complaining about the impact of the Raisman formula on their expenditure pattern. In 1964, Mr. K. J. Binns[29] was therefore commissioned to head a Revenue Allocation Committee to make recommendations for fiscal adjustments. The Binns committee was to make recommendations with particular reference to sharing, 1) mining rents and royalties; 2) export, import and excise duties; and 3) revenues in Distributable Pool Account (DPA); as well as identify the sources of revenue available to the five governments in Nigeria in relation to their legitimate responsibilities. It was also to take into account the creation of the Midwest region and the experiences of various governments under the Raisman formula.[30] The Binns Commission was important because it was the first independence revenue allocation commission.

In the memorandum to the commission, the federal government opposed any further allocation of federal revenue to the regions, but argued strongly "in favour of increasing its own shares of mining rents and royalties (at the expense of the regional governments)." On the other hand, all the "regions …were unanimous in asking for an additional share of federal revenue — partly on the grounds of growing regional need."[31]

The North felt that the reduction in federal revenue limited "the spending capacity of the federal government for low-priority projects."[32] To the Eastern Region, federal revenue should be allocated to the regions in full on the basis of derivation. This is interesting because, by 1964, cocoa prices had dropped in the world market and oil was becoming a major factor in Nigeria's revenue. The Eastern Region suggested that, for losses incurred by the federal government as a result of revenue allocation on the basis of derivation, the latter should levy a "capitation tax of £1 or more on every adult" in the country.

The interesting point about these regional clamours for greater revenue to them at the expense of the federal government is that they reflected the politics of regionalism we have discussed in chapters 2 to 3. The regions wanted to be financially stronger at the expense of the federal centre. The Eastern Region's pressure for revenue allocation fully on the basis of derivation[33] was directly the result of the oil resources in the Eastern Region, at that time 65.4% of total oil output in Nigeria. Hitherto, the Eastern Region had stood for revenue allocation on the basis of "national interest" when the Western Region was enjoying revenue increase from "cocoa-boom" in the world market.

In its report, the commission rejected ideas of Nigeria as a "loose federation" because any doubts with regard to the "primacy of the federal government are immediately dispelled by considering the importance of its responsibilities which are set out clearly in the Exclusive Legislative List of the Federal Parliament, and also …the concurrent Legislative List of the Federal Constitution."[34] It further noted that the "financial stability of the federal centre must be the main guarantee of the financial stability of Nigeria as a whole,"[35] even though it observed that the federal government was quite financially strong and that some federal funds should be transferred to the regions.

On the basis of the commission's report, the revenue allocation formula between federal and regional government and among regional governments, which operated from 1965 to 1967, when states were created, is shown in Table 5.

Table 7
The Binns Formula for Revenue Allocation:
1965-67 (A Summary)

Items (Duties)	To Federal Govt.	To Regions By Derivation	DPA	Remarks
A. IMPORTS				
Tobacco, Motor Spirits & Diesel Oil	–	100% Consumption	–	Proceeds of DPA to be shared. North 42%; East 30%; West 20%; Midwest 8%.
Beverages (beer, wine & spirit)	100%	–	–	
General (other than tobacco, m/spirits, diesel oil)	65%	–	35%	
B. EXPORTS				
Produce, Hides & skin	–	100% Production		
Animals, birds, etc.	–		* 100%	
C. EXCISE				
Tobacco Motor Spirits & Diesel Oil	–	100% Consumption	–	
D. MINING RENTS & ROYALTIES				
Petroleum Oil	15%	50%	35%	

* This is not statutory

Source: *Report of the Fiscal Review Commission* (Lagos: Federal Ministry of Information, 1964)

On the inter-regional or horizontal dimension, in their presentations to the commission, the regions (with the exception of the Midwest) criticized the Raisman formula. The North claimed to have been unable to close the gap in its services and investment in comparison with the other regions (particularly the Eastern Region), which derived more revenue under the existing formula. The Western Region saw the Raisman formula as a "check" on its rate of economic growth and as a "perpetual victimization and penalization." The Eastern Region, which seemed to have improved its revenue under the Raisman formula, described the latter as "extremely unreasonable, unfair, and inequitable."[36] It is important to stress again that by 1964, petroleum oil in the Eastern Region had become an important factor in that region's revenue. It therefore opted for more emphasis on derivation, pressing that all proceeds from mining rents and royalties be returned to the regions.

The Binns Commission, in its recommendation, expressed support for the idea of promoting the welfare of the whole federation. Hence, it recommended that each region be placed in a *comparable financial position* (given allowances for differences in financial policies) "to make equivalent contribution from its recurrent budget towards the financing of its capital development programmes."[37] Therefore, the commission rejected the principles *of derivation* and of *financial need.*[38] The commission, in adhering to the principle of "comparable financial position" (or principle of comparability)[39] among the regions, considered a number of factors: 1) the general cash position of the regions; 2) recurrent budget prospects; 3) the relationship of regional-to-local government finances; and 4) the effect of regional corporations on regional finances.

Having admitted that these criteria were difficult to operationalize in quantitative terms, the commission went on to depend on its judgment in making recommendations. To achieve the above objective of comparability of regional finances, Binns recommended the retention of the contents of the DPA as recommended by the Raisman Commission. He amended the regional shares of DPA funds from fractions of 95ths to read:

Northern Regions	42%
Eastern Region	30%
Western Region	20%
Midwestern Region	8%
Total	100%

The regions opted for getting additional federal revenues through the DPA. Although the commission rejected derivation as a basis for revenue sharing, derivation remained part of the system, as it was under the Raisman formula. The regions did not lose any part of their shares of proceeds from mining rents and royalties, which still remained 50%. It was the federal government, which lost 5% of its 20% share of mining rents and royalties, as under the Raisman formula. Proceeds from customs and excise duties were pretty much still on the basis of derivation and consumption (Table 5).

Essentially, the first fiscal review commission in an independent Nigeria, with its emphasis on comparability of regional financial positions, was in the direction of greater equality in distribution. But it was overtaken by events after May 27, 1967, as the creation of additional states further complicated Nigeria's struggle to find a mechanism for more equitable distribution of revenues on the basis of formula.

d) The "Constitution (Financial Provision) Decree", No. 15, 1967

After the creation of twelve states on 27 May 1967, the federal military government found it necessary to arrange transitional payments to the states through the DPA. The states had initially been authorized to assume the powers and functions of the former regions. The problem of how to share funds in the DPA among the new subnational units arose. As a transitional measure, the federal government issued Constitution (Financial Provisions) Decree, No. 15, 1967.

This decree suspended sections 141 and 164 of the Republican Constitution (1963), which dealt with revenue allocation. It went further:

Accordingly, there shall during the continuance of this decree be paid to the states mentioned in this subsection hereunder at the end of each quarter, sums equal to the following fractions set out opposite the names of each of the states of the amount standing to the credit of the Distributable Pool Account at that date, that is to say:

a)	to North-Western State	7/100
b)	to North-Central State	7/100
c)	to Kano State	7/100
d)	to North-Eastern State	7/100
e)	to Benue-Plateau State	7/100
f)	to Central Western State	7/100
g)	to Lagos State	2/100
h)	to Western State	8/100
i)	to Midwestern State	2/25
j)	to Central-Eastern State	7/40
k)	to South-Eastern State	3/40
l)	to Rivers State	1/20

The six states in the Northern Region were to share equally 7% each of that former region's 42% share of the DPA.

This formula, though transitional, was arbitrary. It was not clear what principles were used for such distribution of resources in the DPA among states. If population (in the Northern States) was the principle used, there was no such uniform application throughout the country. For instance, while all the six states in the Northern Region were to share equally 7% each of the former region's 42% share of the DPA, the same formula was not applied in the three states of the former Eastern Region. It can, therefore, be argued that the formula used was based on no logical fiscal principles, even though the Binns formula was retained in other areas. It dealt with the DPA and did not consider the general issue of revenue sharing. The disparities and inadequacies of the formula given the new states structure, necessitated the review of the Binns formula revenue sharing. Therefore, the federal military government appointed a commission under the chairmanship of Chief I.O. Dina to review Nigeria's Fiscal System in 1968.

e) The Dina Commission Review: 1968[40]

In its terms of reference, the Dina commission was to "look into and suggest any changes in the existing system of revenue allocation as a whole." It was to also to suggest new revenue sources for the federal government and for the states. It was to report to the federal government in four months.

In its report, the committee made clear the premise on which its recommendations were made:

> We believe that fiscal arrangements in this country should reflect the new spirit of unity to which the nation is dedicated. No more evidence of this is necessary than the present war to preserve this unity at the cost of human lives, material resources, and the radical change in this country's structure. It is in the spirit of this newly found unity that we have viewed all the sources of revenue of this country as the common funds of the country to be used for executing the kinds of programme which can maintain this unity.[41]

The commission observed that, while the pragmatic formulae of earlier revenue exercise might have suited well the needs of the regions, "they can hardly stand the more complex governmental structure of today against the background of a relatively less prosperous fiscal-resource base, but growing expenditure needs". Former revenue exercises had had to succumb to regional pressures for greater autonomy. A new outlook was required, the commission felt, to minimize aggressive regionalism of the past and effect a shift to a political ethos of "cooperative federalism". The main essence of this cooperative federalism, the commission clarified, was to be found in the emphasis on the "concept of a working partnership between the centre and the states on one hand, and among the states on the other." The commission believed that the problem of aggressive inter-ethnic and inter-state competition could not be solved by allocations alone. But its "solution can be enhanced by rapid economic development and the assurance of all the states and groups of at least minimum national standards in the distribution of welfare".

On these bases the commission made its recommendations. It identified the DPA as the "main bone of contention" in Nigeria's fiscal system. First, there were disagreements among states about the composition of the DPA, and secondly, the sharing of funds in the DPA had always been controversial. In its recommendations, the commission suggested a change from the term "Distributable Pool Account" to *States Joint Account, (SJA)* because of "some unhealthy psychological tinge in the experience of regional rivalry and group conflict" over shares of funds in the DPA.

The commission then proposed ten possible principles for the allocation of revenues.[42] However, it suggested that proceeds from the *States Joint Account* be allocated to the states on the basis of 1) the principle of basic needs; 2) the principle of minimum national standards; and 3) the principle of balanced development.

Another account was to be established: *Special Grants Account (SGA).* This account was to meet the principles of national interests, to provide special grants to states, which were found to need them. It was to be administered by a permanent Planning and Fiscal Commission. This is a totally new element altogether in the system. This account was aimed at fiscal equalization. This provision was not implemented until 1988 under the Babangida administration.

The commission greatly de-emphasized the role of the principle of derivation. The existing distinction between types of imports and between products was to be discontinued. Thus, the states' share of excise and import duty on the basis of consumption was to be discontinued.

Rents and royalties on onshore oil were to be assigned 15% to the federal government, 10% to states on the basis of derivation, 70% to the States Joint Account (SJA), and 5% to the Special Grants Account (SGA). Offshore oil was to be shared 60% to the federal government, 30% to SJA, and 10% to SGA. Essentially, this shifted more money into common pools for the states to share.

The Dina Commission made numerous other recommendations, all of which we cannot deal with here. Among these were the suggestions for a Uniform Income Tax, the introduction of a National Social Security Scheme, and new sources of revenue (such as occupational licenses).

This report was rejected by the federal military government as a result of the controversies, which trailed the report among the various governments in the country, even under military regime. It is therefore, not always correct that subnational governments under military rule do not disagree with the central government when they feel that their perceived interests are threatened. This report "generated so much heated debate among the state governments that the Supreme Military Council adopted a 'compromise' formula based on 50% equality and 50% population" in sharing DPA funds among states.[43]

The federal government, however, adopted many of this commission's recommendations through the back door. The Dina Report has been described as being "too controversial for" and "too far ahead" of its time.[44] Members of the commission had concentrated on the economic aspects of revenue allocation, but the political assumptions embedded in the report led to its rejection by the states and the federal government. As Chief Dina told a conference in 1969:

> It is however my belief that provided the objective of rapid economic development is acceptable to the majority of our people, what may seem politically unpalatable in the short run, but economically desirable in the long run, would be pursued in the long-term interest of Nigeria.[45]

For the first time, the principle of derivation was reduced in its application to go to only one item: 10% of proceeds from mining rents and royalties were going to the state of origin.[46] The federal government came very close to this in its October 1974 formula. The concern for the general economic development of the country and balanced development of its component political units led the commission to use various mixtures of principles: *need, minimum national standard,* and *balanced development* for sharing funds in the DPA. The recommendation for an SGA to offer special grants to states for specific purposes was based on the principle of national interests and fiscal equalization. Essentially, the Dina Commission was aimed at making the states share revenue from a common pool to avoid great inter-state imbalance created by the derivation principle. Again, this was what General Gowon tried to do in October 1974. As one military governor remarked, five years after the rejection of the Dina Commission Report, "... I believe that the Dina Report is the best one I have ever read on how revenue should be divided in Nigeria; I personally recommend that."[47] But Nigeria was not ready for it in 1968, and the struggle for a more equitable revenue-sharing formula continued.

f) Revenue Formula between 1 April 1969 and 31 March 1975

Having rejected the revenue-sharing formula recommended by the Dina Commission, the federal military government worked out another formula, in consultation with the state governments. On 1 April 1969, a new formula came into existence. The principles on which this formula was based were not clear. No revenue allocation formula review commission had been appointed since Dina. One thing came out of the new formula introduced in 1969. The states were still conscious of their autonomy even under military rule and the derivation principle remained very much part of the system.

As of 31 March 1969, export duties on produce, hides and skin were returned to states in full, on the basis of derivation. This continued after 1 April 1969. However, the duty on produce was increased from 10% to 15%, and three-fifths of this increase was to go to the states (in addition to the former 10%), while two-fifths of it was paid into the DPA.[48]

Table 8
Arrangement for Revenue Allocation (1971/72)

Type of Tax	Fed. Govt	States	DPA*	Remarks
Statutory Allowance				
A. Import Duty				
Tobacco products is 1/lld	_	On basis of Consumption by state	_	The duty on petroleum Gallon.
Beverages: beer, wine, spirit	100%	_	_	

226

Motor Spirit-1/9d, Diesel Oil-1/11d per gal.	–	–		Authority Decree of 1970 and Legal Notice No. 25 of 1969.
Motor Spirit, Diesel Oil, 2d per gal.	–	–	100%	
Unspecified	65%	–	35%	–

B. Exports

Produce, Hides & skin	–	2/3 on basis of derivation i.e 60% on basis of derivation, 86.66% of 1/3	40% of 1/3 = 13.66%	Decree No. 13 of 1970 Customs Tariff No. 27.09/10. This affects only additional proceeds from Export duty on product attributable to the 5% inc. in rate of duty made by the Customs Tariff (Duties &Exemptions) (#2) Order 1969. All export duty revenues were allocated on basis of derivation by export ratios.

C. Excise Duty

Tobacco, Motor Spirits Diesel Oil Unspecified	50%	–	50%	–

D. Mining Royalties & Rents

Offshore	100%	–	–	Decree No. 9, 1971
Onshore	5%	45% to state of origin	50%	–

E. Non-Statutory Allocation	–			

F. Export Duty				
Animals, Birds, Reptiles, etc	–	–	100%	All Northern States: 7% each Lagos State: 2.0% Rivers State: 5.0% South-Eastern State: 7.5% Midwestern State: 8.0% East Central State: 17.5% Western State: 18.0%

Note:* DPA = Distributable Pool Account. This account was shared on the basis of a) 50% equality of states, and b) 50% population.
Source: *Various Budget Estimates and Decrees 1969-1971,* from the Budget Division, Federal Ministry of Finance, Lagos.

Import duties on tobacco, motor spirit, and diesel oil were to be returned to the states on the basis of consumption. The federal government retained import duty on liquor. The distinction between types of import duties continued in spite of Dina Commission recommendations. General or unspecified import duties (excluding tobacco, motor spirit, diesel oil, and liquor) were to be allocated 65% to the federal government and 35% to the DPA. There was no substantial change in the percentage of proceeds on import duties, which went into the DPA from those recommended by Binns in 1964. But, as of 1 April 1969, an increase in import duty on petroleum products by 1.5 kobo became payable to the DPA.[49]

Before 1 April 1969, excise duties on tobacco, motor spirit, and diesel oil went fully to the states on the basis of derivation, while the federal government retained proceeds from all excise duties. As from 1 April 1969, proceeds from all excise duties were to be allocated 50% to the federal government and 50% to the DPA. This deprived the states of their shares of excise duties. There was an increase in the DPA (greater than the Dina recommendation of 30%). Here, derivation was de-emphasized.

The principle of derivation still showed its presence prominently in the distribution of proceeds from mining rents and royalties. In the new formula, revenues from mining rents and royalties were

228

distributed as follows: 45% to state of origin of mineral, 5% to the federal government, and 50% to the DPA (instead of the existing 35%). The federal government lost 10% and the states 5% of their shares to the DPA. This was a slight improvement on the situation in the past.

Generally, the contents of the DPA grew more than it ever had. The DPA comprised, from 1 April 1969: 1) 2% of the increase in duty from produce; 2) 100% of special duty of 1.5 kobo per gallon levied on petroleum products; 3) 50% of proceeds from excise duties; 4) 35% from duties on unspecified imports; 5) 50% from mining rents and royalties, and 6) 100% of export duty on animals, birds and reptiles.

Thus, from two items in the DPA under the Binns formula, there was an increase to six items. There was also a general increase in the percentage of allocations to the DPA. To this extent, it may be said that the federal government was moving gradually in favour of the DPA. The DPA was still to be shared among the states on the basis of two criteria. The first is the logic of federalism, i.e., the political equality of all states in the country; half (or 50%) of the funds in the DPA were to be shared equally among the states, regardless of their population. The second is the principle of need, defined essentially as population. The other half of the funds in the DPA was to be shared on the basis of population of the states. One criticism of this formula has been that the logic of federalism favoured the smaller states at the expense of the more populous states.

However, between 1969 and 1972, a number of measures were taken to improve upon this formula. The federal government gradually implemented many of the items in the Dina Report through the back door, as mentioned earlier. In some cases, it went beyond the Dina recommendations, and by Decree No. 9, 1971, 100% of the royalties and rents from offshore oil went to the federal government. The formula as it operated in 1971 and 1972 is summarized in Table 8.

Between 1972 and 1974, a number of other reforms in the formula were undertaken to reduce the disparity among states. Many of these were in line with the Dina Report, even though some exceeded Dina recommendations. The reform in marketing boards is one of these. As of 1 April 1973, all export duties on marketing board produce were abolished, except for those on rubber. The federal government made available an estimated ₦34 million to compensate the states, which

229

were to suffer losses of revenue as a result of this. The states thus lost an important source of revenue allocated by derivation. In April of 1974, the export duty on rubber was abolished; so also was the produce tax levied by states.[50]

Apart from these changes, the formula in Table 8, hereafter called the 1971-72 formula, remained in operation until 31 March 1975. Generally, there was a gradual move towards greater equity in the distribution of revenue allocation among the states after 1969. The creation of additional states and the necessity to provide additional resources to the new and weaker states might have contributed to the greater allocation of resources into the DPA. But more important seems to be the fact that the military rulers took a more technocratic approach to the problem of revenue sharing. That even the military leaders could not ignore political considerations was seen in the rejection by the SMC of the Dina Report. Similarly, the creation of states did not seem to have changed the concern of various subnational units about the nature of the distribution of resources among component units of the federation. The reported opposition of the states to the Dina Report was indicative of this continuing phenomenon.

However, as states' concern for more equitable distribution of federal resources continued, so also continued the controversy over the existing revenue allocation formula. The increased petro-revenues or *petro-naira* accentuated the controversy over revenue allocation formula. The great increase in petroleum revenues and the use of the principle of derivation as a basis for distributing revenues from mining rents and royalties among states led to greater disparity among states. Although the Dina Commission had recommended that states' shares of mining rents and royalties be reduced to 10%, the formula between 1969 and 1974 fixed it at 45% for on-shore oil.[51] The result of this was disparity among states in their shares of federally derived revenues. The statutory allocation from the federal government to the state governments in 1974/75 years illustrated this point.

On balance, the 1969-74 formula could be said to have been a greater movement in the direction of equitable distribution of federal revenues among states than earlier formulae. However, the adherence to high percentages of revenues on mining rents and royalties derivable to the states of origin distorted the general move towards equity. Thus, the Midwestern State, with a population of 2.5 million (4.5% of Nigeria's total population), got 23.7% (₦139.9m) of federally allocated revenues. Similarly, the Rivers State, with a population of 1.5 million (2.8% of Nigeria's population), had 17.13% (₦101.1m) share of statutory allocations to the state.

On the other hand, the Western State, with a population of 9.5 million (17.0% of Nigeria's population), and the North Eastern State, of 7.8 million people (14.0% of Nigeria's population), got 8.03% (₦47.4m) and 7.07% (₦41.7m) of statutory appropriations to the states, respectively. Put another way, while both the Rivers and Midwestern States, comprising 7.3% (4 million) of the country's total population, shared between themselves 40.83% (₦241.0m) of the total allocation to the states, the ten other states, accounting for 92.7% (51.6milion) of the country's population, shared among themselves 59.17% (₦349.2m) of the statutory allocations.

It was therefore not surprising that the publication of the 1974-75 federal statutory allocation to the states by the *New Nigerian* of 10 April 1974 drew great attention to the existing revenue allocation system. Revenue allocation among states had become a very controversial issue – assuming a higher importance as public moot point for several months in 1974. The adherence to the principle of derivation (with high percentages) created greater financial inequality among states, as oil revenues increased in importance.

Table 9
Federal Statutory Allocations to States During 1974-75 Financial Years

	A	B*	C**
State	Population (1963) (Million)	Allocation (xm)	Percentage of Each State's Share of Total Allocation
North-Western	5.7	34.9	5.91
North-Central	4.1	29.1	4.93
North-Eastern	7.8	41.7	7.07
Kano	5.8	35.0	5.93

Benue-Plateau	4.0	30.1	5.10
Kwara	2.4	23.9	4.05
Lagos	1.4	20.7	3.51
Western	9.5	47.4	8.03
Midwestern	2.5	139.9	23.70
East-Central	7.5	58.3	9.88
South-Eastern	3.4	28.1	4.76
Rivers	1.5	101.1	17.13
Total	**55.6**	**590.2**	**100.00**

*Source: *New Nigerian,* 10 April, 1975*
** Percentage found on the basis of each state's share over total of all states' shares.

There were various arguments in 1974 about the principle to be used in sharing revenue among the states. Many people in Rivers and Midwestern States were angry that many of the proponents of the principle of *need* now had strongly supported the derivation principle of revenue sharing in the past when it favoured them. This seems to be an apparent reference to the Western State, particularly. There seemed to be a feeling that the principle of derivation has fallen out of favour in the Western State by 1974. The Western State now occupied the unenviable position, which the former Eastern Region occupied before 1959.

Arguments by some leaders and commentators in the Western State about the necessity to emphasize the principle of need is to be found in the nature of petroleum which they argued, did not involve direct human labor of individuals as was involved in cocoa farming in the 1950s.

On the other hand, the oil-producing states complained about the damage done to their roads by heavy equipment for oil exploitation, the pollution of rivers where their citizens used to fish, and the destruction of farmlands in the areas of oil exploitation. They argued that their states needed more revenues returned to them in order to cope with these problems created by oil exploitation.

To the Governor of the old Midwestern State, Brigadier Ogbemudia, the Midwestern State was prepared to accept any formula of revenue allocation "provided there is justice and consistency in the application."[52] He assured Nigerians that his state "would continue to make any sacrifice that would be in the national interest."

> ...if they say let us share the revenue by using the principle of need, they will have our hundred percent backing; if it is on derivation, they will equally have our full backing.[53]

Brigadier Ogbemudia agreed that there were glaring disparities among the states, looking at the "figures in relation to the population without other available evidence." However, he continued, "I think that in order to carry out an objective analysis, one has to go to the origin of the formula itself." This was an obvious reference to the clamour by some of the old regions for emphasis on the principle of derivation.

While this governor supported a review of the revenue allocation formula, his Commissioner for Finance, Mr. Edwin Clark, was less enthusiastic. In an NBC-TV radio programme on 25 May 1974, Mr. Clark declared: "What the Federal Military Government and the Supreme Military Council had approved should be regarded as fair and reasonable".[54] He claimed that only 6% of the total revenue derivable from oil was being paid to the states of origin. He asked what then happened to "the remaining 94% the nation gets from the oil?" He observed that the originators of the present derivation system were today the same people opposing it. "There has been no change in the formula since 1958", he claimed.

Mr. Clark also had an answer for those who argued in favor of emphasis on population as an index of need in revenue allocation. He argued:

> You cannot say that because a state has 10 million people, therefore its needs are more than a state with three million people. For example, in the Midwest State alone, we have over 500,000 pupils and students

233

> whereas, some state with a population double that of the Midwest State haven't got one-quarter of that number of pupils and students.[55]

Mr. Clark was thus arguing that population was not necessarily the only important factor in determining need, the level of social services to which a government was committed was, to him, a more important variable. After all, Mr. Clark concluded, whatever formula was adopted "we can never bring two states to the same standard of living."

However, there seemed to have been a general feeling among most, if not all, the state governors that the revenue formula be reviewed. Brigadier Abba Kyari of the North Central State and Colonel David Bamigboye of Kwara State called for the review of the formula in May 1974.[56] Although the system of revenue allocation in operation was an improvement on what had existed, Mr. J.D. Gomwalk of Benue-Plateau State observed that this did not mean it was satisfactory. He felt that it should be reveiwed.[57] Brigadier Esuene the Governor of the South-Eastern State noted that although the system of revenue allocation was "alright," the country needed a more objective system.[58] On the other hand, Mr. Usman Faruk of the North-Western State condemned criticisms of the controversial 1974-75 allocations since the decision was taken unanimously by the SMC. "This year's revenue allocation was agreed to by all of us."[59] He advised people to focus their discussions, on which of the two principles, derivation or need, which should be used for revenue-sharing.

Other calls for the review of the revenue formula by state governors came from Brigadier Johnson of Lagos State[60] and Brigadier Rotimi of the Western State. Brigadier Rotimi called for a revenue system that would guarantee responsible and stable government in Nigeria. Although various revenue systems had been played up in the past, the present pressures, he argued, were for a system of revenue based on the principle of balanced development, task efforts, and fiscal efficiency.[61]

We have gone to this extent to show the feelings of some Nigerian military leaders at subnational level on the revenue formula between 1969 and 1974, which the Federal Commissioner for Finance had described as temporary.[62] Temporary as this had been meant to be, it lasted five years.

Table 10
The October 1974/75 Revenue Allocation Formula:
1 April 1975 (A Summary)

Items (Duties)	Federal	To Regions By Derivations	DPA	Remarks
A. IMPORTS				
Tobacco	–	–	100%	
Beverages (beer, wine & spirits)	100%	–	–	See also "Constitution (Financial Provisions, etc) Decree 1975, Decree No. 6 1975" in Laws of the Federal Republic of Nigeria (Lagos: Federal Government Printer, 1975) pp. A19-21.
Motor Spirits & Diesel Oil	–	–	100%	
General Imports (other than tobacco, m/spirits, diesel oil, liquor)	65%	–	35%	
B. EXPORTS				
Animals, Birds, etc	–	–	100%	
Produce, Hides, & Skins	–	–	100%	
C. EXCISE*				
Tobacco	50%	–	50%	
Motor Spirit				
Diesel Oil				
Unspecified				
D. MINING RENTS & ROYALTIES				
Offshore	–	–	100%	
Onshore	–	20%	80%	

X   **Note**: increase of funds in DPA and decrease of funds shared by derivation among states.

X   **Source**: *compiled from documents from Federal Ministry of Finance, Lagos.*

g) The October 1974-75 Formula[63]

The amendments to the existing revenue formula from October 1974 seemed to have been partially the result of the public clamour for a review of the existing revenue allocation formula. It was also the result of the feeling in the central government that the states should be given enough funds to meet the cost of their projects under the Third National Development Plan: 1975-1980. In his broadcast to the nation, General Gowon accepted the fact that the formula, which existed then, was inadequate for carrying out various capital projects in the new development plan. In fact, as he observed, "No state government except two will be in a position to finance even a single year's programme on the basis of projected budget surplus" under the existing revenue formula. General Gowon went further:

> ...to give credibility to the development programmes of state governments, the Supreme Military Council has considered it necessary that the existing revenue-sharing arrangements should be modified to ensure that each state government is enabled to finance at least sixty-six and two-thirds percent of its programmes from its own independent tax effort and from federally collected revenues.[64]

Whatever gap existed after would be bridged, as in the past, through a combination of loans and conditional grants from the federal government or its financing agencies. This seemed to be recognition of the principle of financial need in revenue sharing among states.

General Gowon announced, that in the future there would be regular review of the revenue allocation formula to "ensure that all levels of government are enabled to perform their allotted development and governmental functions subject only to the totality of the resources available to the government".[65]

However, the Head of State went on, the Supreme Military Council was "satisfied that revenue allocation should be properly conceived not as a constitutional exercise, but as a means of financing development programmes".[66] Hence, plan periods as approved from time to time by the government were to be "adopted as a logical time frame for reviewing the sharing of revenues among governments of the federation". Thus, the old notion of embedding percentage and fractional shares in the constitution was to be "regarded as obsolete and therefore to be discarded". Future revenue-sharing formula as approved by the government would be incorporated "in appropriate decree or legislation".

The objective of the revenue-sharing exercise was to "augment substantially the revenues destined for the DPA". This was to be done by "de-emphasizing the derivation principle in respect of oil and non-oil revenues by transferring revenue from the federal government to the states via the DPA". Therefore, all customs and excise duties, which used to go to the states on the basis of derivation, were to pass to the states through the DPA. The federal government "surrendered" its 100% share of offshore oil revenues to the state through the DPA.

The only revenue still shared on the basis of derivation was mining rents and royalties. It would seem that in a gesture of "sacrifice", the Rivers and Midwestern States acquiesced to the reduction of their shares of mining rents and royalties from 45% to 20%. This formula went very close to implementing the major items of the Dina Report. Like the Dina recommendation, derivation virtually ceased to be an important principle in revenue allocation, except with regard to mining rent and royalties. The difference, though, is that while the Dina Report fixed states' shares of this revenue at 10%, the new formula fixed it at 20%. Even then, it was understood that the reduction of this percentage to 20% was as a result of a compromise struck in the Supreme Military Council.

We argue here that the de-emphasis of the principle of derivation in revenue allocation is a movement towards greater equality in distribution of revenues than had existed in Nigeria prior to this time. The contents of the DPA increased (Table 10) more than under any other revenue formula.

Revenues in the DPA were still to be shared: half equally among the states and half among the states on the basis of population. But one old problem had taken a greater salience. This is the principle of sharing the proceeds of the DPA. The problem of sharing funds in the

237

DPA was not new. It had become a more important issue because most revenues from the federal government to the state governments, unlike in the preceding formulae, now went via the DPA.

The more populous states complained about the logic of federalism, which distributed half of the proceeds of the DPA equally among the states. Secondly, there was still the feeling among many Nigerians that 20% share of mining rents and royalties by derivation were too large a revenue to go to any single state because of the enormous oil revenues which came from two out of twelve states.[67] Yet others who felt that the figure of 20% short-changed oil-producing states without adequate compensation. The struggle for an appropriate revenue formula, which would form the basis of greater inter-state equity in revenue sharing, continued.

On balance, a number of issues had become clear about revenue sharing under the military. First, the central government had become stronger financially, especially through profit tax on oil. It had also become an interventionist, apparently technical force in the distribution of resources among the component units of the federation. Secondly, while military rule did not prevent the issue of resource sharing from becoming tension-charged, the nature of military rule made it easier to moderate piecemeal solutions over time. Finally, the military administration, in its desire for a more even or 'balanced' development had de-emphasized the role of derivation in resource allocation. Is this fair? Are there other ways of dealing with the problems of inequality among component units of the federation, vertically and horizontally? Let us see what happened in subsequent years.

h) The Aboyade Commission, 1977[68]

With the exit of General Gowon, a new military regime came in with a transition to civil rule programme. Part of the transition programme was the Constitution Drafting Committee and subsequent Constituent Assembly. It had therefore become necessary, (given the transition to the Second Republic) to review the existing revenue-sharing formula, which after all, comprised a series of actions taken by decrees issued by the Federal Military Government. The Federal Military Government set up a Technical Committee on Revenue Allocation under the Chairmanship of Professor Ojetunji Aboyade in

1977. This committee was to review the tax process of the three tiers of government and work out revenue-sharing formula, which would enhance fiscal federation, and enable the polity to cope with the challenges of development. Issues such as the equality of states, adequate revenue for each tier of government to carry out its functions, population, needs, even development, derivation and national interest were all to be considered.

The Aboyade committee was more concerned about "administrative and fiscal control"[69] The Committee recommended resource distribution along vertical and horizontal level. Among its recommendations was that all federally collected revenue, except for personal income tax of the Armed Forces, external affairs officers and the Federal Capital Territory should be in one account, to distribute among federal, state and local governments on the basis of the formula below:

Level of Government	Shares %
•Federal Government	57
•State Governments	30
•Local Governments	10
•Special Grants Account	3
Total	100

A major development that was reflected in the recommendations of the committee was the recognition of local government as a "guaranteed tier of government," entitled to statutory allocations from a federally collected pool of funds. In addition to the 10% allocated to local governments, an additional 10% was to be contributed by state governments from their total revenue receipts, to the funds shared among local governments in the state.

In order to cater for special problems such as ecological degradation, national emergencies, disasters and pollution in oil producing areas, the Special Grants Account (SGA) was to be set up to address for these.

On the horizontal level, the committee suggested five criteria for the sharing of revenue among states and local governments. These were:

Principles	Shares (%)
•equality of access to development opportunities	25
•minimum standard for national integration	22
•absorptive capacity	20
•independent revenue and minimum tax effort	18
•fiscal efficiency	15
Total	100

This recommendation obviously de-emphasized the derivation principle, even though it was indirectly covered under other principles. The government of Alhaji Shehu Shagari, in the Second Republic rejected this committee's report for being too technical and not easy to operationalize in practice. The Shagari government therefore set up another Presidential Commission in November 1979 under Professor Pius Okigbo to revisit the issue of revenue sharing or distribution.

i) The Okigbo Commission 1979[70]

The Okigbo Commission was to collate and harmonize the inputs of various governments and deliberations at the Constituent Assembly, as well as review the revenue allocation formula, and make necessary recommendations.

In its recommendation, the commission felt that on the basis of the levels of expenditure (recurrent or capital) the vertical sharing of the Federal Account among tiers of government should be:

Tiers of Government	Shares (%)
•Federal Government	53
•State Government	30
•Local Government	10
•Special Fund	7
a) initial development of FCT–	2.5
b) minimal producing areas -	2.0
c) ecological and other disaster	1.0

240

d)	revenue equalization of fund	1.5
Total		100

On horizontal allocation, the Commission used four principles in the distribution of resources. These are:

Principles	Shares (%)
•Minimum responsibilities of government	40
•Population	40
•Social Development	
Primary School enrolment	
a. direct enrolment	11.5
b. inverse enrolment	3.5
•Internal Revenue Effort	5.0
Total	100.00

After a government White Paper and the subsequent heated debates as well as nullification by the Supreme Court of the Commission's report, the 1981 Revenue Allocation Act was passed in January 1982. On the vertical plane, the Act made the following allocations among tiers of government:

Tiers of Government	Shares (%)
•Federal Government	55.0
•State Government	30.5
•Local Government	10.0
•Special Funds	4.5
- Development of FCT	
- Mineral Producing State	
- (On the basis of derivation)	2.0
- Development of Mineral producing areas	1.5
- General Ecological problems	1.0
- Revenue Equalization	1.5
Total	100.00

Interestingly, the Act did not provide for any revenue equalization fund, as recommended by the Okigbo Commission and the Government White Paper, based on the above principles. These principles were also to be used for sharing revenue among local governments within a State. There was to be established State Joint Local Government Account (SJLGA) for the distribution of revenue among local governments. Each state was to contribute 5% (unlike the 10% in the Aboyade Commission recommendation) of its total government revenue to the SJLGA.

A number of state governments took the federal government to court over this revenue-sharing formula but lost out. This revenue formula remained in operation, except for amendments under the military regime, until 1989. However, given the complaints of states for additional funds, the Military Government of General Muhammadu Buhari amended the formula to increase the states share of the federation account to 32.5%, i.e. "less 2% of the mineral revenue component of the 32.5% of the federation Account."[71]

j) The National Revenue Mobilization Allocation and Fiscal Commission, 1988

The Babangida administration, as part of its transition to civil rule programme, established the *National Revenue Mobilization Allocation and Fiscal Commission* (RMAFC), under Decree No. 49 of 1989. Its first Chairman was Lt-General T.Y. Danjuma.

The RMAFC was established to design and effectively mobilize all resources; carry out periodic review of allocation principles and formulae; ensure full compliance with established revenue-sharing arrangements; submit regular annual reports to the federal government; and the administration and suspension of all loans (internal and external) by all tiers of government[72] This became a permanent institution on fiscal federalism among other functions.

In its submission to the Armed Forces Ruling Council (AFRC) in 1989, the RMAFC recommended vertical revenue allocation as below:[73]

Tiers of Government	Shares (%)
• Federal government	47
• State government	30
• Local government	15
• Special funds	8
• - FCT	1
• - Stabilization	0.5
• - Savings	2.0
• - Derivation	2.0
- Development of Oil	
▪ Mineral Producing Areas	1.5
- Development of non-oil	
Producing areas	0.5
• - General Ecology	0.5
Total	100.00

On the horizontal dimension, the commission recommended:

Principles	Shares (%)
• Equality of State	40.0
• Population	30.0
• Social development factor	10.0
(including education, health,	
• water, landmass and terrain)	
• Internal Revenue effort	20.0
Total	100.00

Table 11
Vertical Allocation of the Federation Account, 1981-1992 (%)

Recipients	1981 Act	1989	Jan. 1990	Jan. 1992	From Jan.
i) Federal Government	55	55	50	50	48.5
ii) State Government	30.5	*32.5	30	25	24
iii) Local Government	10	10	15	20	20
iv) Special Funds	-	**2.5	5	5	7.5
a) Federal Capital Territory	_	_	1	1	1
b) Stabilization	_	_	0.5	0.5	0.5
c) Savings	_	_	_	_	_
d) Derivation	2	#2	1	1	1
e) Development of Oil Mineral Producing Areas	1.5	1.5	1.5	1.5	3
f) General Ecology	1	1	1	1	2
Total	**100**	**100**	**100**	**100**	**100**

Source: *National Revenue Mobilization, Allocation and Fiscal Commission (RMAFC),* Revenue Allocation: "Notes on the Role and Activities of the RMAFC," presented at the seminar for states and local governments, Central Hotel, Kano, 29-30 June, 1992; and T.Y. Danjuma, "Revenue Sharing and the Political Economy of Nigerian Federalism" in J. Isawa Elaigwu, P.C. Logams, and H.S. Galadima (eds), Federalism and Nation-Building in Nigeria (Abuja, NCIR, 1994) p. 103.
Note:
*   What is shared among states is 32.5% of the Federation Account.
\#   This 2% is not of the Federation Account but of the mineral revenue component of the 32.5% of the Federation Account.
**   The Special Fund comprises of 1.5% for development of oil mineral producing state and 1% ecological fund.

The Armed Forces Ruling Council made amendments to these recommendations and the approved formula came into effect in January 1990.

On vertical allocation, the AFRC increased the federal government's share from 47% to 50%, but confirmed state and local governments' shares at 30% and 15% respectively. Special funds were reduced from 8% to 5%. Horizontal allocation was basically confirmed except for internal revenue effort, which was reduced from 20% to 10%, while landmass and terrain, was allocated 10% by the AFRC.

Derivation principle was pegged at 1% for mineral producing states to share in the Federation Account. The total allocation of 1.5% was devoted to the development of oil mineral producing areas. This allocation was raised to 3% from June 1992.[74]

It is interesting that even under military rule, revenue sharing attracted so much attention. Clearly over time, the military administration increased the shares of the federal centre, and de-emphasized the principle of derivation in its formula for sharing revenues. It is also a bit surprising that the AFRC rejected the 2% of the Federation Account, which the commission recommended should be set aside as National Savings. The Commission's recommendation of a *Stabilization Fund* was designed to cushion the system against unexpected economic disturbances, which would affect the Federation Account, and therefore the capacity of the various tiers of government to sustain "acceptable levels of activities."[75] From 1990, the allocation of 0.5% was made for this purpose. However, conflicts arose later over the access of various tiers of government to this fund, especially between state and local governments on the one hand, and the federal government on the other.

In 1992, the formula for the vertical allocation of federally collected revenue was revisited. In the new formula, the allocation was as below:[76]

Tiers of Government	Shares (%)
• Federal government	48.5
• State government	24
• Local government	20

• Special funds	7.5
• Federal Capital Territory	1.0
• General Ecology	1.0
• Stabilization Fund	1.5
• Derivation (Mineral)	1.0
• Development of mineral -oil Producing Areas	3.0
Total	100.00

In this formula, both the federal and state governments lost revenue to local governments, even though loss by states of revenue was higher than the federal government's. Additional funds were given to local governments because they were to take on primary education (following the dissolution of the National Primary Education Board), and Primary Health Care. It is interesting that revenue distribution under the military had, unusually, taken notice of the legislative list and functions of tiers of government. Generally, military regimes in Nigeria gave little attention to conciliation of the functions of tiers of government and the tax powers or revenues of each tier, except during the General Gowon's preparation of the *Third National Development Plan*.

k) Revenue Allocation since May 1999

The 1999 Constitution sections 31-32 of Part 1 of the Third Schedule, recognizes the RMAFC. Its powers are also clearly stated in section 32 of the above schedule. In the Fourth Republic and pursuant to the above constitutional provisions, President Olusegun Obasanjo inaugurated a 37-member commission on September 20, 1999, with a member from each state and the FCT.

The commission had public hearings and received memoranda from various stakeholders, after which it submitted its first report under the 1999 Constitution to the President in August 2001, to be placed before the National Assembly. The recommendations by the commission for vertical revenue distribution are stated below:

Government/fund	Shares (%)
•Federal government	41.3
•State government	31.0
•Local government	16.0
•Special funds	11.7
Total	100.00

However, this report was withdrawn in May 2002 as a result of the Supreme Court judgment in Suit No. SC 28/2001 of 5th April 2002 on Resource Control in which the allocation to "Special Funds" from the Federation Account was declared illegal.

As a result of this Supreme Court judgment, President Obasanjo (by an executive order through a letter to the RMAFC) absorbed the 7.5 % Special Funds, in May 2002. This made the Federal Government's share 56%. The Governors of States and Chairmen of local governments reacted angrily to this Presidential order, which they considered as most unfair, partly because they had not been consulted.

In response to these protests, President Obasanjo issued another executive order, in July 2002, which revised the vertical allocation as:

Tiers of Government	Shares (%)
•Federal government	54.68
•State government	24.72
•Local government	20.60
Total	100.00

Thus the federal government's share was reduced by 1.32%, while state and local governments gained 1.32% in their share of revenue from FA.

Following the Supreme Court judgement on the on-shore and offshore oil dichotomy by the Supreme Court, politicians tried to find a political solution to the issue. If the Supreme Court judgement had confirmed offshore oil as belonging to the federal government, the only political decision available was to repeal the law. The Peoples Democratic Party government at the centre then championed the cause for the abrogation of the on-shore/off-shore oil dichotomy. The *On-*

Shore/Off-Shore Oil Dichotomy Abrogation Bill was passed by the National Assembly and signed into law by the President in 2003.

However, aggrieved 19 Northern states governors went to court to declare the abrogation as unconstitutional. These Northern Governors believed that dichotomy between on-shore and offshore oil should be maintained. This matter has not been disposed of by the Supreme Court at the point of writing.

In December 2002, the commission completed its review of the 2002 Main Report on Revenue Allocation, including in the new report the implications of the Supreme Court judgment. The new Revenue Allocation Formula was submitted to the President for onward transmission to the National Assembly in December 2002. The President tabled it before the National Assembly in January 2003. According to this proposal, the vertical allocation among tiers of government was:

Tiers of Government	Shares (%)
•Federal government	46.63
•State government	33.00
•Local government	20.37
Total	100.00

In a surprise move, President Obasanjo withdrew the Revenue Allocation Bill from the National Assembly supposedly because as he claimed there were many versions of the Bill in circulation at the National Assembly. Shortly after this, President Obasanjo appealed to the RMAFC to review the federal government's share of the allocation, because there was an improper weighting of some constitutional responsibilities of the federal government such as internal security, salaries, pensions of the Armed Forces and the Police, and energy. The President felt that the adoption of "net effort analysis"[77] put the federal government at a disadvantage.

Again state governors and other stakeholders bombarded the commission's office with requests for adjustments. As the Chairman of the commission, Alh. Hamman Tukur put it while delivering the 2004 Revenue Formula Allocation recommendations to President Obasanjo:

...the Governors urged the Commission on behalf of themselves and their Local Governments to, instead, represent an authenticated copy of the Revenue Allocation Formula to Mr. President for onward transmission to the National Assembly, which according to them, was the only body constitutionally empowered to review and amend or pass the new formula.[78]

However, the commission decided that in the interest of equity, justice and fair play, it would consider the view expressed by any stakeholder. The point the governors were making was that the President was misusing his office by withdrawing the bill from the National Assembly and returning it to the commission, with its reservations. The platform for debate was the National Assembly. By returning the formula to the commission, the President was taking undue advantage of his position as the sponsor of the bill at the National Assembly. The state and local governments felt short-changed, and believed that the federal government's reservation should have been part of the debate at the National Assembly.

Thus on September 20, 2004, the RMAFC submitted to the President a reviewed Revenue Allocation formula, which included the December 2002 Main Report and an addendum on changes made in the Vertical Revenue Allocation Formula, as an integral part of the 2002 report. According to the proposed vertical allocation formula,

Government	Shares (%)
•Federal government	53.69
•State government	31.10
•Local government	15.21
Total	100.00

Of the Federal Government's 53.69%, share of the FA, 6.5% was to go to the Federal Republic of Nigeria for the following purposes:

•National Ecological Problems	1.5
•Diversification of the National Economy (in solid minerals and agricultural development)	3.5
•National Reserve Fund	1.5
Total	6.5

According to the Chairman of the Commission, the state governments were supposed to be mainly responsible for primary schools, even though local governments were to be participants in this function. It therefore transferred some funds from the local governments to state government. In addition, the commission again created *special funds*, but was careful to allocate these to the Federal Republic of Nigeria or the federation because these cut across responsibilities of all tiers of government. These special funds include – national ecological problems; the diversification of the national economy in solid minerals and agricultural development; and the National Revenue Fund. These special funds of the Federal Republic were to be "under the supervision of the Executive President of the Federal Republic of Nigeria."[79] Thus, federal government's actual share recommended was 47.19%.

Thus *"The Reviewed Revenue Allocation Formula comprising the December2002 Main Report and its Addendum,"* as well as a draft bill, were passed on to the President on September 20, 2004, after which the President passed it to the National Assembly.

Table 12
Vertical Revenue Allocation Formula May 1999 – 2005

Formula (Proposed and Operational)	REVENUE ALLOCATION (%)			
	Federal Government	State Government	Local Government	Special Funds#
RMAFC (operational till April 2002)	48.50	24.00	20.00	7.50
RMAFC Proposal (August 2001)*	41.30	31.00	16.00	11.70*
Executive Order (May 2002)	56.00	24.00	20.00	–
Executive Order (July 2002)	54.68	24.72	20.60	–
RMAFC Proposal (December 2002)	46.63	33.00	20.37	–
RMAFC Proposal September 20, 2004	53.69	31.10	15.21	–

*The Supreme Court ruling in April 2002 nullified the allocation for *special funds* which the federal government previously monopolized.
Source: *compiled from the documents of RMAFC 1999-2004*

It has been very difficult under the Fourth Republic to get a Revenue Allocation Act. No doubt the interest generated by the issue is a reflection of the current mood of the nation. At no time in Nigeria's history did the vertical allocation generate so much political heat except in the Second Republic. Horizontal allocation had always been the source of intense conflicts. It does seem that vertical allocations are more controversial under democratic regimes than under military probably for obvious reasons.

The RMAFC also made proposals for the horizontal distribution of revenues. The September 2004 formula recommendations, also clearly stated the criteria for *horizontal revenue* sharing:

Principles		Shares (%)
•Equality	-	45.23
•Population	-	25.60
•Population Density	-	1.45
•Internal Revenue Generation Efforts		8.31
•Landmass	-	5.35
•Terrain	-	5.35
•Rural roads/Internal waterways	-	1.21
•Potable water		1.50
•Education	-	3.00
•Health		3.00
Total		100.00

On balance, the history of revenue distribution has been affected by 1) the various changes in the federal structure, especially in the number of subnational units—states and local governments; 2) the nature of military rule; 3) the advent of petronaira and the attendant politics of derivation; 4) the problem of fiscal equalization, vertically and horizontally; 5) persistent demand for the review of the legislative list and expansion in the tax powers of subnational units; and 6) the imperatives of equity and national development.

3) Salient Issues In Nigeria's Fiscal Federalism

From the history of revenue distribution in Nigeria, it is clear that the exercise is not just economic. It is also highly political. A number of salient issues need to be briefly identified.

The first is the various *changes in the federal structure*— especially in the number of subnational states, from three or four (if you include Southern Cameroon's) in 1960 to thirty-six in 1996— have affected the process of revenue sharing. Each new exercise in the creation of additional states reduces the internal resource base of the new states. Thus, while the old Midwest Region or State was an oil rich state, with the creation of additional states in 1996, the current Edo state (still with the capital in Benin) is no longer an oil-producing state. It now has the burden of looking for internal revenue from other sources, in Nigeria's monocultural economy. Similarly, additional states created *new*

252

majorities and *new minorities,* with greater exhibition of self-determination. The implications for political stability are clear. The additional states created greater pressure on the Federation Account, especially as the horizontal allocation of revenue still uses the equality of states as a principle of distribution. Thus, as the creation of additional states produced financially weaker states, the centre got financially stronger.

Secondly, the *nature of military rule* through decree and edicts, and its hierarchical administrative structure, made it easier for military regimes to handle the issue of resource distribution. Often they distributed resources in favour of the centre, giving reasons of national security and interests as paramount considerations. While the military regime, between 1967 and1978, could handle the explosive issue of revenue allocation formula, with little scars, it has been difficult for Obasanjo to get any revenue formula passed since 1999. There are those who believe that the problem is more President Obasanjo's ego problem, than one of type of regimes. They point out that President Shagari got the 1981 Revenue Allocation Act out in two years. Whatever position one takes, it is clear the centralization of political and fiscal powers in Nigeria today has to do with the nature of centripetalism, which the military represents in the Nigerian federation.

Thirdly, the advent of *huge resources from petroleum resources (i.e. petronaira)* had changed the nature of resource distribution in Nigeria. From early 1970s, Nigeria's economy gradually became monocultural. As an illustration, between 1990 and 2004, over 70% of Nigeria's total earnings came from oil resources, thus demonstrating an unduly high dependence of the economy on the oil sector.[80] Over the years, many governments had paid lip-service to the diversification of the economy. In practical terms, nothing significant has changed. The Obasanjo regime went even further than his predecessors to include the regular increase in the pump price of petrol as an economic tool for development. From June 1, 2000, when his government raised the pump price of petrol from ₦25 to ₦30 per litre to August 2005 when his government raised the pump price from ₦50.50k per litre to ₦65 per litre, there have been increases of pump prices, ten times—an average of about two times a year.[1] Many Nigerians have wondered aloud if Nigerian leaders had run out of ideas about effecting positive economic change except in tinkering with aspects of the oil sector.

Another dimension of this over-dependence on oil is that the proceeds of the Federation Account are also heavily oil-derived. Governments at all tiers have become complacent about *revenue generation from internal sources.* They tend to wait for statutory allocation from the Federation Account for their budgetary allocations and development programmes. The level of dependence on statutory allocations from the Federal Account by states, between 1990-1996, has ranged from an average of 30.4% in Lagos to 87% in Niger state.[82] The situation is worse at the local government level. Not even the federal government is really breaking away from this dependency pattern. The result of this is that since internally generated revenue efforts are poor or minimal, the priorities of state governments as autonomous units get skewed. In addition, many subnational units lack the resources to carry out their own activities.

This leads us to the fourth issue—*the problem of fiscal equalization.* The federation, like many others, experiences fiscal imbalances. The greatest number of complaints relate to how the federal government is suffocating the states with its financial powers, with little effort at fiscal equalization. Since the 1980s, there has been "an absence of a clear cut inter-governmental fiscal relations in Nigeria".[83] Given the background of military rule, succeeding civilian 'democratic' regimes have not adequately conciliated the assigned constitutional responsibilities and fiscal resources of component units. The situation did not change in Nigeria even after 1999. The responsibilities of each tier should be relatively marched by corresponding revenues. This had created tension among tiers of government.

The unnecessary politicization of the revenue allocation process had also affected inter-governmental fiscal relations. Ideally the grants-in-aid provision of the 1999 Constitution, section 164(1), makes it clear that:

> The Federation may make grants to a State to supplement the revenue of that State in such sum and subject terms and conditions as may be prescribed by the National Assembly.

The federal government should transfer funds to states, which cannot meet their expenditure needs. In the 1970s, such grants-in-aid were very acceptable. Under the Second National Development Plan, 1970-74 a total of x279 million was disbursed to state governments by the federal government as non-matching grants for specific projects in education, agriculture, commerce and finance and others. In the 1975-80 plan period, ₦1.3 billion was transferred as specific grants to state governments.[84] Over time, grants-in-aid declined as federally collected revenue declined. In addition, the grants-in-aid are disbursed at the discretion of the federal government making it easily too subjective. Perhaps, there is need to formalize the process as done in Canada and Australia, even though both countries have different techniques. The formalization of fiscal intergovernmental relations would make the process more transparent, and rob the federal government of the excessive use of discretion in the dispensation of grants-in-aid.

The other instrument of inter-governmental fiscal transfer is *Loans;* this is usually part of macro-economic stabilization. The power of public borrowing resides with the federal centre; and in the case of internal borrowing can be effected through development stocks, treasury bills and certificates. The accruals can then be shared by the tiers of government. However, only the federal government has the power for external borrowing. Subnational units can only borrow if such loans are guaranteed by the federal government. The Debt Management Office has frightening figures of external debts owed by the 36 states of the federation. Federal and State government internal and domestic debts payments detract from the fiscal capacity of governments to provide desirable services.

On the horizontal level (i.e. within each tier) the biggest problem has been one of agreeing on the appropriate principle for sharing resources. As we have shown above, these principles have shifted from time to time without ever satisfying everyone. Below, Table 11 shows the various principles used over time for horizontal allocations:

Table 13
Horizontal Fiscal Allocation Principle

Year	Fiscal Commission/Committee Decrees. Principles/Factors	Principles/Factors
1946	Phillipson Commission	i. Derivation ii. Even Progress iii. Population
1951	Hicks – Phillipson	i. Derivation ii. Need iii. National Interest
1953	Chick	i. Derivation ii. Fiscal Autonomy
1958	Raisman	i. Need (with indicator) ii. Derivation
1964	Binns	i. Derivation ii. Financial comparability iii. Need iv. Even Development v. Tax Effort
1967	Decree No. 15, 1967	i. Equality (in the North) ii. Population
1968	Dina	i. Basic needs ii. Minimum National standards iii. Balanced Development iv. Derivation
1970	Decree No. 13. 1970	i. Population ii. Equality of States
1977	Aboyade	i. Equality of access to Development opportunity ii. National minimum standard for national integration iii. Absorption Capacity iv. Independent Revenue and Tax Effort v. Fiscal Efficiency.

1979	Okigbo	i) Minimum responsibility of government ii) Population iii) Social Development Factor iv) Internal Revenue Effort
	National Revenue Mobilization, Allocation and Fiscal commission	i) Equality of states ii) Population iii) Social Development iv) Internal Revenue Efforts v) Land Mass and Terrain
2004	RMAFC	i) Equality of states ii) Population iii) Population density iv) Internal Revenue Effort v) Landmass vi) Terrain vii) Rural Road/Inland waterway viii)Potable Water ix) Education x) Health.

Source: Compiled from various reports and documents.

From this table, it seems that by 2004, the principles of allocation had increased to about ten. Does this mean a greater sensitivity to complaints, or does it mean greater equality? The struggle for greater equality in resource distribution is taking on greater saliency as oil mineral producing areas are strongly pressing for 'resource control' — another term for distribution of resources on the basis of the principle of derivation.

Another important issue is the persistent demands for a *review of the Legislative lists*. The pressure for the review of legislative list had been on since 1997. Many groups, as discussed in chapter 10, had felt by 1999 that Nigeria was not running a federal system, or at best, was running a federal system with high unitarist streaks. The centre was accused by various groups of suffocating the subunits. In addition, reactions to the Abacha regime by some groups had led to demands for a review of the federal association. While some had called for a 'sovereign national conference', others had demands for a national conference, to discuss the state of the federation.

Nigeria's federation is highly centralized. The *exclusive list* of the federal government contains 68 items. These include citizenship, immigration, defence, policing, external affairs, mining, nuclear energy, regulation of political parties, and the public debt of the federation. The *concurrent list* of shared powers includes allocation of revenue, electoral law, universities, technological and post-primary education, scientific and technological research, and industrial commercial and agricultural development. The *local government functions* include roads, sewage and refuse disposal, registration of all births, and marriages, primary adult and vocational education, agriculture, health services, and any other functions conferred by the State House Assembly.

Candidly, the federation is heavily centralized. In Chapter Five we discussed this process of centralization. The pressures for a review of the legislative list seem understandable. The federal government has no business directly getting involved with agriculture, rural development, traditional matters, water supply, primary education and others. In many of these areas, beyond national policies for purposes of uniformity, it should give specific grants-in-aid to support activities of state and local governments' activities. Years of military rule have boldly given unitary streaks to the Nigerian Federation. It is however, likely that the legislative lists would be reviewed in favour of the states and local government.

It is hoped that with such reviewed lists would be a review of fiscal and monetary powers. Currently, the federal government raises revenue from mining rents and royalties, the petroleum profit tax, the personal income tax, import and export duties, and capital gains tax. State governments raise revenue from land taxes, estate duties, license fees, betting, and sales taxes. Local governments raise revenue from entertainment taxes, property tax, and trading and marketing licenses. It is hoped that state and local tax powers would be meaningfully expanded to enable each tier of government to meet its expenditure needs.

Conclusion

Candidly, Nigerians are so concerned with the distribution of resources, they often forget that it is even more important to produce what is to be shared. The argument is like a chicken and egg story, after a point. Some people feel that there is no need to help in the production of resources because those who contributed little, gain more. Yet if you do not produce, there is nothing to share. However, as long as you live in the same political community, you need to work out a mechanism for sharing resources through compromise. This is because of the realization that all are equal stakeholders in the process of nation building. It does seem that a number of actions need to be taken in the Nigerian federation:-

1.The revision of the legislative list in favour of the states and local governments seem to be a political imperative. Similarly, the *tax powers should be correspondingly reviewed*. This is not always the easiest exercise.

2.On the *distribution of oil resources*, it may be suggested that there may be a need to go back to the old dichotomy between *on-shore* and *offshore* oil. Fifty percent of the on-shore oil revenues should go to the states of origin on the basis of derivation principle while the other 50% goes to the DPA. However, fifty percent of the offshore oil revenues should go into a *stabilization fund* for fiscal equalization among tiers of government and among non-oil producing states. This should be used to relatively close any gaps between oil and non-oil producing states. Ten percent of the offshore oil revenues should go to the rehabilitation of mining areas (solid minerals and oil). Ten percent of the offshore oil should go to the social development (education, health, e.t.c.) of the oil mineral producing areas; while the remaining thirty percent of offshore oil revenue should go to the federation account for the usual distribution.

3.The RMAFC should be tasked with `the functions of monitoring and working out formal mechanism for fiscal equalization, vertically and horizontally. This can be periodically reviewed, and should rob the central government of the subjectivity involved in the grants it makes to *subnational* units, often with political overtones.

4.Greater inter-governmental interaction may reduce the problems associated with inter-tier conflicts. Under the Obasanjo administration, states and local governments were treated as virtual extensions of the federal government. Some of the avoidable conflicts in the federation under the Fourth Republic derive from the hangover of the military regime in which the centre had grown titanic. Curbing the unnecessary adventures of the centre has become a problem.

There are many arenas of cooperative inter-governmental relations. Politicians at this stage of Nigeria's development are either ill-equipped to deal with these problems or are unwilling to establish normal inter-governmental relations, even when so constitutionally provided.

Like most things in nation states, there is a need for mutual compromise to enable **fairness, justice** and **relative equity** lubricate the wheels of the federation. It is hoped that with more discussions and collective experience, the politics of distribution will not be a danger to the federation.

Notes and references

1.Allison Ayida, *The Nigerian Revolution, 1966-1976,* (Ibadan: Ibadan University Press, 1973), p. 7.

2.Joseph L. *LaPalombara,* "Distribution: A Crisis of Resource Management," in L. Binder, J. Coleman, J. LaPolombara, L. Pye, S. Verba and M. Weiner. (eds.), *Crises and Sequences in Political Development, op. cit.* (Princeton: Princeton University Press, 1971), p. 233.

3.David Easton, *The Political System* (New York: Knopf, 1953), pp. 129-34.

4.David Easton, *A Framework for Political Analysis* (Englewood Cliffs, New Jersey: Prentice Hall, 1965), p. 50. quoted in *LaPalombara, loc. cit.,* p. 234.

5.Harold D. Lasswell, *Politics: Who Gets What, When and How?* (New York: Meridian Books, World Publishing, 1936). Also, M. Abramowitz, *et. al., The Allocation of Economic Resources* (Stanford: Stanford University Press, 1959); H. Lasswell and A. Kaplan, *Power and Society* (New Haven: Yale University Press, 1950); J. D. Montgomery and W. J. Siffin (eds.) *Approaches to Development: Politics, Administration, and Change* (New York: McGraw-Hill, 1966).

6.James Coleman, "Education and Political Development," in J. S. Coleman (ed.) *Education and Political Development* (Princeton: Princeton University Press, 1965), p. 31.

7.*ibid.*, pp 31-32; also, A. Hirschman, *The Strategy of Economic Development* (New Haven: Yale University Press, 1958); Gerald Meier (ed.) *Leading Issues in Development Economics* (New York: OUP, 1964), Chapter V. These authors argue that concentration of resources in a few sectors creates disequilibria, which are positively functional to later attainment of equilibrium. This argument could be extended to the geographical dimension of the country.

8.See an economic argument on investments by Ragner Nurske, "Balanced Growth" in G. Meier, *op. cit.*, p. 250, that increased investment and productivity in one sector "will certainly not have favorable repercussion elsewhere in the economy." He argues for "balanced growth" in order to establish a pattern of mutually supporting investments over a range of industries wide enough to create a forward momentum."

9.Rustow, *op. cit.*, p. 80.

10.Paul Boothe, "Taxing, Spending and Sharing In Federations: Experience from Australia and Canada" in Paul Boothe (ed.) *Fiscal Relations In Federal Countries: Four Essays* (Ottawa: Forum of Federations. 2003), p.11.

11.*LaPalombara, loc. cit.* p. 236.

12. Justice R. Else-Mitchell, *Foreword*, in Commonwealth of Australia, *Equality in Diversity: Fifty Years of The Common Wealth Grants Commission* (Canberra: Australian Government Publishers Service, 1983), p. v.

13. In this chapter, we recognize that the issue of distribution transcends revenue sharing of federally derived resources. Other indices include the allocation and location of development projects as well as statuses. Given limited space and our effort to deal extensively with revenue allocation among *subnational* units (which is a "hot" issue in Nigeria); we shall not discuss the other aspects of distribution, thus confining ourselves to revenue sharing among states. This is in order to make it possible to handle the subject matter more effectively.

14.Adebayo Adedeji, *Nigerian Federal Finance: Its Development, Problems and Prospects* (London: Hutchinson Educational, 1968), p. 220. Also see Akpan H. Ekpo and Enamidem U. Ubok-Udom, (eds.) *Issues In Fiscal Federalism and Revenue Allocation* (Uyo: University of Uyo, 2003).

15. Adedeji, A. *op. cit.*, p. 12.

16. Nigeria, *Administrative and Financial Procedure under   the New Constitution: Financial Relations between the   Government of Nigeria and the Native Administration,   1946* (Lagos: Government   Printer, 1946). This was Phillipson's Report.

17. J.P. Mackintosh, *op. cit.* p. 561.

18.Nigeria, *Proceedings   of   the   General   Conference,* (Lagos: Government Printer, 1950), p. 239.

19. Nigeria, *Report of the Commission on Revenue Allocation* (Lagos: Government Printer, 1951). Other members of   the commission were D. A. Skelton and Sir Sidney   Phillipson.   Mr. Skelton died by drowning in the Lagos harbour   and   so   did   not participate.

20. Adedeji, (1969) *op. cit.,* p. 81.

21.Nigeria, *The Report of Fiscal Commission on Financial Effects of Proposed New Constitutional Arrangements* (Lagos: Government Printer, 1953). Sir Louis Chick was appointed the Sole Commissioner.

22.*ibid.,*

23. Adedeji (1969), *op. cit.,* p. 117.

24.The Commission comprised of Sir Jeremy Raisman (Chairman) and R. C. Tress. Its report was entitled *Report of Fiscal Commission* (London: HMSO, 1958), (Cmd. 481). The report is usually called the Raisman Report.

25.*Report of the Nigerian Constitutional Conference* (1957 Cmd. 207), p. 28.

26. Olu   Akaraogun,   "Revenue   Allocation   -   Debate   in   Nigeria: A Chapter of Opportunism", *Newbreed,* Lagos   (Dec 1970), p. 28.

27. Application of the derivation principle to the other import duties had been a source of dissatisfaction among the   regions. In allocating 30% of revenue from general import duties in the DPA, the commission was attempting to share federally derived revenues in the interest of more equality in distribution. The commission remarked that "this use of general import duties is quite different from the use made of other import duties in the existing system. The latter was intended to be deployed as a further application of the principle of derivation. Our own principles for the allocation of general import revenue involve a departure from derivation.

28. Raisman Report, p. 25.

29. This Commission's report was known as *Report of the Fiscal Review Commission* (Lagos: Federal Ministry of Information, Printing Division, 1964). This report is hereafter referred to as Binns Report, and its revenue formula referred to as the Binns formula.

30.Nigeria, *Official Gazette of the Federal Republic of Nigeria* (Lagos), Vol. 52, Government Notice No. 1072, p. 911.

31. A. Adedeji (1969) *op. cit.*, p. 233.

32.*ibid.*,

33. The principle of derivation refers to a system whereby federally collected revenues on regional produce are returned to regions on the basis of each region's production or consumption of particular items on which customs and excise duties are levied.

34. Binns Commission Report, p. 17.

35.*ibid.*,

36. Adedeji (1969), *op. cit.* p. 233; Binn Report, p. 14.

37. Akaraogun, *loc. cit.*, p. 34.

38. The Eastern Government opposed the principle of need "on the grounds that it would tend to impede national economic development by restraining the free flow of factors of production in those areas of greatest potential economic growth." (Adedeji, *op. cit.*, p.235), Binns Report, p. 20. But it was exactly the principle of the need, which suited the Eastern Region in 1958. This is reflective of the degree of autonomy of the regions and lack of mutual trust as well as the unwillingness of the various *subnational* units to share their resources with one another. The concept of "Nigeria" had not yet gone beyond mere rhetoric. The commission rejected the principle of need; 1) because of the problems it raises in a federation like Nigeria; and 2) because of the expectation of significant change of the economic position of some regions in the future (Binns Report, p. 20).

39. This is very close to our "logic of federal equality" which became adopted later. Essentially, however, this principle may be regarded as one of relatively "even" or "balanced" growth among *subnational* units.

40. Federal Republic of Nigeria, *Report of the Interim Revenue Allocation Review Committee* (Lagos: Federal Ministry of Information, 1968). Other members of this commission were Prof. Aboyade, Mr. A. E. Ekukinam, Mr. Ibrahim Tahir, Mr. P. O. A. Dada, Mr. F. M. C. Obi, Mr. Ahmed Talib, Prof. T. M. Yesufu andMr. D. O. Ogunyemi. All

members of this commission were Nigerians. Hence, A. Ayida remarked:

> The high quality and the objective nature of the Indigenous Dina Report show that there is no need in future for an expatriate expert or experts to be invited for subsequent Revenue Allocation Commissions. Ayida, op. cit., p. 9.

41.Dina Report, paragraph 77.

42.The ten principles are: 1) independent revenue, 2) derivation, 3) basic needs, 4) minimum national standard, 5) population, 6) tax effort, 7) financial prudence, 8) fiscal efficiency, 9) balance development, and 10) national interest.

43.Decree No. 13, 1969. See *Supplement to Official Gazette*, 12, Vol. 57, 12 March 1970. By this decree, outstanding credit of the DPA at the end of each quarter should be distributed among the states thus:a) One half shall be divided equally among the states, and b) The other half shall be divided among the states proportionately to the population of each state."*Laws of the Federal Republic of Nigeria, op. cit.*, p. 50.

44.Ayida, *op. cit.*

45.Chief I. O. Dina, "Fiscal Measures" in Allison Ayida and H.M.A. Onitiri (eds.) *Reconstruction and Development in Nigeria: Proceedings of a Conference*, (Ibadan: Oxford University Press, 1971).

46.At the same conference, Chief Dina expressed his dissatisfaction with the derivation as a principle of revenue-sharing:

> The derivation principle has bedeviled the development of a rational and equitable system of revenue allocation in Nigeria. It has poisoned inter-governmental relationship and has exacerbated inter-regional rivalry and conflict. Perhaps more than any other single factor, it has hampered the development of a sense of national unity or common citizenship in Nigeria.
>
> Moreover, its application has been arbitrary, lacking in consistency. It is applied in full to some tax revenues and partially to others, while a different set of formulae is applied in the allocation of revenue from some other taxes.

Chief Dina went further to suggest that the "principle of derivation should therefore be discarded as quickly as possible and a system of allocation of revenues designed essentially for a dynamic development policy evolved." Also in Akaraogun, *loc. Cit.*, p. 36.

47.Mr. J. D. Gomwalk, Governor of Benue-Plateau State in *The Nigeria Standard* (Jos) 26 May 1973, 9.18.

48.Midwestern State Government, *Revenue Sources in Midwestern Nigeria* (Benin: Ministry of Home Affairs and information, 1970), p. 5.

49.*ibid.*, p. 6.

50.Federal Government of Nigeria, *"Budget Broadcast, 1973-74, loc. cit.* p. xiv.

51.Federal Government of Nigeria, *"Budget Broadcas"t*, 1974-75, *loc. cit.* p. 7.

52.*The Nigerian Observer* (Benin) 4 May 1974, p.1.

53.*ibid.*,

54. *The Nigerian Observer*, 28 May 1974, p.1.

55. *ibid.*,

56. *The Nigerian Herald* (Ilorin) 23 May 1974, p.1.

57. *The New Nigerian* (Kaduna) 27 May 1974, p. 8.

58. *Daily Times* (Lagos) 14 May 1974, p.31.

59. *The Nigerian Observer*, 18 May 1974, p.1.

60. *The Nigerian Observer*, 25 May 1974, p. 1 and 3.

61.*New Nigerian* 27, June 1974, p. 10.

62. *The Nigerian Observer*, 21 January 1974, p. 1. Alhaji Shehu Shagari announced that the "present system is a temporary one" and that it "would be reviewed by the proposed allocation commission," after which the 50% equality and 50% population basis of sharing the DPA "would then cease to exist."

63.This formula was announced by the Head of the Federal Military Government and Commander in Chief of the Armed Forces in his 1 October 1974 Broadcast. *Daily Times*, 2 October 1974, p. 7 and 16.

64. *Daily Times*, 2, October 1974, p. 7.

65.*ibid.*,

66. *ibid.*,

67.The *Daily Sketch* (Ibadan) editorial of 14 May 1974 suggested that revenues from petroleum oil be distributed 20% to state of origin, 5% to federal government, and 75% to the other eleven governments of the federation (Adaraogun, *loc. cit.*,p. 45).

68.The Aboyade Commission comprised, Prof. O. Aboyade (*Chairman*), Prof. G.O Nwankwo, Mallam M. Daura, Dr. J.S. Odama, Dr. O. Omoruyi, Prof. F.A. Teriba and Mr. C.E. Olumese.

69.T. Y. Danjuma, "Revenue Sharing and the Political Economy of Nigerian Federalism" in J. Isawa Elaigwu, P. C. Logams and H. S. Galadima (eds.) *Federalism and Nation-Building In Nigeria: The Challenges of the Twenty-First Century* (Abuja: NCIR, 1994), p. 91.

70.The members of the Okigbo Commission were; Dr. P.N.C. Okigbo (*Chairman*), Alh. U. Bello, Alh. B. Ismaila, Dr. G.B. Leton, Prof. A.O. Philips, Alh. A. Talib, Dr. W.O. Uzoaga and Mr. A.A. Feese (Secretary).

71.T. Y. Danjuma, *loc. cit.*, p. 93.

72.T. Y. Danjuma, *loc. cit.*, pp. 94-95.

73.T. Y. Danjuma, *loc. cit.*, p. 100.

74. *ibid.*, p. 101.

75. *ibid.*, pp. 104-105.

76. *ibid.*, p. 103, Table 5.

77.Hamman Tukur, "Speech of Engr. Hamman Tukur, Chairman RMAFC at A Public Lecture Organized By Lagos State House of Assembly on July 29, 2004 at Sheraton Hotel, Lagos." p. 5; and Hamman Tukur, "Address by the Chairman of the Revenue Mobilization Allocation and Fiscal Commission... to The President on the Occasion of the Presentation of the Reviewed Revenue Allocation Formula", September 20, 2004, p. 1.

78.Hamman Tukur, *ibid.*, p.1.

79.*ibid.*, p. 2.

80.Hamman Tukur, Speech of July 29, 2004, *loc. cit.*

81.*Newswatch* Magazine (Lagos), p. 30-31.

82.Sec L. N. Chete, "Fiscal Federalism and Macroeconomic Management in Nigeria", *Journal of Economic Management* Vol. 5, No. 1, 1998. Hamman Tukur, speech of July 29, 2004, p. 6; Akpan H. Ekpo, "Fiscal Federalism: Nigeria's Post Independent Experiences, 1960-1990", *World Development Report* Vol. 22, No 8. 1994; and Bade Onimode, "Federalism and Resources Management in Nigeria," Conference paper, 2002, (unpublished).

83.Also see Olufemi Fajana, "Three-and-A-Half Decade of Fiscal Federalism In Nigeria," in J. Isawa Elaigwu and R. A. Akindele (eds.) *Foundations of Nigerian Federalism: 1960 -1995* (2nd Edition) (Jos: IGSR, 2001), pp. 105-124.

84.Fajana, *loc. cit.*, pp. 114-115.

10

FEDERALISM IN NIGERIA'S NEW*
DEMOCRATIC POLITY

Nigeria returned to civil democratic rule on May 29, 1999, after many years of military rule. As the country embarks on a new democratic journey, what are the challenges faced by the Nigerian Federation? What problems have arisen in the federal process? How are these being resolved or tackled? What are the prospects of federalism in the new century — especially in the first decade of this century? In order to answer these questions, it is suggested that:

i) the Nigerian federation, at the dawn of the 21st century, is characterized by strong unitarist streaks as a response to almost three decades of military rule;

ii) there are, therefore, intense pressures for a review of the legislative list to devolve many of the powers concentrated at the centre to subnational units;

iii) the issues of resource distribution and/or management have become important issues of debate as Nigerian groups reassess the federation;

iv) in the context of the new democratic polity, new issues have emerged as part of the politics of federalism in response to the explosion of subnational identities; and

v) the quality of leadership is important in effecting necessary compromises in Nigeria's reconciliation system.

Federalism in Nigeria's New Democratic Polity

When the military handed over power to the civilian politicians in 1999, the federation was characterized by a very strong central government; popular agitation for a more decentralized structure; dissatisfaction with the distribution of scarce but available resources; Communal conflicts; and demands by some subnational groups for greater self-determination. What has been the nature of Nigeria's federation since May 1999? What are the new challenges for the Nigerian federation at the beginning of this millennium?

In the terminal days of Nigeria's transition to civil rule, a number of issues had become evident in the political horizon. Given many years of military rule, the Nigerian polity was like a bottle of wine, properly corked and airtight. With the dawn of democracy and the opening of the bottle, the wine explosively popped up. Some Nigerians wonder why, six years after, the bubbles have not settled down.

The Nigerian federation faced a number of challenges by May 1999. Among these were: i) issues of centralization and decentralization in the relations among the three tiers of government; ii) resource distribution and/or management; and iii) the politics of federalism and aggressive subnationalism. There are many issues of interest in the current dynamics of Nigerian federalism, but let us concentrate on these three major points to illustrate the trend in the operation of the Nigerian federation.

1) Decentralization and Centralization

The military had left behind a highly centralized federation. Some Nigerian observers have argued that if the centre gets decentralized in its functions and accompanying powers, there would be less to fight among politicians for the centre, and there would be greater political stability in the system. This is not really as simple as it seems. It does seem that the federal government will continue to attract politicians who feel that their political stature and ambitions transcend the state level.

Relations among the three tiers of government illustrate how the political operators of each tier perceive the other. The current debate is illustrated by these summaries of perceptions:

i) *State government*: the federal government's powers are too sprawling and it is carrying out functions it has no business carrying out: its powers should be curbed to allow the federal system to breathe a new lease of life from the squeeze imposed by years of military rule; the revenue formula must be reviewed to reflect these changes in functions; afterall, we are closer to the grassroot and should have more resources to carry out development programmes: the fiscal dominance of the centre has made it so priced that politicians would do anything to get there;

ii) *Federal government*: remember the period between 1960 and 1966? Do you want a weak federal centre unable to give the country a sense of security? The trend all the world over is to have a strong federal government which can intervene to carry out fiscal and developmental equalization among the component units of the federation; the states and local governments are complacent about revenue generation and must realize that autonomy in a federal association presupposes fiscal autonomy;

iii) *Local government*: state governments are still living in the past; they have not realized that local governments are now constitutionally guaranteed third tier of government and are therefore autonomous of state governments; state governors must stop removing local government chairmen as if they are bureaucrats; states should release appropriate statutory allocations to the local governments promptly: in fact, states should be abolished because they have outlived their usefulness;

iv) *State governments*: local governments are the most problematic tier in the federation; they lack executive capacity; their leaders are inexperienced and mistake federally desirable autonomy for independence or sovereignty; they even forget the provision that the State House of Assembly can make laws specifying additional functions for them; they generate no revenue from internal sources and expect to be autonomous; really they need education on their roles; they have so much money which they are unable to manage properly partly because of their lack of executive capacity; money spent on local government is money thrown down the drain-pipe; give such money to the state government for a more productive performance; autonomy for the local government is autonomy for excellence in wastage and mismanagement.

These summaries reflect the current state of debate on the vertical structure of the federation and the powers and functions of each tier in the context of the politics of power sharing.

In the relations among Federal State and Local Governments, there are signs of *residual militarism* in the actions of political executives. The ghost of the military's politics of control has had difficulty leaving the scene. Federal officials treat state and local government officials with overbearing arrogance. In similar ways, state governors patronizingly relate to local government chairmen.

In federal-state interactions, the relations between President Olusegun Obasanjo and state governors have oscillated between 'hot' and 'cold'. The State Governors are not pleased with the president's way of operating as if he is still a military President.[11] They accuse him of taking actions in flagrant disregard of federally desirable and constitutionally guaranteed autonomy of state governments— especially as provided in the legislative lists. Let us illustrate these concerns with three cases.

The first source of conflict between both tiers of government was the National Minimum Wage (NMW). On Labour Day (May 1, 2000), President Obasanjo announced a national minimum wage of 5,500 for state governments and 7,500 for the federal government.[12] Apparently under pressure from the Nigeria Labour Congress, the President did not consult the state governors or the National Assembly. The governors were livid with anger and reminded the President that the era of centralization under military rule was over.[13] They insisted that only the states could negotiate wages with their employees. While recognizing the powers of the federal government to set the minimum wage, they held that the President could not announce such a wage without due consultations with state governments (as employers of labour) and without sending a bill to the National Assembly.

For almost a year the country was gripped by wage crises[14] and strikes because many state governments could not afford to pay the new wages and arrears as demanded by their labour force. Some analysts believe that the President hastily announced the National

Minimum Wage in order to court the support of the labour force against the National Assembly with which he was having problems. General Obasanjo's military background and unilateral actions goaded him into a number of political hot waters with the state governments.

In a similar manner, the federal government introduced the Universal Basic Education (UBE) programme. This programme is aimed at providing free universal basic education from primary school to the first three years of Secondary School. The federal government announced this programme and went ahead to launch it in Sokoto, before a bill was sent to the National Assembly. State governors complained of lack of consultation. They claimed that the matter was under the concurrent legislative list, and that since the federal government was going to depend on states for the implementation of the programme, states should have been adequately consulted.

In addition, some state governments are controlled by political parties different from the one at the federal level. Each political party has its own programme on education. They therefore frowned on the 'military' fashion in which federal programmes were announced in areas of concurrent legislation, without regard to the priorities of states, especially where states were to be the implementing agency. The state governors and the Vice-President later met to harmonize areas of disagreement over this programme, but many grey areas remained. Adequate political consultations could have reduced tensions in federal-state relations. While, the federal government accused state governments of sabotaging the UBE programme, state governments felt that they could not abandon their programmes in order to execute federal programmes. The federal government had similar problems in getting the cooperation of state governments in the implementation of its Poverty Alleviation Programme (PAP), now replaced by the National Poverty Eradication Programme (NAPEP). Again the states reminded the federal government that each government had its own poverty eradication programme. If the federal government desired the cooperation of states in the implementation of its programmes, it should carry state governments along. Unlike the German Basic law, the Nigerian Constitution of 1999 does not provide for states as implementors of federal laws.

There is also the issue of the Nigeria Police Force and the maintenance of Law and Order. Given the ineptitude and inefficiency of the Nigeria Police in the maintenance of law and order, governors of states with large urban centres and high rates of crimes, found themselves helpless in dealing with crimes. Police is a federal matter, even though the Governor of a state is the Chief Law Officer of the State. As happened in the Second Republic, many governors complained that State Commissioners of Police ignored orders from them but took orders only from their boss, the Inspector-General of Police.[15] In frustration, some state governors demanded for a review of the Constitution to enable the states establish their own police forces. However, some state governors are opposed to the idea of establishing state police forces and have said so. They expressed their reluctance to spend their meagre resources on maintaining state police. These governors opted for a greater level of decentralization of the Nigeria police to enable it respond to problems on the ground more effectively and promptly. In some states, the government officially resorted to using vigilante groups to maintain law and order.[16]

The issues of Revenue Allocation and local governments have also been areas of conflict between the Federal and State government. Only recently, (December 10, 2004) the Supreme Court gave judgement in favour of the Lagos State government making it clear that the federal government had no power to withhold the funds of state governments which had created additional local councils.

Nor has the relations between the National and State Assemblies been smooth. In view of the confusion over the actual tenure of Chairmen of Local Governments, State Houses of Assembly had made laws limiting the term of office of these chairmen to two years in some states, and three years in others.

In an attempt to sort out the problem, the Senate had set up a committee to make recommendations to the National Assembly. The State Houses of Assembly felt that this was a usurpation of the powers given to them under Section 7 of the Constitution that the "Government of every state shall... ensure their existence under a Law which provides for the establishment, structure, composition, finance and functions of such councils." They went to court.[17] In its judgement, the Supreme Court upheld the position of the Draft on local government.

Similarly, some state governments created or tried to create additional local governments in their states. Bayelsa State, for example, created new Local Government Councils, and deployed the chairmen of the old local governments to new local governments. The Senate of the Federal Republic declared this action a nullity because it violated Section 8(3) of the Constitution which provided elaborate processes for the creation of new local governments including a referendum.[18] In addition, the Senate argued that unless the list of local governments as contained in the First Schedule, Section 3, Part 1, was duly amended, no new local government was legal. The action of the Senate was declared a nullity by the Supreme Court. In case of Lagos State vs Federal Government, the Supreme Court declared that while state had the power to create local governments, they should send these to National Assembly for constitutional amendments. President Obasanjo withheld the statutory allocations due to all local governments in Lagos State until the state reversed to the old local governments. Lagos State again sued the federal government to release the allocations due to the old 20 local government councils. The Supreme Court declared that the President had no authority to withhold the statutory allocations due to Lagos State local governments, the President continued to ignore court order. Attempt to reach a political accord with the Lagos State government, only led to the release of a part of the fund by the Presidency. The Presidency, having goaded the Lagos State government into an apparent political solution, turned round to insist on elections to be conducted into the 20 Local governments, before the rest of the funds would be released. The Presidency was trying to score a political victory out of an illegal act. At the time of writing this chapter, this issue had not been resolved. The former Chief Justice, Muhammed Uwais had indicated his frustration with the situation in his valedictory speech. He had wished that it had been possible to arrest President Obasanjo for contempt of court. In state-local government relations, there have also been cold wars. Local Governments complain about undue interference from State Governments. As an illustration, the Sokoto State government was taken to court by 15 Local Governments Councils in the State and the court restrained the state government from deducting 3% of its statutory allocation for funding the Sokoto Emirate Council as passed by the State House of Assembly.[19]

In addition, local government chairmen have argued that state governors, (especially where the chairman comes from a party different from the Governor's) plot to remove such chairmen by using the Audit powers of the state. State Governors have also been accused of plotting with the State Houses of Assembly to shorten the tenure of elected local government officials to three years in order to put their supporters in office. In some states there have been protests by elected local government officials to three years against attempts by State Houses of Assembly to reduce their term to two years. Thus, in Imo State, the police arrested 11 Local Government Councillors along with 300 others who had gone to the State House of Assembly to protest the reduction of their tenure from three to two years.[20] In the case of Bayelsa State where new local governments were created, some councillors took the Governor and Chairmen of the Local Government Councils to court because they believed that it was 'illegal' to share funds from the Federation Account with new and illegal local governments. Similarly, these chairmen also went to court to protest their deployment to new local governments as a form of illegality and disenfranchisement of the people, being perpetrated by some state governments.[21]

However, many governors claim that a majority of chairmen and councillors of local governments only sit down to share money drawn from the Federation Account and hardly embark on development projects. President Obasanjo had publicly chided the chairmen over this issue. The governors are at pains to point out that the chairmen of local governments do not have the powers they had under the 1989 Constitution, and that they should be enlightened on this matter. In addition, the governors are angry that the federal government relates directly with local government councils, which operate under them. They argue that the 1999 Constitution, section 162(6) provides for the *state joint local government account* into which Statutory allocation from federal and state government accruing to the local governments should be deposited.

The states are therefore opposed to what they perceive as attempts by the Federal Government to relate directly to local governments under them. They cite the case of the federal government aiding the local government chairmen to buy security vehicles and gadgets for the maintenance of law and order at local level without the knowledge and involvement of state governors, as evidence of federal government's interference in matters under state governments. The state governors are the chief security officers of the state and should be involved in this kind of arrangement.

The leaders at both federal and state levels of government have so far, demonstrated some caution in their interactions in order not to endanger Nigeria's new democratic polity. It does seem that personality clashes and the lack of adequate culture of relations among the component tiers of government, after long period of military rule, have bedeviled relations among tiers of government. President Olusegun Obasanjo has been accused by some Nigerians of early targeting his opponents in his anti-corruption crusades. They easily quote the cases of Governor Dariye of Plateau and Governor Alamieyesiagha of Bayelsa as examples. These two governors were apprehended by the metropolitan police in London, with regard to money laundering offences, with the prodding of the federal government. This critics point to the cases of some other governors who are close to the President and are reputedly very corrupt, but have not been apprehended. It is hoped that as a new democratic culture of consultations and the rule of law take root in the polity, and as new patterns of inter-governmental relations are established, unnecessary and abrasive conflicts will give way to cooperation and interdependence among tiers of government.

Let us turn briefly to the issue of centralization and decentralization of power in the federation. Federalism presupposes non-centralization of powers among the component units of the federation.[22] No one component—federal, State or (as in the 1999 Constitution) local government—is superior to the other. They all act directly on the people. If there is no superior government, which tier devolves powers to the other? Herein lies the difficulty of devolution of powers in the Nigerian federation, like some others in the world. A review of legislative list is one effective way of dealing with the devolution of powers. It is hoped that the process of constitutional review/amendments will take care of some of these issues.

Given the post-military rule situation and the emergence of a very strong central government, some Nigerians have called for *true federalism*. By *true federalism*, the protagonists of a weak central government refer to a confederation or what they claim to be the classical model of federalism delineated by K.C. Wheare. This is evident in the 1995 *Report of the Constitutional Conference Containing the Resolutions and Recommendations*, Volume 11, which recommended 'innovation' to Nigerian federalism thus:

> It should be true federalism with clear demarcation of powers and functions among the levels of government. In the exercise of those powers and functions assigned by the Constitution, each level of government should be autonomous.[23]

However, as Ranjit Sarkaria of India correctly observed:

> The classical concept of federation which envisaged two parallel governments of coordinate jurisdiction, operating in isolation from each other in watertight compartments, is no where a functional reality now. With the emergence of the Social Welfare State, the traditional theory of federalism completely lost its ground. After First World War, it became very much a myth even in the old federations... By the middle of the twentieth Century, Federalism had come to be understood as dynamic process of cooperation and shared action between two or more levels of government, with increasing interdependence and centrist trends.[24]

In essence, the old sense of autonomy of component units in their areas of jurisdiction, have given way to cooperation, interdependence and interaction. That there is still a call for a return to a nostalgic classical model of federalism, however, is a reflection of the extent to which centrifugal forces are at work in the current Nigerian federation, as groups seek greater autonomy or self-rule at *subnational* state level in order to control their destiny. Paradoxically, the greater the number of states, the less autonomous the content of this self-rule, and the stronger the federal centre.

However, the prospects of a review of the legislative list in favour of subnational units are high. The future is most likely to witness a relatively less strong centre than Nigeria has now. But it is unlikely that

Nigerians would revert to the loose federation they had between 1960 and 65, or even adopt a confederal constitution.[25]

It can be argued that the federal legislative list (or the Exclusive List) is overloaded. It does seem more appropriate that the federal government should make policies for agriculture, health, education and others. Thus, there should be no need for a Federal Ministry of Agriculture, for example. A unit should be responsible for agricultural policies. It can also provide for federal forms of intervention in research, capacity and funding. On the other hand, given the peculiar development of Nigeria's formal western education, the recommendation by the 1995 constitutional conference on education may be unworkable. The Report left primary education to local governments; and transferred education at secondary and tertiary levels to states' legislative lists. The intention of such action is understood, but Nigeria's experiences show that the problem with the educational sector is not just funding. These are human problems of capacity and attitude. The gross anti-intellectual posture in the country is part of these. May be, universities should continue to be in the concurrent list. But they should be rationalized. There is no reason why seven good Medical Schools, six Faculties of Law; six or seven Faculties of Engineering; seven Faculties of Information and Computer Services, as well as Architecture and others—spread out across the country, properly staffed and appropriately funded—should not serve as centres of excellence for the country. No single state can handle these problems. It lies squarely at the door of the federal government. Paradoxically some state governments are requesting the federal government to take over their universities, while new universities are springing up in other states of the country.

In essence, the democratic pressures in the Nigerian federation, is likely to respond to the current centrifugal swing in the federal pendulum. It seems unlikely that Nigeria will eventually have a federation with a weak centre in the next decade, unless something dramatic happens. In addition, as political leaders imbibe greater democratic values, as democratic institutions get grafted and embellished by the federal grid, and as new cultures of tolerance and cooperation in intergovernmental relations are imbibed, Nigeria may witness a gradual adjustment in its vertical federal structure in favour of more appropriate power-sharing formulae among the levels of government. For now, centrifugal forces are likely to continue to push for a drastic reduction in the strength of the central government, beginning with the revenue sharing formula in the federation.

Another important challenge to Nigerian federation is the issue of resource distribution and management.

2. Resource Distribution and Management

Resource distribution includes both statuses and material resources. In fact, it includes the distribution of all scarce but allocatable resources. The locations of government projects as well as the pattern of recruitment into political offices and the public services are also yardsticks for measuring the fairness of leaders in the distribution process in Nigeria.

In order to ensure relative fairness in the appointment of people from various groups into the Federal Public Service, government established the *Federal Character Commission* to monitor the pattern of appointment into all the public services of federal, state and local governments, in order to give Nigerians, a sense of belonging to the nation. Cries of discrimination and marginalization by groups have not abated since the establishment of this commission. But, at least, there is an office to which complaints can now be addressed for redress.

The 1999 Constitution provides in Section 162 (2) that the Revenue Mobilization, Allocation and Fiscal Commission (RMAFC) has the function of tabling before the National Assembly a draft revenue allocation formula. The National Assembly shall then deliberate on this document, taking into account the principles of "population, equality of states, internal revenue generation, landmass, terrain as well as population density". The National Assembly shall note that the principles of derivation applied on all proceeds from all natural resources will not be less than 13%. Since the advent of the new democratic polity, State Governors have argued that a new allocation formula should be put in place giving the states, at least 40%. As a matter of fact, a delegation representing state governors made the same point to the members of the RMAFC. This point was reinforced by the resolution of the Governors' Forum's Meeting in Abuja in August 2000.

Generally, given the centralization of political power under the military, the centre became a financial titan, as military rulers altered the revenue formula[26] as they deemed fit. They did not need to debate the formula at any legislative forum, except at the Armed Forces Ruling Council or the Provisional Ruling Council. There have been calls for the revision of the legislative list and accompanying tax powers in favour of local governments and states. The argument is that the federal centre has too much funds at its disposal, thus encouraging it to engage in policy adventures into areas it should not, and into activities reserved for other tiers of government.

On the horizontal level, there have been cries of 'marginalization' by all groups. The oil producing states of Niger-Delta are angry that the dividends of oil produced in their area, go to other parts of the country, without adequate concerns for their own interests. Basically while oil accounts for over 80% of the country's annual revenue, it has not changed the lives of the Niger-Delta peoples. While the Constitution provides for at least 13% revenue (on the principles of derivation) to the oil producing area, the governors of these states argue that the federal government only agreed to pay these funds to the oil-producing states from January 2000, and has failed to do so between May 29 to December 1999. In response, the governors of the South-South Zone decided to demand for 100% control of their resources. As Governor Ibori of Delta State puts it:

...the Federal Government has not, and we believe does not intend to resolve that very provision of the constitution, so we are not asking for 13 per cent any more, what we are taking now is everything, the 100% per cent control.[27]

The point is that, as in Canada and Australia, the Revenue Commission should be tasked to carry out two functions, in addition, to its current functions. It should carry out fiscal equalization on a vertical dimension, to ensure that funds are available to all three tiers of government to carry out their functions. Furthermore, its fiscal equalization measures on a horizontal level, should carry out relative equalization among states in order to ensure some political stability.

In response to the complaints of neglect in the Niger-Delta, a new body the *Niger-Delta Development Commission* (NDDC) has been established, to replace the old (OMPADEC). The NDDC is designed to alleviate poverty in the Delta area and embark on development projects aimed at improving the quality of lives of the average Niger-Delta person.

Similarly, states with solid minerals also complain that inspite of environmental degradation as a result of mining activities in their areas, they have not been adequately compensated. They are therefore calling for the establishment of the *Solid Minerals Producing Area Development Commission* (SOMPADEC). Interestingly, all the states from which hydroelectric power is generated have also called for the establishment of *Hydro Power Producing Areas Development Commission* (HYPPADEC) to compensate them for the consequences of any environmental damages caused by the activities associated with the generation of hydro-related energy.

Since the current quarrels are over the nature of distribution and not over the recognition of claims by contending parties, compromises will continue to be found. While the federal government went to court to seek the definition of the on-shore and offshore minerals (or oil) in the context of resource distribution, there have been pressures for a political, rather than a legal solution of the matter. This was done when a law was passed merging offshore and on-shore. Since then, however, some Northern states have gone to court to challenge this law. In addition, the politicians are likely to strike compromises over the percentage of resources in the Federation Account, which should be allocated on the basis of derivation. Currently, all mineral resources belong to the federation, and the 13% of the proceeds return to the state of origin of such minerals (including petroleum). Given the centrifugal pulls in the federation, the percentage of the derivation principle may go up gradually in the decade.[28]

One disturbing trait in the politics of leadership and resource distribution is the extent to which actions of leaders (military and/or civilian) can be easily ethnicized. It is very easy for a leader's mandate to be ethnicized or geoethnicized by his people, by the way they lay claim to him. It is also easy for a leader to ethnicize his mandate by his policies and actions. Usually, a leader's mandate being ethnicized by his people becomes more dangerous if the leader also ethnizes his mandate through his official actions in government. The qualities of fairness and justice in a leader cannot be over-emphasized in the process of nation building in a federal context. Let us now turn to the politics of Nigerian federalism and the challenges of aggressive subnationalism.

3) Aggressive Subnationalism, Democracy and the Politics of Federalism

At the terminal period of transition from military to civil rule in 1998-99, there were signs of resurgence of aggressive subnationalism, which had been suppressed under the regime of General Abacha. After May 29, 1999 when the military handed over power to civilians, latent aggressive subnationalism exploded into violence.

One effect of the overcentralization of power by various military regimes was the emergence of strong centrifugal forces, which felt disadvantaged in the system. Many subnational groups felt that if the Nigerian federation were not as centralized as it was, they would have had a fairer deal in the federation.

On the horizontal dimension, there were many expressions of dissatisfaction with the federation by many groups. The summary of positions expressed below, reflect the nature of concerns by various groups:

i) why should one group of Nigerians tend to monopolize the leadership of Nigeria, (that is the presidency or head of government)? We must have it this time or we will re-assess our relations within the federal association;

ii) why is it that the major resources which gives blood to the Nigerian federation comes from my area and yet there is no evidence of the impact of this wealth on the lives of my people? We would like to control resources from our area in order to improve the quality of lives of our people. We must discuss the adequate sharing of this and other resources now or pack it up;

iii) what makes some parts of Nigeria attract more federal presence in terms of industrialization and the location of major federal projects to the exclusion of our area? Is this a federation? If so, should there not be more equitable distribution of resources? Should the federal presence not be felt all over the country? Or are we federally pariah?

iv) why is it that some Nigerian groups think that they must concentrate political and economic powers in their hands? Do they realize that federal compromise involves sharing and not concentration? If we lose our political guarantee against their economic powers we shall have to re-assess our position in this federation;

v) in the context of a relatively primitive capitalist system with a dominant state role in the economy (inspite of efforts at privatization), the powers of the centre are very important, therefore, you cannot divorce political from economic power; to rob us of the access to political power is tantamount to undercutting our economic power; this we shall not accept; the principles of June 12 must therefore be adequately addressed or we shall pull out of the federation;

vi) those of us who fought over the nature of the federal association are not fools; we are watching the greed of others as they share political and economic powers; we shall not originate the excision from the polity this time, but we shall not allow anyone to go; those who betrayed us the last time, cannot do it twice, and if they try to go, we shall force them to stay; to 'keep Nigeria one' is a task that was accomplished, and must continue to be done, so let us sit down and discuss; and

vii) what makes our bigger brothers behave as if they do not need this country anymore, and that only those of us who are small need it; are they saying they have milked the system enough and now that there is nothing to exploit, they must quit? What have we gained in our areas from this federal association—nothing; yet the smaller groups are in the majority; we must discuss our new pattern of relationship in the federal system to take account of our grievances.

Under this *democratic* polity, the suppressed *angst* of various groups with the Nigerian federation found expressions in many ways. The emergence of a fiscally and politically titanic centre had questioned the basic sense of security of groups. Let us illustrate this with some cases.

As a result of the Constitutional Conference of 1994/95, Nigeria was informally divided into 6 geopolitical zones.[29] These zones were regarded as development zones and zones for sharing resources among Nigerian groups. The Southwest zone, from the Abacha days had pressed for a Sovereign National Conference to discuss the restructuring of Nigeria. In essence, it was asking for a return to the old regions with their accompanying autonomy. This demand was partly predicated on the assumption that the federation was too centralized and that those who controlled political power at the centre also controlled resources, including their extraction and distribution. They therefore opted for the old regional autonomy (between 1960 and 65) in order to control their resources and pace of development.

After May 1999, the *O'dua People's Congress* (OPC) declared its stand for the freedom of Yorubas to go it alone as an independent unit. It declared its desire to protect and defend Yoruba interests anywhere in Nigeria. The first eruption of crises was in Shagamu between OPC-backed group and Hausa settlers. Many people were killed and goods were destroyed. The corpses of Hausa men, which were carried back to Kano, generated a retaliatory wave of violence in that city against Yorubas. In response, Northern youths formed the *Arewa People's Congress (APC)* to challenge OPC violence.

OPC violence at Ketu and other places in Lagos angered the Ibos, who also set up the *Igbo Peoples' Congress* (IPC) to deal with what they considered OPC's unwarranted meddlesomeness and violence. The OPC violence in Lagos got to a point at which the President threatened the Governor of Lagos State with a declaration of a State of Emergency in the State, unless he could restore law and order. Lagos had become extremely unsafe. Many people saw OPC's espousal of Yoruba nationalism as the reason for OPC leaders who had been declared wanted being shielded from the police.

If OPC activities were not properly curbed by President Obasanjo, because of the logic of federal autonomy of Yorubas espoused by that group, why should President Obasanjo deal with political manifestations of autonomy in other states? Some Northern states, then chose to use *Sharia* law to declare their federally desirable autonomy. Since May 1999, it was clear that the old North had lost political power, even though it had voted massively for General Obasanjo. The announcement of the introduction of the *Supreme Sharia* in Zamfara State, introduced a new factor in the politics of federalism. Up till then, state governments had operated *Sharia* law as provided in the Constitutions of 1979, 1989 and 1999—it was applicable only to civil proceedings involving Islamic personal law (such as inheritance, divorce and others). The *Supreme Sharia* expanded the parameters of *Sharia* Law to include criminal matters. As a result of this *Sharia* Law, two thieves were amputated in Zamfara State. A seventeen-year-old girl was also flogged eighty times for fornication in the same state. In Kano and Katsina States a number of people were convicted for consuming alchoholic drinks and were sentenced to varying number of strokes of the cane.

Since its introduction in Zamfara State, *Sharia* Law has been adopted in ten other northern States.[30] News of its introduction in Kaduna State (which is multi-ethnic and multi-religious in nature) led to gross communal violence and death of many Nigerians. The killing of Ibos and others in Kaduna extracted reciprocal killings of Hausa-Fulani Muslims in Abia and Imo States. In fact, the State governors of Abia, Imo, Enugu, Anambra and Ebonyi States (of the Southeastern zone) called for a Confederal Nigeria.[31] The governors were quickly backed by the Yoruba *Afenifere* leader, Chief Abraham Adesanya, who argued that there was hardly any difference between "true federation as demanded by Yorubas" and "confederacy which the *Igbos* are now demanding." In his usually blunt style, President Obasanjo described the call for a confederation as "highly mischievous and extremely unpatriotic."[32] Mischievous or not, the demand for confederation by the Southeast zone sent shivers down the political spine of the North which then sent emissaries to the Southeast on reconciliation trips.

Following closely these developments was the announced intention to declare a *Republic of Biafra* by the Movement for the Actualization of the Sovereign State of *Biafra* (MASSOB), on May 27, 2000. Disowned by Ojukwu and the pan-Ibo *Ohaneze* group, MASSOB hoisted a *Biafran* flag, while the leader escaped on motorcycle during the so-called ceremony. Was the call for confederation, like the *Sharia* a political card? If it was, other zones were soon to put their cards on the political table.

As mentioned earlier, the governors of the South-South had complained about the non-release of 13% derivation fund to their states from May 29 to December 31, 1999. From the days of the military rule, the Niger-Delta had always been an area of violence. Devastated by oil exploration, inadequately touched by the benefits of oil, overwhelmed by an army of unemployed youth, the area has seen violence aimed at extracting positive responses from the federal government and oil companies.

In fact, oil pipelines had been vandalized at various times, while communities involved in illegal oil bunkering had suffered tragic consequences resulting from unexpected explosions and inferno. In a demonstration of anger, Bayelsa youths in Odi had captured policemen, ambushed and killed four soldiers. As reaction, government ordered military action, which razed Odi village. It was a wanton military operation, illustrating clearly the need for Nigeria to establish a para-military unit appropriately trained for dealing with civil disobedience.

With this background of restiveness among the youth and their pressures on state governments, what was seen as the refusal of the federal government to release the 13% derivation fund, due to the states from May 29, 1999 to December 1999, soon took another dimension. The Governors of the states in the South-South Zone, met and issued a communique that they had set the machinery "in motion to assume full control of its resources within the framework of true federalism."[33] Was this constitutional? Could states control mineral resources, when mining is under the exclusive legislative list of the federation? Again, the reaction by State governors of the South-South zone reflects the level of dissatisfaction among Nigerians with the operation of the federation.

Similarly, the Middle-Belt (or the North Central Zone) reacted to a number of issues in the federation. The trigger for the Middle Belt reactions was the complaint by the core North or Hausa-Fulani that the Service Chiefs of the Armed Forces came from the Middle Belt and not the North. There were spontaneous reactions to what was regarded as Northern hypocrisy—using the Middle Belt when it was convenient, to fight its war, and turn around to dump them. The Middle Belt Forum made it clear that it was no longer interested in being part of the old Northern geopolity, or share Northern identity with the Hausa-Fulanis.[34] The Middle Belt supported a federation with a strong centre, with equity of opportunities for all. It called for equity in the distribution of resources and the need to encourage solid minerals, agricultural, and industrial development in the zone. Like the

285

Southeast, Southwest and South-South zones, the Middle-belt or the North-central zone called for a national conference to discuss all outstanding issues in the Nigerian federation.

In essence, the violent protests in the Niger-Delta over perceived injustice in resource distribution; the Itsekiri-Ijaw violence in the Niger-Delta; the resumption of the Ife-Modakeke communal violence; the Odi violence and the sacking of the community by Obasanjo administration; the menace of *Odu'a Peoples' Congress* (OPC) and the accompanying violence in Lagos and Shagamu areas; the formation of the *Arewa Peoples' Congress* (APC) and the *Igbo Peoples' Congress* (IPC); the MASSOB feeble attempt to resuscitate *Biafra;* the *Sharia* crises and the demands for a confederation; the South-South demand for the control of its resources; are all part of the bubbles of the Nigerian federation.

That these political bubbles worried President Obasanjo, is reflected in his address to the members of the Obasanjo Leadership Forum when they paid a courtesy call on him. Obasanjo claimed that the *Sharia*, OPC and Niger - Delta crises were all programmed to destabilize Nigeria. According to the President, "... some people want to secede. Some people want to break away from Nigeria while others want a stronger federation".[35]

The demand for a National Conference or a Sovereign National Conference in which these issues could be discussed had dated as far as 1997. When President Obasanjo assumed office, he declared his opposition to the idea of National Conference. However, when it became clear in the late 2004 that members of Pro-National Conference Organization (PRONACO) were going to hold a Sovereign National Conference, President Obasanjo changed his mind. He then announced that the federal government was going to inaugurate a National Political Reform Conference (NPRC).

In a hasty manner, the federal government moved to establish the machinery for the conference. The idea was obviously an after-thought because there were no provisions made for the conference in the budget proposal, which was before the National Assembly. The National Assembly distanced itself from the conference and refused to appropriate any funds for it. The President had to look for money from somewhere else to fund the conference. Some Nigerians believed that an active National Assembly would have insisted that the President explain the sources of funds used for the conference. It did not.

There were about 400 delegates to the conference made up of 50 nominations from the president, 6 nominations from each of the thirty-six states by state governors, few representatives of special interests such as the retired military, women, professional associations and labour. It is paradoxical that Constituent Assemblies in 1978-9 and 1988 under military regimes, comprised at least 50% of elected members. Yet in 2005, the NPRC held under a supposed democratic polity had no elected member. Many critics of the federal government had alleged that President Obasanjo had a personal agenda for a third term in the office, and intended to use the NPRC for that purposes. An elected assembly would have been most difficult to manage.

The conference was inaugurated on February 21, 2005 by President Obasanjo. The NPRC unanimously endorsed a united, indivisible and democratic Nigeria. The conference deliberated on 187 issues but agreed on 185 issues. The issues of resource distribution and the tenure of the President, led to the breakdown of the conference. The South-South delegation which had pressed for 25% of revenues from mineral rents and royalties going to the state of origin on the basis of derivation, as against the current 13%, walked out of the conference. Its position was that 50% of revenues from oil should return to Niger-Delta on the basis of derivation. However, in the interim, it would accept 25% on the basis of derivation. The conference recommended 17%. The South-South states walked out of the conference and never returned.

The second issue was the tenure of Chief Executives – the president, the governors and the chairmen of local governments. There were suggestions that the incumbents of these offices should be limited to one-term of six years. The current constitutional provision is for two terms of four years. The political temperature of the conference rose sharply in response to a number of issues. The presence of a draft constitution allegedly sneaked into secretariat by the 'president's men', made many members to question the motive of President Obasanjo. It was rumoured in the Press and at the conference that the president, about to serve out his second four-year term was desirous of a third term of six years. While the presidency denied this, many Nigerians believed that utterances of the federal government were at variance with its actions. There was a crisis of confidence as few people seem to trust the government of President Obasanjo. The conference ended as abruptly as it had started.

The Report of the Conference was presented to the National Assembly by the President. What many Nigerians seems to find puzzling, is how a National Assembly which had distance itself from the Conference, would now receive the report of the conference for its debate.

The PRONACO group, comprising prominent Nigerians such as Chief Anthony Enahoro, Prof. Wole Soyinka and Dr. Ransome-Kuti, inaugurated its Sovereign National Conference on October 1, 2005. It has since been bugged down by intra-leadership crisis, some Nigerians wondered whether President Obasanjo should have really bothered so much about PRONACO.

Is Nigeria likely to break up? Let us now turn to the prospects of federation in the Fourth Republic.

Prospects of Federalism in the Fourth Republic

It does seem that given the verdant memory of the last civil war, most Nigerian politicians believe that Nigeria cannot survive a second civil war. Given the new freedom embedded in the democratic polity, after years of military rule, they want to test the system to see the extent to which they can go. They may even go to the precipice before finding a line of retreat into the centre of the polity. However, transforming democratic freedom into democratic licence can be very costly for any system and Nigerian politicians have to watch out.

From our discussions above, it does seem like each geopolitical zone is looking for a political bargaining card. While the Southwest card is *true federalism* or a very loose federation or confederation, the Northwestern and Northeastern card in the *Sharia*. The Southeast has dropped its confederation card on the table. The South-South is hanging unto its resource control card, while the Middle Belt or North Central card is a stronger federation to protect minorities. The constitutional review exercise embarked upon by the National

Assembly[36] and the prospects of a National Conference make such bargaining cards very attractive and important for political leaders.

The reasons for the adoption of a federal system of government in the early 1950s are still very much around. The mutual fears and suspicions among the groups in the competitive political process continue to bug the polity. The issues and the context in which they were acted out have probably changed, but Nigerians are most likely to continue with federation or a federal-type compromise in the management of their conflicts in the next decade.

In the next decade, however, a number of issues will continue to attract the attention of political leaders. The distribution of power among three tiers of government on a vertical level, will continue to engage Nigerian political leaders, irrespective of their political party affiliations.[37] It is most likely that the legislative lists will be reviewed in favour of subnational units. The centre may be less powerful than it is now, but it is probably unlikely that Nigeria will adopt a confederal technique in the management of conflicts arising from its federal association.

Secondly, the issue of resource distribution and/or management will continue to dominate debate in the federation. It may raise the political temperature of the federation. There may be even violent dimensions to the problem. But given the complementarity of the Nigerian economy in the past 80 years, piecemeal compromises are likely to be effected over time.

It is hoped that as democratic institutions take their root; as the political processes get routinized; and as intergovernmental relations improve and a new culture of interdependence and cooperation develop among the operators of the federation; the current bubbles will burst, and Nigerians will develop greater sense of tolerance and accommodation of one another.

Conclusion

We have argued that at the dawn of the 21st century, the Nigerian federation is characterized by strong unitarist streaks as a response to almost three decades of military rule. As a result of overcentralization of the Nigerian federation, there have been numerous reactions by subnational groups for a review of the legislative list.

The Nigerian federation faces a number of challenges in the next decade of the new millennium. Among these challenges is the issue of how to decentralize an overly centralized federation. The next few years are likely to witness a constitutional review including a review of the legislative list. It is most likely that the powers of the centre would be reduced in favour of subnational units.

In similar vein, the distribution of scarce but allocatable resources will continue to dominate debate on the state of the federation in the next decade. As Nigerian groups reassess their benefits from (more often rather than contribution to) the federation, conflicts over distribution of resources will continue to arise. However, given the complementarity and interdependence of the Nigerian economy, political leaders are likely to find appropriate forms of compromise, from time to time. The conflicts of distribution may even reach crises proportions, but are unlikely to threaten the existence of the nation-state.

In the new democratic setting, the politics of federalism has led to the emergence of geopolitical bargaining platforms in anticipation of a National Conference. The explosion of subnational identities and associated aggressive nationalism, are likely to surface over time, without destroying the polity.

Ultimately, it is clear that the reasons for the adoption of federation are very much around. The mutual fears and suspicions of one another by Nigerian groups are likely to continue in the next decade. But it is hoped that as groups interact and establish relative mutual confidence in one another and in the federal system, necessary compromises will be effected and conflicts managed appropriately. For a long while, it does seem that federalism or one-federal-type or the other will continue to provide the desirable compromise for managing conflicts in Nigeria.

Notes and references

1. James Coleman, *Nigeria: A Background to Nationalism* (Berkeley: University of California Press, 1958), p.30. Also see J. P. Mackintosh, (ed.) *Nigerian Government and Politics* (Evanston: Northwestern University, 1966); Adebayo Adedeji, "Federalism and Development Planning in Nigeria" in A. Ayida and H. M. A Onitiri, (eds.) *Reconstruction and Development in Nigeria: Proceedings of a National Conference* (Ibadan: Oxford University Press, 1971).

2. See K. W. Post, *The Nigeria Federal Election of 1959* (London: Oxford University Press, 1963).

3. The term *ethnoregional* is used to refer to the administrative territory in which identities of the major regional ethnic group crystallizes around the regional administrative boundaries.

4. According to Sklar, on the January 1966 coup, "political power had shifted away from the Northern rulers and their allies to a more progressive section of the population. The dangerous imbalance between legal and technological power had been corrected." In other words, the January coup corrected existing imbalance. Richard L. Sklar, "Nigerian Politics in Perspective" in R. Melson and H. Wolpe, (eds.) *Nigeria: Modernization and the Politics of Communalism* (East Lansing: Michigan State University Press, 1970), p.50.

5. This period accounted for about 30 years that is three-quarters of Nigeria's political life.

6. Federal Government of Nigeria, Decree No. 34, 1966, declared Nigeria a Unitary State to be called the *National Government of Nigeria*. The period was short-lived and marked by violence. It was reversed by Decree No. 52 of 1966, which returned Nigeria to a *federal* system— *Federal Military Government*.

7. Under General Gowon, these governors were accused of being too autonomous for a military regime. Succeeding military regimes were more centralizing, even though governors always retained a sizeable measure of autonomy.

8. Some Nigerians believe that about three score years of military rule has overly centralized the federation, and are therefore asking for a federation with a weak centre or a *Confederation*.

9.   For details of these see - J. Isawa Elaigwu, "Military Rule and Federalism in Nigeria" in J. Isawa Elaigwu and R. A. Akindele, (eds.) *The Foundations of Nigerian Federalism: 1960-95, Vol. III* (Abuja: National Council on Intergovernmental Relations, 1996), pp.166-193; J. Isawa Elaigwu, The Military and State Building: Federal-State Relations in Nigeria's Military Federalism; 1966-76" in A. B. Akinyemi, P. D. Cole, and Walter Ofonagoro, (eds.) *Readings on Federalism* (Lagos: Nigerian Institute of International Affairs, 1979), pp.155-181.

10.   From the four old regions by 1966, were created the following States:

Northern Region	Western Region	Eastern Region	Midwestern Region
Sokoto	Lagos *	Anambra	Edo
Zamfara	Oyo	Enugu	Delta
Kebbi	Osun	Imo	
Kaduna	Ondo	Abia	
Katsina	Ekiti	Ebonyi	
Kano	Ogun	Rivers	
Jigawa		Cross River	
Borno		Bayelsa	
Yobe		Akwa -	
Adamawa		Ibom	
Taraba			
Plateau			
Benue			
Nasarawa			
Kwara			
Kogi			
Bauchi			
Gombe			
Niger			

* Lagos was the Federal Capital Territory until 1991, when Abuja became the Federal Capital Territory (FCT)

11.   General Obasanjo was a former Military Head of State (1976 - 78). He came to power as an elected President on May 29, 1999. He has not yet shed his military toga. He is fond of taking actions without sensitivity to due process as required in a democratic polity.

12.   *The Vanguard* (Lagos), June 24, 2000, p.6.

13.   *ibid., The Vanguard,* May 4, p.2.

14.   There were labour crises all over the country. Many state governments could not pay the new wages, thus negotiations with their labour forces failed. In some states, public servants were on strike for between three to six months. See *Vanguard,* May 4, 2000, p.2 in which Governor Dariye of Plateau State expressed his concern—"Our concern is that we don't want to go back to the ugly past when workers were owed several months arrears of salaries."

15.   It has been suggested that the Structure of the Nigeria Police Force be decentralized in order to allow the zonal commands to be more responsive to local situations. Quite a number of Nigerians are apprehensive of the wanton misuse of the local police by local governments, politicians and traditional leaders, in the past.

16.   This is the case of Anambra State where the Bakassi Boys became officially recognized *Vigilante* to complement police efforts. Attempts by the Governor of Lagos to use the OPC have been criticized by the Police, especially since the OPC is a banned organization. See *This Day* (Lagos) August 18, 2000, p.13; August 2, 2000, p.1; July 30, 2000 p.1 and July 27, 2000, p.1.

17.   *The Punch* (Lagos), July 7, 2001, p.1 and 2.

18.   This section (8-3) of the 1999 Constitution states that:
"(3) A bill for a Law of a House of Assembly for the purpose of creating a new local government area shall only be passed if-
(a) a request supported by at least two-thirds majority of members (representing the area demanding the creation of the new local government area) in each of the following, namely-

(i) the House of Assembly in respect of the area, and

(ii) the local government councils in respect of the area, is received by the House of Assembly;

(b) a proposal for the creation of the local government area is thereafter approved in a referendum by at least two-thirds majority of the people of the local government area where the demand for the proposed local government area originated;

(c) the result of the referendum is then approved by a simple majority of the members in each local government council in a majority of all local government councils in the State; and

(d) the result of the referendum is approved by a resolution passed by two-thirds majority of members of the House of Assembly."

19. *The Vanguard* (Lagos), August 23, 1999, pp.1-2.

20. *The Vanguard,* March 9, 2001, p.1.

21. *The Punch,* July 7, 2001, pp.1-2.

22. There are many publications on Nigerian federalism, among which are—Frederich Ebert Foundation, *Constitutions and Federalism: Proceedings of the Conference on Constitutions and Federalism* (Lagos: Friedrich Ebert Foundation, 1997); E. E. O Alemika and Festus Okoye, (ed.) *Constitutional Federalism and Democracy in Nigeria* (Kaduna: Human Rights Monitor, no date); A. Adedeji, *Nigerian Federal Finance* (London: Hutchison Educational, 1969); A. Akanle, *The Power to Tax and Nigerian Federalism* (Lagos: Centre for Business Executives, 1985); E. O. Awa, *Federal Government of Nigeria: A Study of the Development of the Nigeria State* (Berkeley: University of California Press, 1964); Peter P. Ekeh, (ed.) *Nigerian Federalism* (Bufallo: Association of Nigerian Scholars for Dialogue, 1997); *Publius: The Journal of Federalism,* Vol.1, No.1 1994 (on Nigeria); J. Isawa Elaigwu and Erim O. Erim, (eds.) *Foundations of Nigerian Federalism: Pre-Colonial Antecedents,* Vol.1 (Abuja: National Council on Intergovernmental Relations, 1996); J. Isawa Elaigwu and Godfrey Uzoigwe, (eds.) *Foundations of Nigerian Federalism: 1900-1960,* Vol. II (Abuja: National Council on Intergovernmental Relations, 1996); J. Isawa Elaigwu and R. A Akindele, (eds.), *Foundations of Nigerian Federalism: 1960 -1995, Vol. III* (Abuja: National Council on Intergovernmental Relations, 1996); D. Rothchild and Victor Olorunsola, (eds.) *State versus Ethnic Claims: African Policy Dilemmas* (Boulder: Westview, 1983).

23. Federal Government of Nigeria, *The Constitutional Conference Containing The Resolutions and Recommendations*, Vol. II, (Lagos: Government Printer, 1995) p.61.

24. Ranjit S. Sarkaria, "Foreword" in S. C. Arora, (eds.) *Current Issues and Trends in Centre-State Relations: A Global View* (New Delhi: Mittal Publications, 1991), p.3; Government of India, *Sarkaria Report: Commission in Centre - State Relations* (India: Government of India Press, 1988).

25. The nearest Nigeria went to a Confederal Constitution was crisis period 1966-67, when the Federal Military Government issued Decree No. 8, 1967, of March 17, 1967, in response to the Aburi peace accord in Ghana.

26. There had been Revenue Commissions in the past — i) Philipson Commission (1946); ii) Hicks-Philipson Commission (1951); iii) Chicks Commission (1953); iv) Raisman Commission (1958); v) Binns Commission (1964); vi) Dina Committee (1969); vii) the Military governments issued decrees in 1967, 1970, 1971 and 1975 on revenue allocation matters; viii) Aboyade Commission (1978); and ix) Okigbo Commission (1980). The Okigbo Commission formula was amended by subsequent military regimes, as they deemed fit. See T. Y. Danjuma, "Revenue Sharing in Nigerian Federalism" in J. Isawa Elaigwu, P.C. Logams and H. S. Galadima, (eds.) *Federalism and Nation-Building in Nigeria: The Challenges of the 21st Century* (Abuja: National Council On Intergovernmental Relations, 1994), pp. 87-115.

27. *This Day*, July 28, 2000, p.7.

28. After all, between 1964 and 1969, the percentage of mineral rents and royalties, which went back to the States, was 45%. It may go up again beyond the current 13%.

29.   These political zones are-

North-West	North-Central	North-East	South-South	South-East	South-West
Sokoto	Benue	Borno	Delta	Abia	Lagos
Kano	Plateau	Adamawa	Edo	Anambra	Ogun
Jigawa	Kogi	Yobe	Rivers	Enugu	Oyo
Zamfara	Niger	Taraba	Bayelsa	Imo	Osun
Kebbi	Nasarawa	Bauchi	Akwa-Ibom	Ebonyi	Ondo
Kaduna	Kwara	Gombe	Cross-Rivers		Ekiti
Katsina					

30.   These states include, Kebbi, Niger, Sokoto, Kano, Yobe, Bauchi, Borno, Kaduna, Jigawa and Katsina.

31.   *The Vanguard,* March 27, 2000, p.1.

32.   *The Source,* (Lagos) Vol. 6, No.25, April 3, 2000, p.12.

33.   *This Day,* (Lagos) August 16, 2000, p.10; *The Vanguard,* September 26, 2001, pp.31 and 33.

34.   *The Nigeria Standard,* (Jos) August 17, 2000, p.7.

35.   *The Vanguard,* July 19, 2000, p.2.

36.   The National Assembly has a committee on Constitutional Review, which has been collating ideas on review exercise. It is not clear how far this exercise will go in the context of calls for a National Conference. In addition, there is also a Presidential Committee on Constitutional Review, comprising members of the three political parties.

37.   Nigeria has thirty political parties—The Peoples' Democratic Party (PDP) which controls 28 State Governments and the Federal Government; the All Nigeria Peoples Party (ANPP) which controls seven State Governments; and the Alliance for Democracy (AD) which controls one State, after the 2003 elections. All the political parties have splinter groups or factions.

INTERGOVERNMENTAL RELATIONS IN NIGERIA*

As government in most countries get more complex, so have institution of governance. Actors in government have found that there is an increasing need for interaction and interdependence among units and levels of government. This kind of cooperative relationship is even more imperative in federations because:

> The inevitability within federations or overlaps and interdependence in the exercise by governments of their powers has generally required different orders of government to treat each other as partners. This has required extensive consultative cooperation and coordination between governments[1]

It is the "consultation, cooperation and coordination" between and/or among government or units of government which is often referred to as Intergovernmental Relations (IGR). Why do we need intergovernmental relations? What is the relationship between IGR and Federalism? In Nigeria, institutions of IGR are available but how do they operate? What kinds of problems emanate from intergovernmental relations? Let us now make a few suggestions to guide us in our attempts to provide some answers to the above questions. We suggest that:

i) there is an intricate and complex relationship between Federalism and IGR;
ii) IGR is basically a mechanism for managing conflicts while delivering services;
iii) the dynamics of the Nigerian federation and the Nigerian constitution make IGR a political imperative;
iv) while resolving some problems of intergovernmental management IGR does pose some challenges; and

v) unless the political leaders and politicians imbibe the appropriate value of IGR and practise it, the people and/or the political class may lose out.

Federalism and Intergovernmental Relations

Federalism is a technique for managing conflict among heterogenous groups in a state through a system of constitutional division of powers which provide for "shared rule", while also allowing for "self rule"[2] at the subnational level. Federalism assures the delineation of powers between tiers of government and thus provide for "shared rule" among the important units of the federation. But it also makes provisions for autonomy and "self rule" at the subnational level as groups seek to protect their local identities.

In essence, federalism is a mechanism for managing conflicts between two types of self-determination, national self-determination and subnational self-determination.[3] The federal pendulum may swing in the direction of centripetal forces (towards the centre) when there is generally greater mutual trust and less suspicion among component groups and units of the federation. However, the pendulum may swing in the direction of centrifugal forces (towards subnational units) in the context of intense suspicion among groups. In the direction of centripetal forces, the federal centre is likely to be stronger, while in the direction of centrifugal forces, the federal centre is likely to be weaker.

While the classical model of federalism as delineated by K. C. Wheare provides the basis of understanding federalism today in practice, in terms of federal association among component units this model does not exist anywhere, in practice not even the older federations of Switzerland or the United States.[4] Essentially, the old sense of autonomy or independence of component units in their areas of jurisdiction has given way to cooperation, interaction and interdependence. These demands make intergovernmental relations inevitable in federation, even though there may be forms of intergovernmental relations in a unitary system, depending on the extent of devolution of powers in the system. Countries with federal features also utilize different forms and institutions of IGR.

One of our suggestions is that IGR is basically a mechanism for managing conflict and delivering services. Institutions and processes of IGR serve to: i) promote cooperation among governmental units; ii) recognize and manage conflicts; iii) deliver services more efficiently; and iv) to respond to changing circumstances.[5] IGR can take many forms, including informal relations among officers such as "through various means of direct communications (e.g. by letter and telephone), between ministries, officials and representatives of different governments with each other".[6] Formal and constitutional institutions also exist for IGR in many countries, as well as *ad hoc* meetings among members.

The pattern of IGR may differ from one country to the other, to the extent of the separation of powers among the three branches of government – executive, legislative and judiciary. In the Presidential system of government, executive federalism is more intense and the role of executive in IGR at different governmental levels and units, gets more visible and numerous.

To what extent has the Nigerian federation been able to establish institutions and processes of IGR, to carry out the functions above?

Intergovernmental Relations in Nigeria

The dynamics of the Nigerian federation and the Nigerian constitution make IGR a political imperative. With over four hundred lingo-cultural groups, a population of over 120 million, thirty-six states and a federal capital territory, and 774 local governments, IGR in Nigeria is an inevitability. Over the years, the pendulum of federal associations among groups has swung between centrifugal and centripetal forces, as Nigerians sought to adjust the federation. In some cases, violent reactions have followed such adjustments, resulting once in a civil war.

As Nigeria uses the framework of federalism to manage her conflicts, she has found that intergovernmental relations is a necessary mechanism to promote cooperation, manage conflicts, respond to changing circumstances and deliver services more efficiently. There are institutions and processes of IGR. We shall look at some of them. For our purposes, we classify IGR institutions under i) Constitutional, ii) Statutory, and iii) Informal/*ad hoc* institutions. These have changed over time, depending on the constitution and the system of government in operation. Let us turn to the constitutional institutions of IGR.

I) Constitutional

These are constitutionally provided institutions of IGR. They include:

a) *The National AssemblySS*Sections 4(1) of the 1979, 1989 and 1999 Constitutions state clearly that "there shall be a National Assembly for the federation which shall consist of a Senate and a House of Representatives".[7] Representing the whole federation on the basis of population in the (House of RepresentativesSHOR) and on the basis of equality of states (in the Senate), the National Assembly is an open legislative institution of IGR.

Its powers of legislation over appropriation bill[8], control over public funds[9], contingency fund[10], and investigation[11], all makes the National Assembly an important intergovernmental institution in the constitution.

b. *The Supreme Court*[12] has the final power of arbitration in civil, criminal and constitutional matters. In Nigeria's Second Republic, state governments took the federal government to court over revenue sharing formula and the Agricultural Development Basin Authorities.[13] Individuals and corporate groups also went to the court to seek redress. Thus, on government ownership of private schools, Archbishop Okogie took the Lagos State Government to court[14].

c. *The Council of State*[15]

This is essentially one of the advisory executive bodies contained in the Constitutions of 1979, 1989 and 1999. Its functions include advising the president with regard to the conduct of national census; prerogatives of mercy; award of national honour; the Independent Electoral Commission; the National Judicial Commission; the National Population Commission, and on public order.

The membership of this body also reflects its intergovernmental nature. It comprises - a) the President as Chairman; b) Vice-President as Deputy Chairman; c) all former Presidents/Heads of States; d) all former Chief Justices of Nigeria; e) President of senate; f) Speaker of the House of Representatives, all governors of States of the federation, and the Attorney-General of the federation.

d) *The Federal Character Commission*[16] is another constitutionally guaranteed executive IGR agency. The functions[17] of this agency include — working out equitable formula for the distribution of all cadres of posts in the federal and state public services; promoting, monitoring, and enforcing compliance of proportional sharing of public offices; and taking measures to enforce such compliance. Given various complaints about injustices/unfairness in the distribution of public service positions among component units of the federation, the importance of this commission cannot be over emphasized.

The membership of the commission consists of Chairman and one member appointed from each state of the federation. This agency is expected to carry out the constitutional provisions in section 14(3-4) of 1979; 15(3-4) of 1989; and 14(3-4) of 1999 Constitutions which states that -"the composition of the government of the federation or any of its agencies and the conduct of its affairs shall be carried out in such manner as to reflect the federal character and the need to promote national unity..."

The commission has an office in each state of the federation and the Federal Capital Territory (FCT), Abuja.

e) *The Independent Electoral Commission (INEC)*[18] has the function of organizing, undertaking and supervising all elections. There is a provision for State Electoral Commission in each state of the federation. It also has the function of registering political parties; monitoring the organization and operation of political parties; and annually examining and auditing of the funds and accounts of political parties. This commission registered the three political parties—the Peoples Democratic Party (PDP); the All Nigeria Peoples' Party (ANPP); and the Alliance for Democracy (AD)—which formed the crux of Nigerian's Fourth Republic from May 29, 1999. It has since registered a total of 30 political parties in Nigeria.

Its membership comprises of a Chairman, 12 members and a resident Commissioner per state of the federation. In practice the resident commissioners are usually not posted to their states of origin.

f) *The National Economic Council (NEC)*[19] has the powers to advise the "President concerning economic affairs of the federation and in particular on measures necessary for the coordination of the economic planning efforts or economic programmes of the various governments of the federation"[20]. It's members include the a) Vice President (Chairman), b) Governor of each State, and c) Governor of the Central Bank.

g) *The National Judicial Council*[21] has the power to recommend appointments to the bench at federal, and state levels and FCT. It can also recommend the removal from office of the judicial officers, and exercise disciplinary control over members of the judiciary. Its membership comprises -

a) Chief Justice of Nigeria (CJN) (Chairman);
b) next most senior Justice of state court (Deputy Chairman);
c) President, Court of Appeal;
d) 5 retired Justices selected by the CJN-from Supreme Court or Court of Appeal;
e) Chief Judge of the Federal High Court;
f) 5 Judges, appointed by CJN from among Chief Judges of States and high Court of FCT, in rotation for 2 years;
g) 1 Grand Khadi appointed by CJN from among Grand Khadi of States and FCT in rotation for 2 years;
h) 1 President of the Customary Court of Appeal appointed by CJN from among Presidents of Customary Court of Appeal-2 years rotation;
i) 5 members of Nigerian Bar Association (NBA) with 15 years qualification, at least one of whom is a Senior Advocate of Nigeria, appointed by CJN on recommendation of the Executive Council of Nigerian Bar Association—for 2 years, subject to re-appointment; and
j) 2 persons,—not legal practitioners, who in the opinion of the Chief Justice of Nigeria - are of unquestionable integrity.

h) *The National Population Commission*[22] has the function of undertaking periodic enumeration of population through sample surveys, census etc.; continuos registration of birth, deaths; advising the President on population matters, and providing data/information on population for national planning and development. Its members are a) Chairman and b) a person from each State of the Federation and FCT.

i) *The Revenue Mobilization, Allocation and Fiscal Commission.*[23] is responsible for - monitoring accruals to and disbursement of revenue from the Federation Account; periodically reviewing the revenue allocation formula and principles in operation to ensure conformity with changing reality; advising federal and state government on fiscal efficiency and methods by which their revenue can be increased and determining the remuneration of the President, Vice-President, Governors, Deputy-Governors, Ministers, Commissioners, Special Advisers, Legislators and holders of public offices mentioned in section 84 and 124 of the constitution[24]

Its membership comprises a) Chairman, b) one member from each state of the federation and FCT.

All these executive IGR institutions are constitutional. The long period of military rule "froze" the activities of some of these agencies, but they are again operational. Ironically, many of these agencies were created by various military administrations, but they are now operating fully to carry out their mandates. There are other institutions of IGR, which are statutory (i.e. established by law), but not in the constitution.

II) Statutory Agencies

These institutions of Intergovernmental Relations are usually backed by law, and most of them were established under military rule. This is evidence that even under the military's 'hierarchical' structure of authority, it was still necessary to establish institutions of IGR in order to resolve conflicts and/or deliver services. Among such IGR institutions are:

a) *The Directorate of Food, Road and Rural Infrastructure.*[25]
In 1986, the federal government, under Babangida administration, introduced the Directorate of Foods, Road and Rural Infrastructure (DIFRRI) to open up rural areas, provide essential services such as water supply through boreholes, rural electric power supply and roads. Essentially, this programme was aimed at making the rural areas more attractive and thereby reducing the rural-urban drift. Rural development is really the function of state and local government. Since the federal government's intervention in these areas was deemed necessary, DIFRRI was established as an IGR institution. State governments were to contribute 25% of the total fund for DIFRRI projects, while the rest came from the federal government. While DIFRRI headquarters managed the funds, state governments and state DIFRRI Offices (under state governments) executed these projects. A

Presidential inspection group usually monitored performances of the agency in different states.

Between 1986-1989, DIFRRI had opened up 30,000km-untarred road to rural communities, supplied potable water to 250 communities and had reached advanced stages of installation of rural electrification in 227 communities. This agency exhibited successful performance for about five years, after which it became bureaucratized and suffered from corruption on the part of the operators at state and local levels. DIFRRI was later dissolved by the Abacha government in 1994.

b) *The National Council on Intergovernmental Relations (NCIR)* [26] was established July 1992 to closely monitor the operation of the federal system, giving continuing attention to intergovernmental relations in the Nigerian federal system; study, conduct research and maintain data", recommend solutions to problems of intergovernmental relations and necessary forms of improvement; play mediatory roles in resolving conflicts; and establish contacts with other organizations with similar objectives.

The membership of the Board of Governors was such that each tier of government and each arm of government at each tier of government is represented. The membership included, a chairman, the Director-General and Chief Executive, three private citizens, four State Governors, two federal Ministers, two Senators, two members of the House of Representatives, the Accountant-General of the Federation, two speakers of the state Houses of Assembly, two chairmen from local governments, two councillors, and the mayor of Abuja, the federal capital. NCIR was also mandated to constantly review the legislative list and send its recommendations to the National Assembly and to all tiers of government. In its short life-span, NCIR published a number of research works, including the three-volume major works on Nigerian federation.[27] It also successfully mediated in the conflicts between the Andoni and Ogoni in the Rivers State; Abia and Imo States; Oyo and Osun States; and Adamawa and Taraba States, over assets-sharing after the creation of states.

NCIR was dissolved in March 1996 by the Abacha government. Among the reasons for its dissolution was the nature of military rule, which did not need it very much, and therefore did not provide the ambiance for it to operate. Secondly, there were civil servants who did not understand the nature of autonomy granted the institution nor did they want to understand it. They were more concerned about bringing the institution under the office of the Secretary to the Government of the Federation (SGF). Thus, a major problem of NCIR was bureaucratic suffocation, which even starved it of funds. In addition, NCIR had no independent source of funds, which was necessary if it was to mediate among tiers of government, and to remain neutral. Its funds came from the federal government. Finally, the political setting lacked a democratic grid within which it was to work or operate, such as the existence of a National Assembly.

c) *Boundaries Commission*[28]

This commission has the function of determining and intervening "in any boundary dispute that may arise between Nigeria and any of her neighbours or between any two states of the federation with a view to settling such disputes"[29] With the increase in the number of states from four in 1963 to thirty-six in 1996, there have been many instances of boundary disputes, which needed resolution. Again the membership of this commission reflects the intergovernmental nature of its role. Its membership includes the Vice-President who is the Chairman; the Minister of Defence; the Inspector-General of Police; the Minister of Justice; the Ministers of External Affairs, Internal Affairs, Works and Housing, and National Planning; the Director-General of the National Intelligence Agency; the Governors of the states involved and two members appointed by the President from the public or private sector. This agency has made tremendous efforts in settling boundary disputes among states and communities within the country. It has also successfully carried out boundary disputes with the Republic of Benin, even though the Bakassi Peninsula with the Cameroons defied its capability and the case had to be decided by the International Court of Justice.

d) *The National Directorate of Employment (NDE)*[30]

This was established in order to organize employment, especially self-employment for graduates of higher institutions. It gives loans to any unemployed youths to begin self-employed life. It has offices in all states of the federation.

e) *The National Planning Commission (NPC)*[31]

This commission has at one time or the other been a full-fledged government ministry. It is in charge of development and rolling plans for the country and is very much in control of annual budgetary processes, especially, capital votes.

f) *The National Primary Education Commission*[32]

The functions of this commission include prescribing "minimum standards of primary education throughout Nigeria," collating, "after consultation with all the state governments, periodic master plans for balanced and coordinated development of primary education" in Nigeria and the allocation of the National Primary Education Fund to relevant agencies in the states and Abuja. It was dissolved in 1993, was re-established, and was dissolved again to make way for a more effective control by state and local governments, as well as setting the stage for the re-introduction of the Universal Primary Education (UPE). This commission has again been re-established.

In addition to these statutory institutions of inter-governmental relations, there are also other more informal institutions/agencies. These are more *ad hoc* in nature, even if they are not mandatory for the members.

III) Ad Hoc or Informal Bodies and Agencies

These informal bodies/agencies are also useful in bringing together federal, state and local officials in a particular policy area. They also help to smoothen intergovernmental relations and encourage cooperation among component units of the federation. The various National Councils on Education, Agriculture, Health, Industry, Information, Tourism and Finance, are usually meetings among ministers at federal and state levels, to bring state and federal political executives together to harmonize policies in the interests of the federation. As an illustration, the Federal Minister of Education and his counterparts in the state (called commissioners) meet periodically to review educational programmes in the country and harmonize their policies.

Other non-executive but informal agencies of Intergovernmental Relations also exist. The informal meetings of the Association of Speakers of State Houses of Assembly are a get-together of leaders of state legislatures. Similarly, informal meetings of the Governors' Forum are very useful for comparing notes and cooperation. While these meetings are more informal than the Australian Premiers' conferences, they are useful in lubricating the engine of federalism in Nigeria. The conference of Chairmen of Local Governments, or the Association of Local Governments of Nigeria (ALGON) serves the same purpose at the local level.

All the above institutions of IGR are important in managing conflicts and responding to changing circumstances in the Nigerian federation. While IGR institutions are useful, they also carry with them a baggage of their own problems, which need careful attention.

Intergovernmental Relations and the Politics of Federalism

Some of the tensions, which arise in the Nigerian federation, emanate from the overlap of functions among tiers of government. They are derivable from the kind of pulls, which we discussed earlier — the tension arising from attempt at delicately striking a balance between centripetal and centrifugal forces. These become very evident in the relations between federal and state governments, state and local governments, and even in the relations among state governments.[33]

One of the most pronounced complaints about Nigeria's intergovernmental relations is that there are too many institutions/agencies of Inter-government Relations whose functions overlap. It is argued that these myriads of structures can create new bureaucracies, which end up defeating the purposes of establishing these institutions/agencies. Except in so far as the constitution delineated some institutions/agencies, rational cases have been made for streamlining these agencies. Often the interpretation of the laws establishing these agencies also generates new crises of autonomy in the system, thus calling for attention. One of the problems of evaluating intergovernmental relations institutions/agencies is that there is a need to balance conflict-management functions of these institutions with their efficiency in the delivery of services. There are times when efficiency in the delivery of services need to be compromised for conflict resolution. Federal systems and systems with federal features are not known for the greatest efficiency. But the functions of conflict management they serve are indispensable to the system.

In the context of the politics of federalism, the logic of self-determination cuts both ways. It can either encourage secession as Nigerians have witnessed, or centralization of political power as Nigeria also experienced under military rule. The tensions are such that it takes skills in leadership to manage them. At times, the pressures of federalism are such that they push for the creation of a union without accompanying pressures for unity among the component units of the federalism. As the former Canadian Prime Minister, Pierre Trudeau aptly observed:

> ...the principle of self-determination which makes federalism necessary makes it rather unstable. If the heavy paste of nationalism is relied upon to keep a unitary nation-state together, much more nationalism would appear to be required in the case of a federal nation-state.[34]

Nigerians have learned from hard experience that federalism is a paradoxical *elixir* to be purchased from any political market. Yet, there is currently no viable political alternative to federalism for Nigeria's aggressively heterogeneous society.

Another interesting aspect of IGR, which often generates tensions, is the relationship between the demands of autonomy and finance. What is the fiscally desirable level of autonomy? To what extent can a component unit claim federally desirable autonomy? This is an on-going problem, as unequal federal units as Canadian and Australian experiences show. In such cases, a process of fiscal equalization may help the operators to manage such tensions.

Another important aspect of intergovernmental relations is the quality of operators. Operators or leaders at different levels must learn to make a transition from *the politician to the statesman,* with the interest of all constituents and the nation at heart. Such leaders are likely to reduce the intensity of tension between and among component units.

Conclusion

In this chapter we have argued that there is an intricate and complex relationship between federalism and intergovernmental relations. Our suggestion is that intergovernmental relations are basically a mechanism for managing conflicts while delivering services.

The dynamics of the Nigerian federation and the Nigerian Constitution makes intergovernmental relations a political imperative—with many institutions/agencies of intergovernmental relations. While appreciating the functions of intergovernmental relations institutions/agencies, we argued that these institutions/agencies pose some challenges of their own, which attract attention of operators. Finally, we argued that unless the political leaders and politicians imbibe the appropriate value of intergovernmental relations and practise it, the people and/or the political class might be worse for it.

Notes and references

* An earlier version of this paper was published in the *Indian Journal of Federal Studies,* Vol. 2, No. 2, pp. 65-78.

1.   Ronald Watts, *Comparing Federal Systems In The 1990s* (Ontario: Queens University, 1996), p.51.

2.   *ibid.,* p.7.

3.   Adebayo Adedeji, "Federalism and Development Planning in Nigeria", in A. Ayida and H.M.A Onitiri (eds.) *Reconstruction and Development in Nigeria: Proceedings of a Conference* (Ibadan: Oxford University Press, 1971).

4.   Ranjit S. Sarkaria, "Foreword" in S.C. Arora (ed.) *Current Issues and Trends in Centre-State Relations: A Global view.* (New Delhi: Mittal Publications, 1991), p.3; *Sarkaria Report: Commission in Centre-State Relations* (India: Government of India Press, 1988) Part 1, p.11; see also Christine Fletcher and Cliff Walsh, *Intergovernmental Relations in Australia: Managerialist Reform and The Power of Federalism* (Monograph) No. 4, September 1991 (Federalism Research Centre, Australian National University).

5.   Watts, *op. cit.* identifies two functions of *Intergovernmental Relations* (IGR) - "Conflict resolution and a means of adapting to changing circumstances." (p.51).

6.   Watts, *ibid.,* p.51.

7.   Federal Republic of Nigeria, *Constitution of the Federal Republic of Nigeria,* 1979, Section 47; Constitution, 1989, Section 45; Constitution, 1999, Section 43.

8. Federal Republic of Nigeria, *Constitution of the Federal Republic of Nigeria,* 1999, Section 59.

9. *ibid.,* Section 80 (1-4).

10. *ibid.,* Section 83.

11. *ibid.,* Section 88.

12. *ibid.,* Section 230.

13. The *Nigeria Standard,* (Jos) February 4, 1981, p.1; *The Punch* (Lagos) February 8, 1981, p.16.

14. J. Isawa Elaigwu, *Nigeria's Federal Balance: Conflict and Compromises in the Political System,* Postgraduate Lecture Series, vol.1 (No. 4) (Jos: University of Jos, 1984), pp.19-20.

15. Constitution; 1999, Section 153(1) and Third Schedule, Part 1, Federal Executive Bodies, B.

16. Constitution 1999, Section 153, Third Schedule, Part 1, C.

17. The functions are: 8-(1) in giving effect to all the provisions of Section 14(3) and (4) of this Constitution, The Commission shall have the power to:

a) work out an equitable formula subject to the approval of the National Assembly for the distribution of all cadres of posts in the public service of the federation and of the states, the armed forces of the federation, the Nigeria Police Force and other government Security Agencies, government owned companies and parastatals of the States;

b) promote, monitor and enforce compliance with the principles of proportional sharing of all bureaucratic, economic, media and political posts at all levels of government;

c) take such legal measures, including the prosecution of the head of staff of any ministry or government body or agency which fails to comply with any federal character principle or formula prescribed or adopted by the commission; and

d) carry out such other functions as may be conferred upon it by an Act of the National Assembly.

18. Note that this agency has different slants to its functions under different constitutions—*Federal Electoral Commission* (FEDECO) under 1979 Constitution; National Electoral Commission (NEC) under 1989 Constitution and Independent Electoral Commission (INEC) under the 1999 Constitution.

19. Third Schedule (1999 Constitution) Section 153, Part 1, H.

20. Third Schedule (1999 Constitution) Section 19.

21. Constitution 1991, Section 153, Third Schedule, Part 1.

22. *ibid,;* Part 1 J.

23. *ibid,;* Part 1 N.

24. *ibid,;* Section 32 part 1 N.

25. DIFRRI was established in 1986 for details of its functions, see Air Vice-Marshall L.D. Kionyan (rtd), *Why Rural Development Is a Must* (Lagos: DIFRRI, n.d). Official Gazette, vol.74, No. 19, 1987, pp.263-81.

26. Decree No. 89, 1992 establishing the council also stipulated its many functions which for space constraints cannot be included here.

27. J. Isawa Elaigwu and Erim O. Erim (eds.) *Foundations of Nigerian Federalism: Pre-colonial Antecedents* (Abuja: NCIR, 1996); J. Isawa Elaigwu and G.N. Uzoigwe (eds.) *Foundations of Nigerian Federalism, 1900-1960* (Abuja: NCIR, 1996); J. Isawa Elaigwu and R.A. Akindele (eds.) *Foundations of Nigerian Federalism 1960-1995* (Abuja: NCIR, 1996).

28. For their activities, see the *Boundary News*, a bulletin of the Boundary Commission, especially *Boundary News*, Vol.2, No.1, January-March 1999.

29. It should be noted that with the creation of many local government areas, there are also boundary problems among local governments.

30. NDE was established to help unemployed youth. It has done quite an appreciable job, even though unemployment rate has defied its efforts. The Obasanjo government established the Poverty Alleviation Programme (PAP) which was replaced by the National Poverty Eradication Programme (NAPEP), the impact of which has been minimal or hardly noticeable.

31. Decree No. 12 of March 1992.

32. Decree No. 31 of 1988 established the commission and it was incorporated into the 1989 Constitution.

33. Please see a discussion of this in J. Isawa Elaigwu and Victor Olorunsola, "Federalism and Politics of Compromise" in Dornald Rothchild and Victor A. Olorunsola (eds) *State Versus Ethnic Claims: African Policy Dilemmas* (Boulder, Colorado: Westview Press, 1983), pp.281-303.

34. Pierre Trudeau quoted by Shridath Ramphal, in A. B Akinyemi, P.D Cole and Walter Ofonagoro (eds.) *Readings on Federalism* (Lagos: Nigerian Institute of International Affairs, 1979), p. xxii.

12

CONCLUSIONS

In this book we have argued that federalism and militarism are not necessarily incompatible bedfellows. The major differences in the operation of federalism under civilian and military regimes in Nigeria are to be found in the style and structures of administration. In fact, all military regimes in Nigeria have always given a semblance of running Nigeria as a federal system. The only occasion, in which a military regime abolished the federal system, there was a violent response, in May 1966. Thus, given Nigeria's complexity, a form of federalism, no matter how warped, had always been used as a medium for effecting desirable compromises in the polity.

That Nigeria opted for federalism in the terminal colonial period was not surprising. The reason for the adoption of a federal compromise, as we have shown, is historical and multidimensional. If federalism is a mechanism for effecting political compromises in a multinational state, the Nigerian experience has shown that federalism is embedded with its own seeds of discord. If it encourages "shared rule," the subnational self-determination, which it encourages through "self-rule," may work against national self-determination. Nigeria's civil war experience, which followed the *Biafran* secession in 1967, clearly illustrates the above point.

In Nigeria's federal structure, there is a delicate balance between the centre's demand for control and the demand by the subnational units or states, for autonomy. As the federal pendulum swing between centripetal and centrifugal forces in the polity, Nigerians made desirable adjustments. By 1999, years of military rule had swung the federal pendulum in favour of the federal centre. Many Nigerians then reacted to what was regarded as the bold unitary streaks in Nigerian federalism, by calling for a revision of the legislative list and tax powers, among tiers of government.

On the horizontal plane, the echoes of the past are still very much around even if these may be heard today within different structures, and these seem to detract from the goals of national unity or integration. Some of the issues in Nigeria's past which simmer to the surface occasionally include – resource distribution, differential social mobilization among Nigerian groups, the creation of additional subnational states and local governments, the majority-minority dichotomy; ethnoregionalism as illustrated by North-South divide; religion and the 'federal character' provision in the constitution.

We have also argued that the future threat to the survival of Nigeria, if any, may not come from the vertical relations between the federal centre and subnational states, but from the horizontal relations among Nigerians as the centre become increasingly a big political prize to win, especially as the crises of allocation of scarce and allocatable resources increase in tempo and aggressiveness.

The reasons for the adoption of a federal system of government in the early 1950s are still very much the same today. The mutual fears suspicions among the groups in the competitive political process continue to bug the polity. The issues and the context in which they were acted out have probably changed, but Nigerians are most likely to continue with federation or a federal-type compromise in the management of their conflicts in the next decade.

In the next decade, however, a number of issues will continue to attract the attention of political leaders. The distribution of power among three tiers of government and on the horizontal level will continue to engage Nigerian political leaders, irrespective of their political party affiliations. It is most likely that the legislative lists will be reviewed in favour of subnational units. The centre may be less powerful than it is now, but it is unlikely that Nigeria will adopt a confederal technique in the management of conflicts arising from its federal association.

In addition, the issue of resource distribution and/or management will continue to dominate the debate in the federation. There may even be violent dimensions to the problem. But given the complementarity of the Nigerian economy in the past 80 years, piecemeal compromises are likely to be effected over time.

It is hoped that as democratic institutions take their root; as the political processes get routinized; and as intergovernmental relations improve and a new culture of interdependence and cooperation develop among operators of the federation, Nigerians will develop greater sense of tolerance and accommodation of one another.

In all federal systems there is a continuing process of adjustment and compromise. No federation has attained a perfect balance between centrifugal pulls (towards self-determination for subnational groups) and centripetal pulls (toward control by and sovereignty of the centre). Adjustment in one area may affect another area in the federal scale. In Nigeria the politics of compromise in the federal context have been complex.

Out of the various shocks to the Nigerian political system, only federalism has survived. Both parliamentary and presidential systems have been experimented with federalism. Nigerians have not yet been patient and tolerant enough to learn about both political systems and imbibe the values, which underwrite them. Perhaps the problem is more among Nigerians, not the system.

Yet, even if the federal system gets shaken up by occasional crises, it is part and parcel of the process of political development. One thing seems clear – that Nigeria is now an *organic state* – it is more than a *mere geographic expression*. Thus, the arenas of compatibility among groups are widening.

Federalism (even given its problems) is likely to be used as a compromise mechanism by Nigerian groups for a long while. The identities of groups are yet to 'coalesce' so as to reduce conflict of total identities (with its ramifications) to less dangerous conflicts of interests. If federalism is to serve Nigeria well, there must be greater commitment to ideals and better understanding of the values of federalism. For as late Martin Diamond correctly observed:

> Whether federalism survives, how it can be adapted and modified so as to deal with contemporary problems etc., all require knowing what it is we want from federalism and what federalism by nature can supply.[1]

Certainly what federalism cannot supply are values of **fairness**, **justice** and **accommodation** of all in the system. Nigerian political leaders must imbibe these values. However, federalism may provide a conducive medium for realizing, in relative forms, the values of fairness and justice in public life, and political leaders must effectively use this medium.

Notes and references

1. Martin Diamond, *The Federal Polity*, quoted by Stephen L. Schechter, "The Present State of American Federalism," *Publius*, Vol. 8, No.1 (Winter 1978), p. 6.

Index